Social and labour practices
of multinational enterprises
in the textiles, clothing
and footwear industries

Social and labour practices of multinational enterprises in the textiles, clothing and footwear industries

International Labour Office   Geneva

ISBN 92-2-103882-3

First published 1984

Printed in Switzerland

PREFACE

This is the fourth in a series of sectoral studies by the ILO on the social and labour practices of multinational enterprises.[1] As is customary, information for the study was obtained through a questionnaire addressed to governments and to employers' and workers' organisations as well as to multinational enterprises themselves[2] in more than 30 countries. Relevant information was also requested from the three major international sectoral union organisations.[3]

At the time this study was conducted, the sector was going through a period of major intenrational restructuring, under the influence of a world-wide recession and redeployment of industry. Thus, although an attempt was made to cover a varied sample of multinationals, not all the major enterprises originally approached found themselves in a position to participate.[4] Still, data could be obtained - through questionnaires and interviews - from a sample of eight parent enterprises and 13 of their subsidiaries operating in both industrialised and developing countries.[5]

In order to put the findings of the ILO survey in the overall context, the report is preceded by an introductory chapter based on available studies and other documentation. Such additional sources have also been used, as appropriate, in the remaining chapters to supplement the survey data.

With the information provided by the enterprises and obtained from other sources, it is believed that a fairly representative picture of the labour and social practices of multinationals in the sector has emerged from the report. The co-operation offered by all the respondents to the ILO survey was essential and is herewith gratefully acknowledged.

The study was co-ordinated by Mr. Paul Bailey of the ILO's Bureau of Multinational Enterprises (MULTI). Close liaison was maintained with various other technical ILO departments, especially the Sectoral Activities Department. Research assistance was provided by Mr. Akira Noro (MULTI), Ms. Möwes and Ms. Madany, University of Geneva, and Mr. Stark and Mr. Konkolewsky, ILO trainees.

---

[1] Earlier studies were as follows: ILO: Social and labour practices of some European-based multinationals in the metal trades (Geneva, 1976); idem: Social and labour practices of some US-based multinationals in the metal trades (Geneva, 1977); and idem: Social and labour practices of multinational enterprises in the petroleum industry (Geneva, 1977). Studies on multinationals in the textiles, clothing and footwear industries have been requested in resolutions adopted by various meetings of Industrial and analogous Committees.

[2] A profile of the participating enterprises and their main characteristics is found in Appendix I.

[3] A list of the governments, organisations and enterprises who replied is found in Appendix II.

[4] Assistance with the selection of enterprises was provided by the IOE and national employers' organisations.

[5] The text of the questionnaires used for the study is found in Appendix III.

CONTENTS

Page

CHAPTER I

Production of textiles, clothing and footwear

The textile, clothing and footwear sector is one which has been undergoing major structural change throughout the world in recent decades. In the industrialised countries the industries in this sector belong to the declining ones facing major problems of structural adjustment to new market conditions, international competition and related technological change. Still, on a global scale, the production of fibres has been increasing since 1950 as is shown in Table I-1 below (whereby the share of man-made fibres has increased from less than one-fifth in 1950 to almost one-half by 1980). However, the distribution of world production has shifted remarkably between 1963 and 1980 with the share of the industrialised market economy countries declining in both textiles (from 58 to 48 per cent) and clothing (from 70 to 51 per cent).[1] As far as footwear is concerned world output grew by some 26 per cent between 1966 and 1975. There was also a change in the location of production within this industry, which has been systematically away from higher-wage countries towards lower-wage ones. The major part of the fall in the share of production of footwear in a number of industrialised countries has been absorbed by increases in other groupings of countries with the largest percentage of growth being accounted for by Asian producers. The shares of the Eastern European, African and other European countries, such as Greece, Portugal, Spain and Yugoslavia have also expanded markedly.[2]

As for the annual percentage rate of change in the volume of production in textiles, it has been observed that between 1973 and 1980 the industrialised and the developing countries were behaving in exactly the opposite manner; the former had a 0.5 per cent decrease while the developing areas had a 2.5 per cent increase. In clothing (including leather and footwear) developing countries demonstrated a higher rate of increase both for the period 1963-73 (5.5 per cent) and 1973-80 (3 per cent) than the industrialised countries which had only a 2 per cent increase for 1963-73 and a decrease of 0.5 per cent for 1973-80.[3] While a variety of factors explain these structural changes in world production as will be seen later, it is obvious that the labour-intensive segments of the sector being considered are particularly responsive to variations and differentials in labour costs.

Taken as a whole, the developing countries have already reached the target of the Lima Declaration[4] for their textile-related production. Likewise, the share of developing countries in the exports of leather, textiles and clothing has increased and now reaches 34, 20 and 45 per cent respectively of the imports of OECD countries (see table I-2).

Table I-1: World production of cotton, wool and man-made fibres (1980-81) (mn kg)

| | Raw cotton | Wool | Man-made fibres | | | | | Total of all fibres |
			Synthetic filament	Staple	Cellulosic filament	Staple	Total	
1950	6 647	1 057	54	15	871	737	1 677	9 381
1960	10 113	1 463	417	285	1 131	1 525	3 358	14 934
1970	11 784	1 602	2 397	2 417	1 391	2 187	8 393	21 779
1971	13 008	1 567	2 891	2 831	1 397	2 201	9 320	23 895
1972	13 669	1 457	3 205	3 245	1 343	2 391	10 184	25 310
1973	13 714	1 432	3 820	3 912	1 361	2 499	11 592	26 738
1974	14 019	1 511	3 780	3 795	1 301	2 465	11 341	26 871
1975	11 809	1 510	3 764	3 672	1 136	2 065	10 638	23 957
1976	12 632	1 446	4 137	4 545	1 183	2 286	12 151	26 229
1977	14 138	1 445	4 332	4 829	1 155	2 379	12 695	28 278
1978	12 970	1 524	4 629	5 546	1 168	2 440	13 783	28 277
1980	14 228	1 608	4 759	5 923	1 142	2 412	14 236	30 060
1981	15 382	1 610	4 877	6 129	1 075	2 434	14 515	31 507

Source: V. Cable: World textile trade and production (London, The Economist Intelligence Unit, 1979), p. 1, based on Organon World Cotton Statistics; and for 1978-81 United Nations: Transnational corporations in the synthetic fibre, textile and clothing industries (New York, Centre on Transnational Corporations, forthcoming 1984), Chapter 2, p. 46.

Table I-2: Percentage share of developing countries in textile-related
            production and trade

	Total world			OECD imports of 1979[3]
	Production (1979)[1]	Exports (1982)[2]	Imports (1982)[2]	
Textiles	25	24	32	20
Clothing	15	41	17	45
Leather	25			34[*]

[*] Includes footwear and fur.

[1] Estimates provided by the International Textile, Garment and
Leather Workers' Federation (ITGLWF) based on GATT (1979) and UNIDO
figures.

[2] GATT: International trade 1982/83 (Geneva, 1983), p. 81. The
figures given are for world trade. If intra-EC trade is excluded, the
developing countries' share in world exports of textiles and clothing
rise to 35 and 59 per cent, respectively, and that of imports in the
textiles and clothing sectors would be 44 and 19 per cent, respectively.
(GATT: Recent trends in production and trade in textiles and clothing,
Report by the Secretariat, COM. TEX/W/135 of 13 Dec. 1982, restricted,
p. 10.)

[3] OECD: "North-South technology transfer: The adjustments ahead",
in OECD Observer, Mar. 1981.

This does not imply, however, that the developing countries do not have
any problems with the industry nor that developments are uniform. As
a matter of fact, many countries and regions see in the further expansion
of the sector an essential condition for their continued industrialisation.

It has been noted that developing Asia alone accounted for three-
quarters of manufactured exports from all developing countries[5] and that
three countries in Asia in turn also accounted for a similar proportion
of the developing world's clothing exports. Developing Asia also
showed the highest growth rate for the production of wearing apparel
from the mid-1960s to the mid-1970s.[6] Production increases and export
shares of developing countries are concentrated furthermore in a few
so-called "newly industrialising countries" (NICs). Data confirms
specifically for cotton yarns and fabrics the advances made by the
developing countries and also by some of the centrally planned economies
in comparison to most of the industrialised market economy countries.[7]

Employment

Against the background of the production changes as described above, the textiles, clothing and footwear industries have been identified as a sector "in trouble"[8] - i.e. marked by rapid employment declines in the industrialised countries in the past decades.

In the early 1960s the textiles and clothing industries were two of the largest employers in the market economy countries. After the significant structural changes in the industries which occurred during this decade, employment in textiles and clothing in the industrialised market economy countries declined by some 0.4 million between 1963 and 1970 and by over one million between 1970 and 1976.[9] The OECD has demonstrated these trends in the context of total industrial restructuring and showed that this sector has undergone the greatest structural contraction in employment terms in the major industrialised countries.

ILO data also indicate a loss between 1970 and 1980 of over some 1.2 million jobs alone in the nine-member European Communities in the textile, clothing and footwear industries. Annex table 1 provides further details of losses and gains in the textiles, clothing and footwear industries in most of the industrialised market economy countries, using figures found in the ILO Year Book of Labour Statistics. This contrasts with often sharp employment increases in the industries of the sector in the developing and Mediterranean basin countries (see Annex table II).[10]

It can be observed that the decline in employment in the sector in the industrialised countries has accelerated in recent years. In addition, there has been a significant shift in the geographic distribution of textile and clothing activity within the industrialised market economy countries. Thus, North America increased its share of employment in textiles and clothing in the OECD area from 24 per cent in 1963 to almost 29 per cent by 1979, while the four southern European countries - Italy, Spain, Portugal and Greece - increased their share from a little over 16 per cent to 23 per cent. Job losses have been concentrated in the other European countries, whose share in the sector fell from 47 to 35 per cent during the same period.[11]

The disruption of international trade through currency fluctuations, protectionism, rising oil and energy prices, growing imports from low-wage countries, technological changes and regional imbalance have been mentioned as factors connected with the employment decline in the sector.[12] Additionally, consumer spending on clothing has generally decelerated in recent years.[13] However, a recent study on the elements responsible for the employment decline in textiles and clothing has identified productivity and technology developments as a major factor in several industrialised countries.[14] Other factors, including international trade, and in particular competition from

developing countries, are thought to be of relatively less importance.
It is evident, however, that competitive pressures, including those from
international trade, have accelerated concentration into fewer and
larger firms as well as the adoption of modern technologies and of
productivity improvements in the industrialised countries.

International trade

Movements in the volume of world trade in textiles and clothing
since 1973 have been characterised by sharp year-to-year fluctuations.[15]

For many developing countries, however, steady increases in the
exports of textiles and clothing have been experienced and ascribed a
pivotal role for their economies.   Thus, the share of textile and
apparel exports in relation to all manufactured exports for the
period 1967-74 tripled, for instance, in Brazil (from 7 to 22 per cent),
doubled in Colombia (from 13 to 26 per cent) and, although it declined
in the Republic of Korea, it remained higher there than in the other
countries (1967: 50 per cent, 1974: 38 per cent).[16]   It is also
remarkable that the exports of clothing from developing countries to
industrialised countries has increased three times as fast as world
trade between 1955 and 1979.[17]

Trade data analysed[18] by GATT demonstrates the general net loss in
most industrialised countries and the general net gains in developing
ones, especially the newly industrialising countries.   A study by the
OECD on the impact of the NICs on production and trade in manufactures
has characterised OECD exports/imports in textiles, clothing and
leather (travel goods and footwear) as follows: (i) although the
internal imports (from other OECD countries) in textiles still account
for a major part, the share of Far Eastern NICs is constantly increasing (except for 1975); (ii) more than half of the OECD imports in
clothing were accounted for by the Far East NICs after 1974; (iii) in
leather, travel goods and footwear imports NICs in total have been a
major supplier since 1975 together with Italy; and (iv) the bulk of
OECD exports in textiles and clothing go to other OECD countries
(internal trade).

It can, therefore, be concluded that while the newly industrialising countries seemed to have had considerable success in penetrating
the markets of the industrialised countries in clothing they were
clearly very small suppliers of textiles.[19]   The share of developing
countries in the textile imports of the industrialised market economy
countries increased between 1968 and 1978 from 1.12 to 2.79 per cent.
The consumption rate of imports from all countries was 1.93 and 4.93 per
cent, respectively.   For clothing imports the corresponding rates were
1.94 per cent (1968) and 11.64 per cent (1978) as regards developing
countries.[20]

According to the OECD, clothing, textiles and leather products from developing countries constituted in 1979 some 10 per cent of consumption in the member countries.[21]

The performance has recently been observed of what is termed the "second-tier" NICs[22] or the "newly exporting countries" (NECs),[23] i.e. a group of 16 newcomers to the scene of exporters of manufactures. Available research suggests that these NECs are basing their rapid export growth on much the same products as did the original NICs. Of the top seven products for NECs in 1979, five were the same as in the top seven list of NICs in 1970, namely clothing, textile yarns and fabrics, electrical machinery, non-metal mineral manufactures and miscellaneous manufactures. Indeed, the reliance of the NECs (exports) on the two traditional products, textiles and clothing, was even stronger (at 39 per cent) in 1979 than it had been for the NICs in 1970 (27 per cent).[24]

Trade and employment

Employment substantially increased in the textile industry in several developing (and socialist) countries both as a result of an increase in exports to industrialised countries and in domestic demand, as noted in the above-mentioned ILO general textile report.[25] The report maintained that it was difficult, and perhaps misleading, to assess the impact of an increase of imports from developing countries on employment in any industry in the industrialised countries thus isolating imports from many other factors which influence employment levels, especially since employment declines were matched by produc- tivity increases. It nevertheless held that import competition certainly had an impact when employment levels in the industry were declining - both directly by suppressing jobs in the least dynamic undertakings producing similar products and indirectly through a reduction in jobs when reorganisation was forced by foreign and domestic competition. This evaluation nevertheless confirms the over- riding importance of productivity development for the job losses referred to above,[26] as does the OECD study on the impact of newly industrialising countries on production and trade, which found the impact of the NICs to be of relatively minor influence on employment in industrialised countries.[27] However, trade competition can have a substantial impact for employment in certain product lines and, therefore, on individual enterprises.

It appears from Annex table III that employment has considerably declined in textiles and clothing over the previous decade (1970-79), for the 12 main industrialised countries covered (Canada, Federal Republic of Germany, Italy, Austria, United States, France, Belgium, United Kingdom, Switzerland, Netherlands, Norway and Sweden).[28] In fact, the reduction in employment during a general economic recession phase was in most countries followed by continued reduction in the recovery phase. This undoubtedly reflects the productivity changes but also changes in the product mix in response to the changing international division of labour and accompanying trade flows.   On the other hand, the correlation between trade expansion and sectoral employment in the developing countries included in Annex table III has been notable.

The role of multinationals in production and employment restructuring in the sector

Although a recent OECD study has contended that, in the past 10-15 years, the bulk of foreign direct investment (FDI) by MNEs in the textile and clothing industries has been directed to other industrialised countries, FDI played a significant role in the years after the Second World War, especially in Latin America and Africa, in building up the petrochemical sector, including the production of synthetic staples and fibres.   In the past 20 years many large projects were undertaken which resulted in large geographical shifts to newcomers.[29]

Certainly, foreign investment is only feasible for enterprises over a certain size.   Smaller nationally operating firms account for the bulk of the output in textiles and even more in clothing, which in general belong to a sector which is less concentrated than other industries such as the metal trades or the petroleum industry.[30] Multinationals have penetrated the sector of textiles, clothing and footwear less than they have other sectors such as the more capital- and technology-intensive industries.[31]   Additionally, many multinationals in the sector have only one or two subsidiaries in other countries.

Table I-3 confirms for indigenous firms (whether national or multinational) that they tend to hold larger shares of either production of employment for the countries listed than do foreign MNEs.[32] However, especially in the developing countries, many of the local firms may be involved via licensing or other arrangements - such as subcontracting - with foreign enterprises.[33]   In certain cases foreign multinationals were instrumental for the build-up of the local textile industry in developing countries.   This has been noted for the Republic of Korea: the successful export performance of its textile industry (exports jumped from $341 million in 1970 to $3,200 million in 1977 - and the textile labour force doubled to reach 700,000) is attributed to the involvement of Japan-based enterprises.[34]

Of the largest 500 MNEs analysed by Stopford and Dunning only 14 were in textiles, apparel and leather goods industries, and for nine of these foreign production represented less than 10 per cent of the world-wide sales.[35]   In only one case did foreign production account for more than 50 per cent of overall sales.[36]

Likewise, textile, clothing and footwear investments usually represent in the major capital-exporting countries between 1 and 7 per

Table I-3: Employment share (percentage) of foreign-owned enterprises in the textile and clothing industries[1] for selected host countries (for various years in the mid-1970s)

Australia	Brazil	Canada	France	Greece	Japan	Republic of Korea	Portugal	Sweden	United Kingdom
15.9	10.9[2]	25.7	8.0	5.5[3]	0.2	6.0	3.1	3.8	2.5

[1] ISIC group 32.

[2] Percentage based on assets data.

[3] Percentage based on production of textiles only.

Source: Adapted from Stopford and Dunning: Multinationals: Company performance and global trends (London, Macmillan, 1983), pp. 26-27.

cent of foreign direct investment, with the notable exception of Japan (22 per cent, see table I-4).   This fact is not surprising though since Japan is a relative newcomer and most of the initial investments by the other industrialised countries had been undertaken years ago.

However, multinationals are not unimportant in the sector and their role in restructuring production and employment is not insignificant. Multinational enterprises account for the bulk of employment in the export processing zones of developing countries in which textiles, clothing and electronics are the most important sectors.   In developing Asia, where EPZs account for more than half a million workers,[37] it can be estimated, for instance, that MNE employment in textiles is in the order of 200,000, i.e. corresponds to 40 per cent of total zone employment.   Export processing zones, however, are increasingly meeting with quota restrictions in importing countries connected with the Multifibre Arrangement (MFA).

As regards the clothing industry, EPZs in India, Malaysia, the Philippines and Sri Lanka have been successful and have attracted a considerable number of multinationals thereby increasing their international competitiveness.   Together with the establishment of subsidiaries in the Caribbean, North Africa, South Africa, South-East Asia and the Far East to manufacture clothing items for marketing in the industrialised countries by the parent company, MNEs due to their internationalisation[38] have contributed to the significant shifts of production observed among the different regions of the world.

The chemicals, pharmaceuticals and synthetic fibres industries all have cross-linkages, as might be expected, in petrochemical processing. While some sectors have been diversifying into others, in the traditional textile industry which has largely stayed within its own confines the reverse has been happening, i.e. it has been faced with intensive competition from chemical producers such as Du Pont, Monsanto, ICI, Hoechst and others, all of which have important stakes in synthetic fibres.   Thus, chemical firms accounted for 38 per cent of all textile sales and reached a percentage almost as high as that of the textile enterprises themselves in their own sector.[39]   However, the interconnection of the textile and clothing industries with the chemical/ synthetic fibre industries had major repercussions on employment in the chemical industries of the industrialised countries.   Thus, the restructuring of a significant part of the Western European textile industry, which is a major consumer of synthetic fibres, had dramatic repercussions on employment in this particular branch of petrochemical production.   In turn, rationalisation and restructuring measures led to substantial reductions in employment in the synthetic fibre plants of major European multinationals.[40]   Annex table IV provides in chronological order some recent employment-related examples of these measures involving several of these major enterprises.

Table I-4: Outward foreign direct investment in textiles, leather,
            clothing and footwear as a percentage of all FDI, 1975

United States		Japan		United Kingdom		Sweden		Federal Republic of Germany	
$million	%	$million	%	$million	%	$million	%	$million	%
1 099	2	918	22	1 038	7	65	1	469	4

Source: Adapted from J. Stopford and J. Dunning: Multinationals:
         Company performance and global trends (London, Macmillan,
         1983), p. 32 (table 2.4).

While the sector being examined is less concentrated than others
as has been noted above, multinationals, especially in the textile
industry, do hold significant market shares and have increased their
influence through integrated marketing networks.   Thus, according to
UNCTAD estimates, some 35 to 40 MNEs controlled in the beginning of the
1980s, directly and indirectly, a significant part of the world's
textile production, in particular synthetic fibres.[41]   A number of
developing countries (such as India, Egypt, Brazil and Mexico) have
actively promoted the textile industry with which multinationals are
however interlinked.   On the other hand, countries such as the United
Republic of Tanzania and Algeria have a strong public sector textile
industry.

As regards the sales of MNEs themselves in textile-related
products, it has been estimated that the three largest MNEs account for
30 per cent of all sales of the 20 most important multinationals in the
industry.[42]   Taking textile, apparel and leather goods enterprises
together, the five largest enterprises (most of them multinationals)
account for 30 per cent of the total turnover of the sector.[43]
Non-capital linkages, such as licences and management contracts, add to
the influence of multinationals in the sector.   This is further
enhanced by the fact that some major multinationals have vertically
integrated operations, covering production of fibres, manufacture of
apparel and retail.

Within the textile industry in particular the role of multinationals is considered as becoming more important according to the 1978
ILO Textile Committee report which refers in this connection to the
growth in numbers, size and foreign location of MNEs, their diversified
production, modern technology and means of communication.   Whereas in

1977 only 5 per cent of a sample of leading textile companies was based
in developing countries, this had risen to 9 per cent in 1981 with these
companies accounting for 14 per cent of the total turnover of the
industry as opposed to 4.2 per cent in 1977.[44]

Table I-5 shows for specific countries and for the 14 larger
textile-related MNEs that both foreign content (defined as overseas
subsidiary production plus home country exports) and overseas production
as a percentage of foreign content have been rising, especially for
European and UK-based MNEs between 1977 and 1981.

The question necessarily arises as to whether the tendency towards
multinationalisation of production and relocation of industries in the
textile, clothing and footwear industries will continue and at what
pace.   While there is no definite answer, as for all projections, a
number of factors would speak for a certain slowing-down, at least in
the years to come - which is in line with research findings that for the
most recent period (1977-82) the number of large textiles, clothing and
leather goods enterprises expecting a higher proportion of sales for
their foreign affiliates has declined (see Annex table V).[45]   It can
also be said that the increasing use of high technology reduces the
share of labour costs and might also reduce the attractiveness of low
labour cost countries.   Additionally, the tendency towards greater
protectionism in the industrialised countries - prominent in the textile
and clothing industry (and which consequently leads to limited growth
prospects in the main export markets) - can be expected to possibly act
as a brake on the shift of industrial production to the developing
countries.[46]

However, the available evidence tends to suggest that proportionate
increases in overseas production by MNEs has been accompanied, during
the period 1977-81, by similar increases in the export ratio with, for
example, the exception of the United Kingdom textiles industry which has
"recorded overseas production gains and export losses".[47]

International subcontracting and
offshore processing

International subcontracting both by multinational and other
enterprises for the manufacture of clothing items is another development
affecting world-wide employment.   Often designs, cuts and fabrics are
provided by multinational enterprises to producing firms located in
developing countries.[48]   Although the employment effects of subcontracting are difficult to separate from other influences, they are certainly
among the significant factors in restructuring the clothing industry.[49]

A special development in this connection is offshore processing,
i.e. the farming out of certain stages of production, especially to
developing low-wage countries and to several European countries with
relatively lower labour costs.   While exact data are not available

Table I-5: Foreign content[1] and overseas production of the major MNEs in the textiles, clothing and leather goods sectors[2] as a percentage of world-wide sales, 1977-81

	Canada		Japan		Europe		United States		Total	
	1977	1981	1977	1981	1977	1981	1977	1981	1977	1981
Foreign content	-	-	26.5	-	57.8	63.4	16.8	18.0	28.4	29.5
Overseas production as a percentage of foreign content	29.0	28.5	-	-	65.5	74.0	82.8	83.7	57.4	60.4

[1] Definition of foreign content: Production of overseas subsidiaries plus exports from parent (home) country.

[2] The following 14 enterprises are covered: Blue Bell Incorporated, United States; Burlington Industries Incorporated, United States; Coats Patons plc, United Kingdom; Courtaulds plc, United Kingdom; Genesco Incorporated, United States; Interco Incorporated, United States; J.P. Stevens and Company, United States; Kanebo Limited, Japan; Kuraray Company Limited, Japan; Levi Strauss and Company, United States; Teijin Limited, Japan; Toray Industries Incorporated, Japan; Toyobo Company Limited, Japan; Unitika Limited, Japan.

Source: Adapted from Stopford and Dunning: Multinationals: Company performance and global trends, op. cit., pp. 71 and 73.

these activities have probably had a substantial influence on the restructuring of the textiles, clothing and footwear sector.

Value-added duties applied by several industrialised countries have considerably facilitated the development of offshore processing. This type of processing is concentrated on clothing and knitwear while there have only been small inflows of fabrics and outflows of yarn.[50]

The relative importance, commodity composition and geographical location of offshore processing in the textile sector varies considerably from country to country and over time. Thus, in the Federal Republic of Germany imports of textiles and clothing subject to value-added duties have increased from DM113 million (3.2 per cent of the total imports) in 1961 to DM961 million in 1973 (8.8 per cent) and DM1,334 million in 1978 (6 per cent). Textiles and clothing have accounted for a steadily rising share of all imports of the Federal Republic of Germany under value-added duties, reaching more than 60 per cent in 1978. Offshore processing for the Federal Republic of Germany is heavily concentrated in Eastern European countries (especially Yugoslavia), as well as in Austria, with developing countries being of only marginal importance.

Likewise, in the United States, there has been a steady expansion of textile and clothing imports under value-added duties with an increasing share in total imports. The United States offshore production under value-added duties is largely concentrated in some Latin American and Asian countries (predominantly Mexico and the Philippines). The bulk of this offshore processing is undertaken by subsidiaries of United States corporations or local enterprises controlled by them.

For France, the share of offshore processing under value-added customs duties in total imports of ladies' clothing had reached 7 per cent by 1979. The suppliers were mainly enterprises in Morocco, Tunisia and Portugal but also in Eastern Europe. French multinationals as well as other enterprises shared in this development. Swiss and Netherlands companies also seem frequently involved in offshore processing while enterprises in the United Kingdom, Italy and Japan have not explored these possibilities as of yet.

General employment trends in multinationals in the textiles, clothing and footwear sector

Some rough indications on these global trends can be obtained from published data contained in available directories of multinational and large enterprises. Stopford and Dunning, basing themselves on their directory published in 1981, have calculated that employment in the 14 major multinationals in the sector has declined between 1977 and 1981 by 2 per cent in the United States and by 35 per cent in Japan.[51] The overall employment decline of these same MNEs world-wide was

13 per cent in the same period while the trend for a greater internationalisation of textiles, apparel and leather goods industries has continued.[52]   For instance, whereas MNEs based in the United States had less than 14 per cent of their production abroad in 1977 this share had increased to over 15 per cent by 1981.   Similarly, European-based enterprises (especially British ones) had 47 per cent of their production in overseas subsidiaries in 1981 while only 38 per cent had been located abroad four years earlier.   World-wide the foreign production of the multinationals surveyed increased from 16 to 18 per cent.[53] This was generally accompanied, as table I-6 shows for selected major MNEs in the sector, by an increase in the employment share in foreign operations.   However, the figures should be interpreted cautiously as many of the enterprises in question are engaged in a variety of production lines and their activities in the sector being considered, especially textiles, cannot be considered separately with the available data.

Overall developments in sector MNEs

Table I-7 was compiled on the basis of data about major enterprises regularly published in Fortune magazine (most of which are multinationals).   The employment data shown in table I-7 relate to the total activities of the enterprises and not only to the products relevant for the sector being studied.   The share of textiles, clothing or footwear in total sales is shown in the table.   (Total employment, world-wide, of the 46 major textile-, clothing- and footwear-related multinationals in table I-7 decreased between 1974 and 1980 by some 5 per cent, although the table sometimes reflects diverse tendencies in the various countries of location.)

Nevertheless, it can be concluded from the available global data for the enterprises in the sector that employment in the relevant multinationals taken as a whole - which overwhelmingly is in the industrialised home countries - has declined especially in the textile-dominated firms (and in the United States in particular).   Similarly, despite expansion of foreign production, most of the clothing enterprises have also had stagnant or declining employment between 1974 and 1980.   As regards synthetic fibre-producing enterprises, their employment has partly increased, stagnated or even decreased.   On the whole, these data fit well with the overall tendencies uncovered for the sector in different countries.

A specific study on the foreign expansion in the 1960s and 1970s of textile and clothing enterprises was undertaken for the Federal Republic of Germany by the Max Planck Institute.   Table I-8 (which is extracted from this study) shows that employment in these enterprises home-based in the Federal Republic more than doubled abroad between 1966 and 1974, while declining at home by one-quarter.[54]   It was found, furthermore, that by 1974/75 just over half of these production facilities in the textile industry, with around 11,000 employees, and

Table I-6: Domestic and foreign employment of major selected textile, clothing and footwear MNEs

Enterprises	1974	%	1975	%	1976	%	1977	%	1978	%	1979	%	1980	%	1981	%
FEDERAL REPUBLIC OF GERMANY																
BASF A.G. (Chemical products, synthetic fibres)																
Total employees	110 989		111 400		112 700		113 800		115 408		115 400		116 518		116 646	
Domestic			89 120	80	89 033	79	88 764	78	87 710	76	87 704	76	87 388	75	87 484	75
Abroad			22 280	20	23 667	21	25 036	22	27 698	24	27 696	24	29 130	25	29 162	25
BAYER A.G. (Chemical products, synthetic fibres)																
Total employees*	134 837		169 400		171 200		170 400		179 000		181 000		181 639		180 900	
Domestic									102 030	57	101 360	56	101 717	56	101 304	56
Abroad									76 970	43	79 640	44	79 921	44	79 596	44
HOECHST A.G. (Chemical products, fibres)																
Total employees*	178 710		182 500		183 000		180 900		179 546		182 700		186 850		184 700	
Domestic			105 850	58	104 310	57	101 304	56	100 545	56	98 658	54	100 899	54	99 738	54
Abroad			76 650	42	78 690	43	79 596	44	79 001	44	84 042	46	85 951	46	84 962	46
FRANCE																
DOLLFUS-MIEG (Textiles)																
Total employees	26 961		25 650		22 681		21 375		20 799		22 269		20 955			
Domestic	20 955	77.8	19 450	76			15 878	74.3	15 054	72.4	13 929	62.6	12 313	58.8		
Abroad	6 006	22.2	6 200	24			5 497	25.7	5 745	27.6	8 340	37.4	8 642	41.2		
RHONE-POULENC S.A. (Chemical products, synthetic fibres)																
Total employees	119 000		115 800		115 000		110 700		107 219		106 700		95 389		89 300	
Domestic			78 744	68	74 750	65	73 062	66	70 765	66	70 422	66	61 049	64	56 259	63
Abroad			37 056	32	40 250	35	37 638	34	36 454	34	36 278	34	34 340	36	33 041	37

* The employment in companies which are less than 50 per cent owned has either been counted entirely or on a prorated basis.

Table 1-6: Domestic and foreign employment of major selected textile, clothing and footwear MNEs (cont.)

Enterprises	1974	%	1975	%	1976	%	1977	%	1978	%	1979	%	1980	%	1981	%
ITALY																
MONTEDISON S.P.A. * (Chemical products, synthetic fibres)																
Total employees	153 200		150 600		144 500		135 300		126 878		110 000		105 532		100 100	
Domestic	144 008	94	141 564	94	135 830	94	125 829	93	117 997	93					94 094	94
Abroad	9 192	6	9 036	6	8 670	6	9 471	7	8 881	7					6 006	6
JAPAN																
KANEBO LTD. * (Textiles)																
Total employees	35 219		33 325		29 205						36 343		22 679			
Domestic											28 897	79.5	14 704	65		
Abroad											7 446	20.5	7 975	35		
TORAY INDUSTRIES INC. (Synthetic fibres, chemicals)																
Total employees	28 650		28 797		28 524				24 866		22 400		22 903		33 100	
Domestic									22 130	89	19 936	89	19 926	87	19 198	58
Abroad									2 736	11	2 464	11	2 977	13	13 902	42
NETHERLANDS																
AKZO N.V. (Synthetic fibres, chemicals)																
Total employees	105 400		98 200		91 000		84 400		83 200		83 200		83 100		77 800	
Domestic			29 460	30	27 300	30	25 320	30	24 128	29	24 128	29	23 268	28	23 340	30
Abroad			68 640	70	63 700	70	59 080	70	59 072	71	59 072	71	59 832	72	54 460	70
UNITED KINGDOM																
COATS PATONS plc (Textiles, clothing)																
Total employees	74 000		71 000		70 000		68 000		66 000		65 000		60 000		49 000	
Domestic	32 560	44	29 980	38	24 500	35	25 160	37	23 760	36	22 750	35	20 400	34	17 640	36
Abroad	41 440	56	44 020	62	45 500	65	42 840	63	42 240	64	42 250	65	39 600	66	31 360	64
COURTAULDS plc (Synthetic fibres, clothing)																
Total employees	155 000		123 675		138 770		107 500		130 000		128 003		153 003			
Domestic	123 701	80	113 800	92	112 000	80.7			103 000	79.2	95 300	74.5	109 000	91.2		
Abroad	31 300	20	9 875	8	26 770	19.3			27 000	20.8	32 703	25.5	44 000	8.8		

* The employment in companies which are less than 50 per cent owned has either been counted entirely or on a prorated basis.

Table I-6: Domestic and foreign employment of major selected textile, clothing and footwear MNEs (cont.)

Enterprises	1974	%	1975	%	1976	%	1977	%	1978	%	1979	%	1980	%	1981	%
IMPERIAL CHEMICAL INDUSTRIES plc (Chemicals, fibres)																
Total employees	201 000		195 000		192 000		154 000		151 000		148 200		143 200		132 400	
Domestic	132 660	66	128 700	66	124 800	65	95 480	62	92 110	61	88 920	60	84 488	59	74 144	56
Abroad	68 340	34	66 300	34	67 200	35	58 520	38	58 890	39	59 280	40	58 712	41	58 256	44
UNITED STATES																
CELANESE CORPORATION (Fibres, chemicals)																
Total employees	38 000		37 000		31 900		32 100		33 200		33 300		46 200		41 500	
Domestic									24 900	75	24 975	75	32 802	71	29 465	71
Abroad									8 300	25	8 325	25	13 398	29	12 035	29
CONSOLIDATED FOODS CORPORATION (Clothing)																
Total employees	75 200		77 300		75 700		75 700		80 900		94 500		88 600		85 300	
Domestic					55 261	73	55 261	73	58 248	72					63 122	74
Abroad					20 439	27	20 439	27	22 652	28					22 178	16
E.I. DU PONT DE NEMOURS AND COMPANY (Chemicals, fibres)																
Total employees	136 886		134 600		132 500		132 000		134 400		136 900		136 300		177 200	
Domestic							104 280	79	107 520	80	108 151	79	106 314	78	141 760	80
Abroad							27 720	21	26 880	20	28 749	21	29 986	22	35 440	20
GENERAL MILLS INC. (Clothing)																
Total employees	46 400		50 100		60 000		60 000		66 600		64 200		66 032		71 225	
Domestic					49 200	82	49 200	82					59 429	90	64 815	91
Abroad					10 800	18	10 800	18					6 603	10	6 410	9

Source: J.M. Stopford, J.H. Dunning and K.O. Haberich: The world directory of multinational enterprises (London, Macmillan, 1980), Vols. 1 and 2; J.M. Stopford: The world directory of multinational enterprises 1982-83 (London, Macmillan, 1982), Vols. 1 and 2; and documentation provided by the participating enterprises in the study.

Table I-7: Major world textile, clothing and footwear enterprises based on Fortune magazine

Enterprises	Total sales 1980	Textile and clothing (or footwear) Sales		Employees	
		%	Total	1974	1980
E.I. Du Pont de Nemours and Company, United States	13 652 000	36	4 505 160	136 886	136 300
Courtaulds, United Kingdom	3 967 639	79	3 141 348	155 000	153 003
Burlington Industries Inc., United States	2 900 649	100	2 900 649	81 000	65 000
Levi Strauss and Company, United States	2 840 844	100	2 840 844	30 141	48 000
BASF A.G., Federal Republic of Germany	15 277 348	15	2 291 602	110 989	116 518
J.P. Stevens, United States	1 915 959	...	...	46 000	41 400
Akzo N.V., Netherlands	6 272 300	30	1 881 690	105 400	83 100
Celanese Corporation, United States	3 348 000	56	1 874 880	38 000	46 200
Toray Industries, Japan	2 644 409	69	1 824 642	28 797	22 903
Interco Inc., United States	2 024 307	81	1 639 688	43 600	50 000
Coats Patons, United Kingdom	1 603 267	95	1 523 103	74 000	60 000
Toyobo, Japan	1 726 435	84	1 450 205	32 026	17 258
Blue Bell Inc., United States	1 397 760	100	1 397 760	25 000	35 000
Kanebo, Japan	2 056 629	68	1 398 507	35 219	22 679
Hoechst A.G., Federal Republic of Germany	16 480 551	8	1 318 444	178 710	186 850
Freudenberg, Federal Republic of Germany	1 237 366	100	1 237 366	23 300	23 900
Northwest Industries, United States	2 876 400	44	1 265 616	30 000	44 000
Unitika, Japan	1 567 598	79	1 238 402	14 831	8 293
Rhône Poulenc, France	7 155 069	17	1 216 358	119 000	95 389
Asahi Chemicals, Japan	3 102 752	37.4	1 157 326	25 519	20 779
Teijin, Japan	1 689 844	67	1 132 195	13 570	10 534
Akzona, United States	1 054 015	...	...	19 515	15 910
Monsanto Company, United States	6 573 600	16	1 051 776	60 926	61 836
Dollfus-Mieg, France	1 136 350	90	1 022 715	26 961	20 955
Spring Mills, United States	937 650	...	...	19 700	22 600
Mitsubishi-Rayon, Japan	933 489	...	...	10 657	3 561
Imperial Chemical Industries, United Kingdom	13 290 347	7	930 324	201 100	143 200
Snia. Viscosa, Italy	1 826 370	48	876 657	33 845	32 000
Genesco, United States	845 338	100	845 338	57 000	21 800
Gulf and Western Industries, United States	5 782 783	15	867 417	75 000	95 520
Cluett-Peabody, United States	745 853	...	...	29 694	20 941
Cone Mills, United States	729 885	...	...	14 100	12 800
Montedison, Italy	9 103 770	8	728 270	153 200	105 532
Consolidated Foods Corporation, United States	5 342 000	13	694 460	71 000	88 600
Hart Schaffner and Marx, United States	674 888	...	...	20 500	21 500
Bayer A.G., Federal Republic of Germany	15 880 596	4	635 223	134 837	181 639
VF, United States	633 770	...	...	18 000	19 400
United Merchants and Manufacturers, United States	621 974	...	...	36 000	15 000
Lowenstein, United States	620 475	...	...	16 000	13 000
Dan River, United States	607 737	...	...	19 000	14 500
Collins and Aikman, United States	599 542	...	...	10 000	10 750
Oerlikon-Buhrle, Switzerland	2 455 607	23	564 789	19 400	37 204
Kellwood, United States	556 334	...	...	17 544	17 900
Warnaco, United States	465 009	...	...	14 250	10 045
General Mills Inc., United States	4 170 000	10	417 000	46 400	66 032
Armstrong World Industries, United States	1 376 290	17	233 969	24 102	22 645

Table I-8: Employment and regional distribution of textile and garment industry MNEs from the Federal Republic of Germany, 1966-74

(a) Employment

	Textile industry			Garment industry		
	1966	1970	1974	1966	1970	1974
Domestic employment	538 500	501 500	393 700	406 400	379 100	310 400
Employment in foreign subsidiaries (estimates)[a]	8 000	14 200	29 500	15 000	24 800	31 000
Employment in foreign subsidiaries as percentage of domestic employment (estimates)	1.5%	2.8%	7.5%	3.7%	6.5%	10.0%

[a] Estimates based on a survey of Federal German production facilities abroad.

Data obtained from Textil-Wirtschaft, 41 (1966), 42 (1970); Statistisches Bundesamt, Statistisches Jahrbuch für die Bundesrepublic Deutschland; and survey of 399 companies.

(b) Regional distribution of foreign subsidiaries

		EEC	Austria, Switzerland, Sweden	Other industrial countries	Mediterranean countries	Latin America	Africa	Asia
Regional distribution according to the number of foreign subsidiaries	T	26	28	13	12	4	13	5
	G	19	27	3	35	3	3	11
Regional distribution according to the number of foreign employees abroad	T	21	26	7	11	1	28	5
	G	21	33	4	23	9	1	10

T = textile; G = garment.

Data obtained from survey of 399 companies with about 300 foreign subsidiaries (about 150 each in the textile and garment industry).

Source: F. Fröbel, J. Heinrichs, O. Kreye: The new international division of labour: Structural unemployment in industrialised countries and industrialisation in developing countries (Cambridge, Cambridge University Press, 1980), p. 113.

over two-thirds of the foreign production facilities in the garment industry, with around 18,500 employees, were producing overwhelmingly or exclusively for the market in the Federal Republic of Germany.[55] These data do not include production expansion abroad or at home of foreign-owned enterprises located in the country.

Similarly, as from the mid-1960s, the Japanese textile industry was engaged predominantly in overseas investment, principally in low-wage countries of Asia, in order to secure and develop its traditional export markets. A second major region was Latin America, with one-fifth of Japanese foreign investment in the textile industry by 1976. The driving forces behind this foreign expansion were the lower wage costs.[56] (Table I-9 in fact shows how Japanese MNEs have tended to concentrate more in developing countries as compared with European or North American companies.) Sales back to Japan by Japanese companies abroad jumped from 2 per cent in 1972 to 20 per cent in 1974, while purchases from Japan decresed from 44 per cent to 39 per cent by 1974[57] and to 37 per cent by 1978.[58] While moving labour-intensive branches of the textile industry to low-wage countries, the Japanese textile industry has concentrated on capital-intensive branches at home and on final-stage production of imported products from industrialising Asian countries.

"Job exports" from industrialised home countries

The significant differences between the development of home country employment of multinationals in the sector and their foreign employment, together with known transfers of certain production lines, leaves little doubt that multinationals - more than in other sectors - have transferred jobs from their industrialised home countries to other countries (in particular to the developing ones). It is difficult, however, to measure these transfers exactly since there is obviously no simple correlation between job losses in the home countries and job gains in the host countries. There is also the even more difficult question of to what extent multinational enterprises may have had viable alternatives, such as exports in particular, instead of foreign direct investment. While there are few studies on the basis of which such hypotheses could have been tested, those that exist have generally concluded that only a fraction of the jobs lost in the home countries might actually have been saved had the multinational pursued different policies. In addition, the methodological basis for any such studies is debatable.

In the context of employment implications of imports, the question also arises as to the role played by exports from subsidiaries abroad, especially those from developing countries, for employment in the home countries of the respective MNEs. While the aforementioned indications for increasing intra-firm transactions for enterprises from the Federal Republic of Germany and Japan would seem to support the hypothesis of increasing displacement of home-country employment in multinationals due

Table I-9: Location of foreign manufacturing subsidiaries of synthetic fibre multinational enterprises in industrialised and developing countries (1980)

Enterprise	Total number of foreign subsidiaries*	Countries of foreign subsidiary location (percentage)		Percentage of developing country subsidiaries in	
		Industrialised	Developing	Asia	Latin America
Japan					
Asahi	13	31	69	67	22
Teijin	11	0	100	82	18
Toray	23	4	96	77	14
Mitsubishi Rayon	23	10	90	NA	NA
Europe					
Akzo	81	68	32	19	50
Courtaulds	24	79	21	0	20
ICI	190	72	28	15	33
Bayer	56	68	32	11	67
Hoechst	38	60	40	27	40
Montedison	60	64	36	9	64
United States					
Du Pont	52	56	44	30	61
Monsanto	16	62	38	17	50

* Includes subsidiaries of firms in all product lines.

Source: L.G. Franko: The threat of Japanese multinationals: How the West can respond (John Wiley and Sons, IRM, Geneva, 1983), p. 123.

to these influences, other available data and more specific calculations seem to be opposed to such a general assumption.

Thus, evidence for the United States pertaining to the degree to which American imports in sectors of notable export performance of developing countries have been "related-party transactions" between subsidiaries and American parent companies (see Annex table VI) indicates that textiles, clothing and footwear show fewer links than other sectors. As far as these industries are concerned, it would therefore be difficult to substantiate the argument that the intra-firm trade of multinational enterprises has been a major factor in the transfer of employment out of the industrialised countries involved, in particular towards developing countries. Apart from the decisive role of productivity and cost developments, to which reference has been made already on various occasions, it must be remembered in this connection that locally owned domestic firms in many developing countries, including Hong Kong and the Republic of Korea, have been very successful in exporting relatively standardised, competitively priced goods; and subcontracting arrangements by non-MNEs as well as MNEs are likewise of relative great importance, as has been shown above. Other industrial agents of change include trading companies and retail and import houses. While taking account of the observations on the question of direct "job exports" by multinationals due to their greater foreign expansion in recent decades, it is still certainly correct to say that MNEs are one particularly visible, but not the major, change agent in world-wide employment restructuring, at least as far as the industries in question are concerned.

However, adjustment problems related to certain industrial imports of textiles, clothing and footwear from developing countries, whether they involve local enterprises or MNE subsidiaries in these countries, are often important at the micro-economic (plant, enterprise, product line) level. Among the sectors most highly penetrated by such imports are clothing, footwear and leather goods which largely require assembly by hand - and they are also among the most labour-intensive manufacturing activities in the industrialised countries. Moreover, labour in this sector is usually female, relatively unskilled and immobile, and therefore difficult to transfer to other occupations;[59] and problems may be compounded where the workers directly affected are occupationally handicapped, e.g. by reason of age, sex, access to retraining, etc., or are unskilled new entrants into the labour force. In this connection, it has been observed that job losses arising from competition from developing countries often require that the workers affected should upgrade their qualifications as otherwise they cannot be absorbed in their declining industries, or elsewhere, with their existing and usually low skills. It is also clear that structural change or job losses, whatever their origin and magnitude, pose greater problems in periods of relative economic stagnation, such as the one which has prevailed over the past few years in many industrialised market economy countries, than in periods of unprecedented growth as was the case in the preceding decades. Thus, although the available global evidence

does not permit one to ascribe to MNEs the main role in structural
employment change and concomitant "job exports" through the world, even
relatively smaller production transfers in these enterprises (irrespective of the question of whether they are necessary by competitive
pressures or not) can, at the present juncture, arouse legitimate
social concern on the part of labour and governments.[60]

Notes

[1] "Textiles and clothing: Economic forces stronger than government
policies", in OECD Observer (Paris), No. 120, Jan. 1983, p. 24.

[2] ILO: The employment implications of technological choice and
changes in international trade in the leather and footwear industry,
Report II, Second Tripartite Technical Meeting for the Leather and
Footwear Industry, Geneva, 1979, pp. 5-10.

[3] GATT: International trade 1980/81 (Geneva, 1981), p. 77.

[4] It will be recalled that the Lima Declaration calls for 25 per
cent of the world industrial production to be undertaken in the Third
World by the year 2000.

[5] R. Maex: Employment and multinationals in Asian export processing zones, Multinational Enterprises Programme working paper No. 26
(Geneva, ILO, 1983), p. 68, Annex table 1.

[6] D. Morawetz: Why the emperor's new clothes are not made in
Colombia (Oxford University Press for the World Bank, 1981), p. 72; and
ILO: General report, Report I, Second Tripartite Technical Meeting for
the Clothing Industry, Geneva, 1980, p. 100.

[7] V. Cable: World textile trade and production (London, The
Economist Intelligence Unit, 1979), based on Organon World Cotton
Statistics.

[8] R. Plant: Industries in trouble (Geneva, ILO, 1981), esp.
pp. 39-54.

[9] OECD: The impact of the newly industrialising countries production and trade in manufactures (Paris, 1979), p. 42. However,
despite experiencing a continuous decline, the industry still remains
the second largest employer in most OECD countries after machinery and
equipment but often ranked together with food and drink.

[10] For the countries and years shown in Annex tables I and II,
a 19 per cent employment drop was recorded for the industrialised
countries and a 43 per cent gain for the developing countries in
question.

[11] OECD Observer, op. cit., p. 26.

[12] ILO: General report, Report I, Textiles Committee,Tenth Session, Geneva, 1978, p. 93.

[13] GATT: International trade 1980/81, op. cit., p. 76.

[14] G. Renshaw: Employment, trade and North-South co-operation (Geneva, ILO, 1981).

[15] GATT: International trade 1978/79 (Geneva, 1979), pp. 65-66. For a description of the recent slow-down in world textile and clothing trade, see idem: International trade 1982/83 (Geneva, 1983), p. 81.

[16] G. Schmid and O. Phillips: "Textile trade and the pattern of economic growth", in Weltwirtschaftliches Archiv (Review of World Economics), Vol. 116, 1980, No. 2, pp. 302-303.

[17] OECD Observer, op cit., p. 26.

[18] GATT: International trade 1980/81, op. cit., table A9.

[19] A.J. Field: Trade and textiles: An analysis of the changing international division of labour in the textile and clothing sector 1963-1978 (Quezon City (Philippines), New Day Publishers, forthcoming 1984).

[20] UNCTAD: Handbook of international trade and development statistics, Supplement 1981 (New York, United Nations, 1982), pp. 424-431. For a discussion of the concept of import penetration, see Cable: World textile trade ..., op. cit., pp. 40 and 52-53.

[21] OECD: Development co-operation, 1982 Review, table IV-2, p. 39.

[22] "A new wave of industrial exporters", in OECD Observer (Paris), No. 119, Nov. 1982, pp. 26-30.

[23] O. Harrylyshyn and I. Al Khan: "Is there cause for export optimism? An inquiry into the existence of a second generation of successful exporters" in Weltwirtschaftliches Archiv, Vol. 118, No. 4, 1982, pp. 651-663.

[24] ibid., p. 657.

[25] ILO: General report, Textiles Committee, Tenth Session, op. cit., pp. 93-94.

[26] Renshaw: Employment, trade and ..., op. cit.

[27] OECD: The impact of ..., op. cit., p. 45 (footnote).

[28] Field: Trade and Textiles: An analysis of ..., op. cit., p. 6.

[29] OECD: Textile and clothing industries: Structural problems and policies in OECD countries (Paris, 1983), pp. 57-62 and p. 94 (footnote 53). See also United Nations: Transnational corporations in the synthetic fibre, textile and clothing industries (New York, Centre on Transnational Corporations, forthcoming 1984).

[30] Previous ILO sectoral studies on more concentrated industries include, ILO: Social and labour practices of some European-based multinational enterprises in the metal trades (Geneva, 2nd impr. 1981); idem: Social and labour practices of some US-based multinationals in the metal trades (Geneva, 1977) and Social and labour practices of some multinationals in the petroleum industry (Geneva, 1977). By way of example, for cotton, 15 large traders control 85-90 per cent of the globally traded cotton (including developing, industrialised and socialist countries). UNCTAD: Fibres and textiles: Dimensions of corporate marketing structure (Geneva, 1981), p. 55.

[31] See in this context J. Stopford and J. Dunning: Multinationals: Company performance and global trends (London, Macmillan, 1983).

[32] By way of illustration it is of interest to note that a recent study of a sample of 30 clothing firms in Colombia found that three-quarters of them were family-owned and that one of the seven firms which exported over 90 per cent of their production only was owned by a foreign parent (the only one in the sample). It and another firm operated under US tariff item 807, re-exporting goods which had originated in the United States. (Morawetz: Why the emperor's ..., op. cit., pp. 58 and 105.)

[33] United Nations: Transnational corporations in the synthetic fibre, textile and clothing industries, op. cit.

[34] This account is largely based upon M. Yoshioka: "Overseas investment by the Japanese textile industry", in Developing Economies (Tokyo), Mar. 1979, No. 1, pp. 3-44.

[35] Stopford and Dunning: Multinationals: Company performance ..., op. cit., p. 54 (table 4.3).

[36] The criteria adopted by Stopford and Dunning of course exclude the vast majority of apparel and leather goods firms, as well as most of the textile firms. This and similar studies thus by definition do not include most apparel, shoe and leather goods firms which are small, including the ones which are multinationals since they are small compared with those in other branches of industry. The same applies also to a lesser extent to textile firms. See in this connection the report by the International Textile, Garment and Leather Workers' Federation (ITGLWF): The MNCs in the textile, garment and leather industries (Brussels, 1976).

[37] Maex: Employment and multinationals ..., op. cit., p. 64.

[38] ILO: General report, Report I, Tripartite Technical Meeting for the Clothing Industry, op. cit., p. 86.

[39] Stopford and Dunning: Multinationals: Company performance ..., op. cit., p. 97, table 5.6.

[40] ILO: General report, Report I, Chemical Industries Committee, Ninth Session, Geneva, 1982, p. 121. The report went on to indicate that "since 1970, one in five factories in the textile and clothing industry in the European Community has closed down ...", (p. 125, footnote 2).

[41] UNCTAD: Fibres and textiles ..., op. cit., p. 66. Also F. Clairmonte and J. Cavanagh: The world in their web: Dynamics of textile multinationals (London, Zed Press, 1981), p. 165. (Note that the latter book is essentially a revised version of the UNCTAD document.)

[42] Stopford and Dunning: Multinationals: Company performance ..., op. cit., p. 99, table 5.9.

[43] J. Dunning and R. Pearce: The world's largest industrial enterprises (Farnborough, Hampshire, Gower, 1981), p. 78, table 4.8.

[44] ILO: General report: Textile Committee ..., op. cit., p. 90, and idem: General report, Report I, Textile Committee Eleventh Session, Geneva, 1984 (forthcoming).

[45] Dunning and Pearce: The world's largest ..., op. cit., esp. tables on pp. 140-143.

[46] OECD: Multinational enterprises and the structural adjustment, IME/83/7 (Paris, OECD, 1983), p. 44.

[47] Stopford and Dunning: Multinationals: Company performance ..., op. cit., p. 65.

[48] ILO: General report, Report I, Second Tripartite Technical Meeting for the Clothing Industry, op. cit., p. 86.

[49] idem: Contract labour in the clothing industry, Report II, Second Tripartite Technical Meeting for the Clothing Industry, Geneva, 1980, pp. 10-13 and 55-57.

[50] Information for this section has been extracted from OECD: Textile and clothing industries: Structural problems and policies ..., op. cit., pp. 58-61.

[51] J. Stopford and J. Dunning: The world directory of multinational enterprises 1982-1983 (London, Macmillan, 1983).

[52] idem: Multinationals: Company performance ..., op. cit., p. 78, table 4.12.

[53] ibid., p. 67, table 4.6.

[54] F. Fröbel, J. Heinrichs, O. Kreye: The new international division of labour: Structural unemployment in industrialised countries and industrialisation in developing countries (Cambridge, Cambridge University Press, 1980), pp. 111-116.

[55] ibid., p. 116.

[56] Yoshioka: "Overseas investment ...", op. cit.

[57] Japanese Ministry of International Trade and Industry (MITI) data as cited in Yoshioka: "Overseas investment ...", op. cit., p. 41, table XXIX.

[58] R. Dore and K. Taira: Flexible rigidities: Industrial policy and structural adjustment in the Japanese economy: 1970-1980 (Geneva, ILO, 1983; mimeographed World Employment Programme research working paper; restricted).

[59] H. Werner: "Probleme der internationalen Arbeitsteilung", in Materialien aus der Arbeitsmarkt - und Berufsforschung (Erlangen), 1979, No. 9, pp. 3-7.

[60] See in this connection ILO: Employment effects of multinational enterprises in industrialised countries (Geneva, 1981), p. 76.

ANNEX TABLE I

EMPLOYMENT GAINS/LOSSES IN SELECTED INDUSTRIALISED COUNTRIES

(in thousands)

Country	Year	(a) Textiles ISIC 321	(b) Wearing apparel [*] ISIC 322	(c) Leather products [**] ISIC 323	(d) Footwear [***] ISIC 324	(a + b + c + d) Total loss ISIC 32
AUSTRIA	1973	70.05	6.66[1]			150.54
	1980	56.48	64.91[1]	5.32		126.71
	loss	-17.35 (-23%)	-5.14 (-7%)	-1.34 (-20%)		-23.83 (-16%)
BELGIUM	1973	107.8	86.6	6.2	7.2	207.8
	1980	66.5	49.8	3.2	2.9	122.4
	loss	-41.3 (-38%)	-36.8 (-42%)	-3.0 (-48%)	-4.3 (-60%)	-85.4 (-41%)
CANADA	1970	68.1	86.6	9.4	17.4	181.5
	1980	65.4	84.7	8.3	14.1	172.5
	loss	-2.7 (-4%)	-1.9 (-2%)	-1.1 (-12%)	-3.3 (-19%)	-9 (-5%)
DENMARK	1970	22.46	20.09	2.4	3.94	48.73
	1978	14.78	12.97	1.51	2.7	31.96
	loss	-7.68 (-34%)	-7.12 (-35%)	-0.73 (-33%)	-1.24 (-31%)	-16.77 (-34%)
FRANCE	1971					864
	1978					669
	loss					-195 (-23%)
GERMANY, FEDERAL REPUBLIC OF	1972					1 084
	1980					792
	loss					-292 (-27%)
GREECE	1971	46.70	10.84	3.52	5.88	66.94
	1977	64.98	27.92	3.80	7.38	104.08
	gain	+18.28 (+40%)	+17.08 (+158%)	+0.28 (+8%)	+1.5 (+26%)	+37.14 (+55%)
IRELAND	1973	21.2	17.5	2.1	4.9	45.7
	1980	17.4	13.8	1.5	3.3	36
	loss	-3.8 (-18%)	-3.7 (-21%)	-0.6 (-29%)	-1.6 (-33%)	-9.7 (-21%)
ITALY	1970	371.1	269.9[2]	27.5		668.5
	1977	276.6	246.5[2]	24.5		547.6
	loss	-94.5 (-25%)	-23.4[2] (-9%)	-3 (-11%)		-120.9 (-18%)

Annex table I (cont.)

Country	Year	(a) Textiles ISIC 321	(b) Wearing apparel* ISIC 322	(c) Leather products** ISIC 323	(d) Footwear*** ISIC 324	(a + b + c + d) Total loss ISIC 32
LUXEMBOURG	1971	0.091	0. 570			0.661[3]
	1977	0.344	0. 473			0.817[3]
	loss/ gain	+0.253 (+278%)	-0.097 (-17%)			+0.156[3] (+24%)
NETHERLANDS	1970	79	62	14[1]		155
	1979	36	23	7[1]		66
	loss	-43 (-54%)	-39 (-63%)	-7[1] (-50%)		-89 (-57%)
SWEDEN	1970	27.07	28.14	3.35	4.31	62.87
	1978	16.71	13.52	1.94	2.63	34.8
	loss	-10.36 (-38%)	-14.62 (-52%)	-1.41 (-42%)	-1.68 (-39%)	-28.07 (-45%)
SWITZERLAND	1970	59.99	61.81	3.99[1]		125.79
	1979	36.68	36.50	2.37[1]		75.55
	loss	-23.31 (-39%)	-25.31 (-41%)	-1.62 (-41%)		-50.24 (-40%)
TURKEY	1970	129.22	6.90[4]	2.58	9.88[5]	148.58
	1980	123	5	1.40	3.84[6]	133.24
	loss	-6.22 (-5%)	-1.9 (-28%)	-1.18 (-46%)	-6.04 (-61%)	-15.34 (-10%)
UNITED KINGDOM	1970	678	360	49	95	1 182
	1980	424	287	35	68	814
	loss	-254 (-37%)	-73 (-20%)	-14 (-29%)	-27 (-28%)	-368 (-31%)
UNITED STATES	1970	975	1 364	107	222	2 668
	1980	864	1 297	77	163	2 401
	loss	-111 (-11%)	-67 (-5%)	-30 (-28%)	-59 (-27%)	-267 (-10%)

ISIC = International Standard Industrial Classification of all Economic Activities.

* ISIC 322 = Manufacture of wearing apparel, except footwear.

** ISIC 323 = Manufacture of leather and products of leather, leather substitutes and fur, except footwear and wearing apparel.

*** ISIC 324 = Manufacture of footwear, except vulcanised or moulded rubber or plastic footwear.

[1] (c) + (d).

[2] (b) + (d).

[3] Total of (a) and (b) only.

[4] 1971.

[5] 1972.

[6] 1976.

Source: ILO: Year Book of Labour Statistics, various issues.

ANNEX TABLE II

EMPLOYMENT GAINS/LOSSES IN DEVELOPING AND MEDITERRANEAN BASIN COUNTRIES

(in thousands)

Country	Year	(a) Textiles ISIC 321	(b) Wearing apparel ISIC 322	(c) Leather products** ISIC 323	(d) Footwear*** ISIC 324	(a + b + c + d) Total gain/loss ISIC 32
ALGERIA	1971	29	6.8[1]			35.8
	1978	35.5	8.3[1]			43.8
	gain	+6.5 (+22%)	+1.5[1] (+22%)			+8 (+22%)
BOLIVIA	1970					7.92
	1980					27.43
	gain					+19.51 (+246%)
CAMEROON	1973	3.35	5.4	0.31[2]		9.06
	1979	5.22	7.39	1.61[2]		14.22
	gain	+1.87 (+56%)	+1.99 (+37%)	+1.3[2] (+419%)		+5.12 (+57%)
COLOMBIA	1971	63.16	28.62	5.19	7.62	104.59
	1978	77.07	46.29	8	8.66	140.02
	gain	+13.91 (+22%)	+17.67 (+62%)	+2.81 (+54%)	+1.04 (+14%)	+35.43 (+34%)
CYPRUS	1970	1.376	5.448	0.336	2.158	9.318
	1980	2.127	8.276	0.789	2.434	13.626
	gain	+0.751 (+55%)	+2.878 (+52%)	+0.453 (+135%)	+0.276 (+13%)	+4.308 (+46%)
EGYPT	1970	249	4	3	5	261
	1976	279	3	4	5	291
	gain/ loss	+30 (+12%)	-1 (-25%)	+1 (+33%)	0	+30 (+12%)
ETHIOPIA	1970	21.105	0.549[3]	0.918[3]	1.272[3]	23.844
	1978	29.958	1.207[3]	1.143[3]	1.569[3]	33.877
	gain	+8.853 (+42%)	+0.658 (+120%)	+0.225 (+25%)	+0.297 (+23%)	+10.033 (+42%)
HAITI	1971	0.99	0.724[4]	0.382	0.237[4]	2.333
	1980	2.044	5.163	1.128	0.431[5]	8.766
	gain	+1.054 (+107%)	+4.439 (+613%)	+0.746 (+195%)	+0.194 (+82%)	+6.433 (+276%)
HONG KONG	1970	127.47	110.97	0.79	3.89	243.12
	1980	127.61	263.68	3.75	6.89	401.93
	gain	+0.14 (+0.11%)	+152.71 (+138%)	+2.96 (+375%)	+3 (+77%)	+158.81 (+65%)

Annex table II (cont.)

Country	Year	(a) Textiles ISIC 321	(b) Wearing apparel ISIC 322	(c) Leather** products ISIC 323	(d) Footwear*** ISIC 324	(a + b + c + d) Total gain/loss ISIC 32
KENYA	1970	7.39	2.96	0.56	1.54	12.45
	1979	20.08	5.31	1.66	2.12	29.17
	gain	+12.69 (+172%)	+2.35 (+79%)	+1.1 (+196%)	+0.58 (+38%)	+16.72 (+134%)
KOREA, REPUBLIC OF	1971	202.7	63.1	3	5.9	274.7
	1978	427.3	204.2	31.2[6]	27	689.7
	gain	+224.6 (+111%)	+141.1 (+224%)	+28.2 (+490%)	+21.1 (+358%)	+415 (+151%)
MALAWI	1970	2.343	1.238	0.036	0.135	3.752
	1979	4.155	2.236	0.071	0.381	6.843
	gain	+1.812 (+77%)	+0.998 (+81%)	+0.035 (+97%)	+0.246 (+182%)	+3.091 (+82%)
MALTA	1970	2.78	1.42[7]	0.19		4.39
	1979	3.438	9.05[7]	1.2		13.688
	gain	+0.658 (+24%)	+7.630[7] (+537%)	+1.01 (+531%)		+9.298 (+212%)
MAURITIUS	1970	0.737	9.374	0.141[8]	0.274	1.526
	1980	2.169	16.484	0.563[8]	0.443	19.659
	gain	+1.432 (+194%)	+16.11 (+4 307%)	+0.422 (+299%)	+0.169 (+62%)	+18.133 (+1 188%)
PORTUGAL	1971	121.16	29.25[7]	4.63		155.04
	1978	135.46	50.15[7]	4.67		190.28
	gain	+14.3 (+12%)	+20.9[7] (+71%)	+0.04 (+0.8%)		+35.24 (+23%)
SIERRA LEONE	1970					0.153
	1980					0.032
	loss					-0.121 (-79%)
SINGAPORE	1970	7.05	9.99	0.71	2.00	19.75
	1979	8.72	27.38	1.21	1.59	38.9
	gain	+1.67 (+24%)	+17.39 (+174%)	+0.5 (+70%)	+0.41 (+21%)	+19.15 (+97%)
SPAIN	1970					514.9
	1979					522.3
	gain					+7.4 (+1%)

Annex table II (cont.)

Country	Year	(a) Textiles ISIC 321	(b) Wearing[*] apparel ISIC 322	(c) Leather [**] products ISIC 323	(d) [***] Footwear ISIC 324	(a + b + c + d) Total gain/loss ISIC 32
SRI LANKA	1971	51.54	5.03	0.73	2.68	59.98
	1979	64.10	6.39	1.04	3.07	74.6
	gain	+12.56 (+24%)	+1.36 (+27%)	+0.31 (+43%)	+0.39 (+15%)	+14.62 (+24%)
YUGOSLAVIA	1970	153	87[9]	20	36	296
	1980	226	121	31	64	442
	gain	+73 (+47%)	+34 (+40%)	+11 (+55%)	+28 (+77%)	+146 (+49%)

ISIC = International Standard Industrial Classification of all Economic Activities.

[*] ISIC 322 = Manufacture of wearing apparel, except footwear.

[**] ISIC 323 = Manufacture of leather and products of leather, leather substitutes and fur, except footwear and wearing apparel.

[***] ISIC 324 = Manufacture of footwear, except vulcanised or moulded rubber of plastic footwear.

[1] (b) + (c).

[2] (c) + (d).

[3] 1976.

[4] 1972.

[5] 1978.

[6] 1979.

[7] (b) + (d).

[8] (c) includes manufacture of rubber products.

[9] 1979.

Source: ILO: Year Book of Labour Statistics, various issues.

ANNEX TABLE III

INDEX NUMBERS OF PRODUCTION, EMPLOYMENT AND TRADE IN TEXTILE AND CLOTHING IN MAJOR EXPORTING AND IMPORTING COUNTRIES 1970-79

Country	Year	1970	1971[3]	1972	1973[2]	1974	1975	1976	1977	1978	1979[5]
Germany, Fed. Rep. of											
Textiles	- Production	100	...	...	109	103	100	108	106.6	105.3	109.6
	- Employment*	(100)	(31.9)	100	95.5	86.4	79.4	78.1	75.9	75.5	...
	- Exports	100	122.1	134.8	203.5	242.0	218.0	257.7	274.7	330.7	...
	- Imports[4]	100	...	150.7	...	207.2	222.4	244.1	280.9	332.1	...
Clothing	- Production	100	...	...	100	92	94	92	90.1	87.3	87.1
	- Employment*	*	*	*	*	*	*	*	*	*	...
	- Exports	100	123.0	152.6	211.6	226.8	265.6	334.6	406.6	492.7	...
	- Imports[4]	100	...	178.9	...	267.1	304.6	358.9	398.3	497.8	...
Italy											
Textiles	- Production	100	...	...	115	113	104	122	116.7	111.2	126.0
	- Employment	100	94.7	80.2	88.4	85.7	80.8	77.2	74.5	...	...
	- Exports	100	117.9	146.2	175.8	204.9	223.6	234.0	284.6	384.7	...
	- Imports[4]	100	...	118.8	...	239.1	195.9	294.7	300.1	343.6	...
Clothing	- Production	100	...	...	93	93	85	105	101.3	89.5	102.4
	- Employment	100	99.4	98.6	100.6	100.3	96.8	94.0	91.2	...	...
	- Exports	100	110.8	141.3	150.2	176.9	213.0	243.3	298.7	387.0	...
	- Imports[4]	100	...	121.3	...	219.8	187.1	237.6	297.1	290.7	...
France											
Textiles	- Production	100	...	...	113	110	99	106	104.5	101.5	103.4
	- Employment*	(100)	(100.0)	(101.4)	(99.8)	100.0	94.1	92.7	89.4	85.2	...
	- Exports	100	111.7	132.0	183.1	207.3	198.7	209.6	242.7	286.7	...
	- Imports[4]	100	...	176.1	...	309.0	328.9	394.4	420.9	505.3	...
Clothing	- Production	...	...	...	...	...	...	...	...	...	...
	- Employment*	*	*	*	*	*	*	*	...	...	...
	- Exports	100	129.7	184.1	238.7	267.1	307.0	287.5	341.5	394.9	...
	- Imports[4]	100	...	168.8	...	237.4	308.9	423.5	451.3	506.0	...
Belgium											
Textiles	- Production	100	...	...	106	101	86	96	816	83.3	83.4
	- Employment	(100)	(96.2)	(93.8)	100	96.9	87.8	83.5	75.7	67.9	...
	- Exports[1]	100	114.8	142.1	188.6	215.9	217.2	239.3	265.8	304.1	...
	- Imports[1]	100	...	154.5	...	268.9	262.9	311.8	238.2	399.7	...
Clothing	- Production	100	...	...	125	132	130	126	117.3	117.3	120.5
	- Employment	(100)	(101.8)	(107.9)	100	96.9	87.6	80.6	71.2	64.7	...
	- Exports[1]	100	124.8	142.1	204.5	215.9	217.2	239.3	266.2	278.8	...
	- Imports[1]	100	...	166.1	...	262.7	320.1	371.3	444.7	524.5	...
United Kingdom											
Textiles	- Production	100	...	...	106	96	91	94	87.1	89.7	94.0
	- Employment	100	86.9	83.4	83.0	81.7	73.9	71.6	71.5	68.7	67.0
	- Exports	100	108.8	116.8	152.2	183.4	162.4	176.0	210.3	243.3	...
	- Imports[4]	100	...	157.6	...	259.6	251.4	282.6	326.3	434.0	...

Annex table III (cont.)

Country	Year	1970	1971[3]	1972	1973[2]	1974	1975	1976	1977	1978	1979[5]
Clothing	- Production	100	...	...	117	112	115	114	116.9	120.9	122.0
	- Employment	100	90.0	89.8	88.0	84.8	81.3	76.5	78.0	76.0	76.3
	- Exports	100	106.9	121.9	148.9	182.3	199.2	250.4	353.4	434.7	...
	- Imports[4]	100	...	172.2	...	291.3	348.3	408.1	432.1	543.6	...
Austria											
Textiles	- Production	100	108	114	121	116	101	108	109	105	110
	- Employment[*,6]	(100)*	(100.7)*	(99.7)*	100	94.7	83.8	81.5	80.3	75.2	76.3
	- Exports	100	...	148.4	...	242.4	225.3	251.9	292.4	353.1	...
	- Imports	100	...	141.6	...	231.3	227.9	260.0	292.9	330.9	...
Clothing	- Production	100	105	115	129	131	126	127	127	121	131
	- Employment	*	*	*	100	107.6	102.5	99.8	100.8	95.0	92.8
	- Exports	100	...	138.8	...	211.3	234.1	268.9	324.8	430.4	...
	- Imports	100	...	177.1	...	348.8	426.7	542.7	669.5	795.5	...
Switzerland											
Textiles	- Production	100	101	110	112	109	91	104	105	105	113
	- Employment	100	95.7	90.4	84.7	80.1	68.7	68.6	66.8	63.8	...
	- Exports	100	...	135.9	181.4	210.4	204.9	237.0	268.9	341.5	...
	- Imports[4]	100	...	126.9	...	206.9	177.1	207.3	237.3	268.9	
Clothing	- Production	100	101	101	98	92	87	106	107	103	102
	- Employment	100	95.6	91.7	84.8	77.5	66.6	65.4	64.1	61.8	...
	- Exports	100	...	120.6	148.5	178.4	201.4	226.4	266.3	358.9	...
	- Imports[4]	100	...	147.2	...	221.0	225.2	261.8	301.6	386.2	...
Netherlands											
Textiles	- Production	100	...	...	96	93	78	78	72.1	69.9	68.1
	- Employment	100	93.7	84.8	77.2	73.4	67.1	60.8	55.7	...	...
	- Exports	100	121.1	138.4	184.9	218.4	206.6	221.9	229.0	266.4	...
	- Imports[4]	100	...	130.9	...	204.5	192.9	212.8	228.4	263.0	...
Clothing	- Production	100	...	...	86	76	69	61	53.1	51.7	54.3
	- Employment	100	91.9	85.5	75.8	64.5	53.2	46.8	41.9	...	...
	- Exports	100	116.0	149.1	197.4	227.5	251.7	256.3	254.9	297.5	...
	- Imports[4]	100	...	158.1	...	236.9	271.3	321.6	364.6	428.8	...
United States[a]											
Textiles	- Production	100	104	119	128	119	109	120	120	123	127
	- Employment	100	97.9	101.9	103.5	98.9	89.0	94.2	93.3	92.3	91.5
	- Exports	100	104.7	129.1	202.2	207.6	269.3	326.7	324.3	373.0	...
	- Imports	100	...	123.3	...	127.0	90.7	125.8	141.2	139.1	...
Clothing	- Production[b]	100	103	108	116	113	106	124	132	132	130
	- Employment	100	98.4	101.3	105.4	99.9	91.1	96.6	96.5	97.7	96.2
	- Exports	100	95.1	109.9	127.8	184.1	185.7	247.3	295.4	330.5	...
	- Imports	100	...	133.1	...	150.6	169.6	249.8	292.4	336.3	...
Hong Kong											
Textiles	- Production[d]	...	...	...	100	95	105	126	110	111	105[c]
	- Employment	100	99.2	94.9	94.4	91.9	105.5	107.7	97.3	96.5	99.4
	- Exports	100	...	131.9	...	255.2	205.2	296.5	268.5	289.8	...
	- Imports	100	...	124.0	...	155.2	159.9	209.4	221.0	254.9	...

Annex table III (cont.)

Country	Year	1970	1971[3]	1972	1973[2]	1974	1975	1976	1977	1978	1979
Clothing	- Production	...	...	...	...	...	...	...	...	...	...
	- Employment	100	118.4	129.0	133.9	152.8	195.9	220.4	207.1	222.6	226.6
	- Exports	100	129.6	153.6	205.7	238.7	288.3	412.6	423.1	481.4	...
	- Imports	100	...	141.7	...	171.5	153.0	221.9	293.9	387.5	...
Korea, Republic of											
Textiles	- Production[a]	100	121	161	201	208	263	345	373	428	478
	- Employment	100	97.8	109.3	135.4	138.3	155.3	...	...	...	...
	- Exports	100	162.5	207.8	518.2	579.8	764.0	1 123.6	1 273.7	1 805.8	...
	- Imports	100	...	93.6	...	175.9	162.2	202.9	219.8	244.9	...
Clothing	- Production[a]	100	142	210	389	510	654	926	1 031	1 284	1 342
	- Employment	100	120.4	151.3	178.0	232.6	290.2	...	...	...	...
	- Exports	100	142.3	207.0	351.1	447.8	537.3	863.8	965.0	1 205.2	...
	- Imports	100	...	705.2	...	315.7	163.1	357.8	405.1	704.2	...
Japan											
Textiles	- Production	100	101	105	111	97	93	100	97	99	97[c]
	- Employment	100	95.8	94.6	93.4	80.5	81.0	...	...	...	...
	- Exports	100	118.1	125.3	140.4	176.2	167.5	189.2	212.7	219.6	...
	- Imports	100	...	174.9	...	425.8	364.2	440.0	401.0	625.4	...
Clothing	- Production	...	...	...	100	89	83	88	88	89	88[c]
	- Employment	100	102.2	112.1	120.3	136.2	128.3	...	...	...	...
	- Exports	100	101.2	92.8	80.0	70.9	71.8	89.8	100.0	105.0	...
	- Imports	100	...	152.6	...	569.8	415.2	637.7	702.9	995.9	...
Tunisia											
Textiles	- Production	...	...	...	...	...	...	...	...	...	...
	- Employment	100	97.2	102.7	109.5	...	...	...	...	...	...
	- Exports	100	...	303.4	...	655.1	668.9	813.7	1 041.3	1024.1	...
	- Imports	100	...	155.3	...	310.2	332.8	500.0	608.0	717.9	...
Clothing	- Production	...	...	...	...	...	...	...	...	...	...
	- Employment	100	62.1	97.2	128.6	...	...	...	...	...	...
	- Exports	100	...	170	...	2 760.0	4 490.0	7 180.0	14 190.0	20 170.0	...
	- Imports	100	...	218.1	...	990.9	1 890.9	3 136.3	4 009.1	5 663.6	...
Philippines											
Textiles	- Production	100	125	118	136	123	127	126	...	...	...
	- Employment	100	116.1	98.3	137.0	140.2	...	...	...	...	...
	- Exports	100	...	168.5	...	372.2	416.6	535.1	624.0	809.2	...
	- Imports	100	...	97.4	...	180.5	164.4	209.6	239.6	278.8	...
Clothing	- Production	100	113	115	128	135	151	188	...	...	...
	- Employment	100	110.8	110.4	175.9	181.4	...	...	...	...	...
	- Exports	100	...	575.0	...	5 925.0	8 275.0	20 000.0	28 425.0	40 025.0	
	- Imports	100	...	50.9	...	66.6	74.5	113.7	164.4	...	...
Brazil											
Textiles	- Production[e]	(100)	(112)	(117)	(126)	(123)	100	106	107	113	...
	- Employment	100	106.2	104.5	109.0	120.0	114.7	...	...	...	...
	- Exports	100	...	342.8	...	956.8	841.9	873.2	1 188.8	1 304.3	...
	- Imports	100	...	161.2	...	495.4	275.8	255.0	282.2	...	...

Annex table III (cont.)

Country	Year	1970	1971[3]	1972	1973[2]	1974	1975	1976	1977	1978	1979
Clothing	- Production[f]	...	...	...	...	...	100	108	103	111	...
	- Employment[f]	100	97.8	113.4	144.4	160.6	169.1	...	...	...	...
	- Exports	100	...	1 016.6	...	4 110.0	3 393.3	3 313.3	3 363.3	4 243.3	...
	- Imports	100	...	100	...	97.5	87.6	81.4	87.5	...	...
Greece											
Textiles	- Production	...	...	...	...	...	...	...	...	...	...
	- Employment	100	106.5	113.2	122.8	131.0	138.3	150.2	...	...	...
	- Exports	100	...	213.2	...	501.3	470.7	655.5	766.9	889.4	...
	- Imports	100	...	130.2	...	201.9	259.0	302.0	369.6	443.2	...
Clothing	- Production	...	...	...	...	...	...	...	...	...	...
	- Employment	100	110.7	122.3	144.2	221.2	236.2	269.3	...	...	...
	- Exports	100	...	216.1	...	891.9	1 251.5	2 016.1	2 191.9	2 588.8	...
	- Imports	100	...	141.1	...	419.6	458.8	600.0	731.3	1 045.1	...
Romania											
Textiles	- Production	100	114	128	147	170	177	206	229	...	...
	- Employment	100	111.9	123.5	134.2	142.9	142.4	150.8	154.7	157.9	...
	- Exports	...	100	146.4	207.1	178.5	214.2		...	...	...
	- Imports	...	...	...	...	...	...	...	...	...	
Clothing	- Production	100	115	136	161	197	220	245	264	...	...
	- Employment	100	100.2	121.2	133.6	143.7	151.1	157.4	160.3	160.8	...
	- Exports	...	100	132.6	175.6	187.5	201.3		...	...	...
	- Imports	...	...	...	...	...	...	...	...	...	
Mexico											
Textiles	- Production	100*	107*	116*	128*	131*	138*	161*	164*	...	...
	- Employment	(100)*	(97.9)*	(101.6)*	(102.8)*	100*	100.9*	103.0*	99.3*	98.5*	102*
	- Exports	100	...	218.9	...	731.0	731.0	458.7	423.3	...	...
	- Imports	100	...	127.9	...	222.8	229.6	225.8	229.4	...	...
Clothing	- Production	(*)	(*)	(*)	(*)	(*)	(*)	(*)	(*)	...	...
	- Employment	(*)	(*)	(*)	(*)	(*)	(*)	(*)	(*)	(*)	(*)
	- Exports	100	...	209.8	...	461.5	461.5	364.8	335.1	...	...
	- Imports	100	...	173.3	...	294.0	325.1	358.3	339.5	379.9	...
Norway											
Textiles	- Production	100	97	95	95	93	87	88	90	...	...
	- Employment	...	...	100	77.8	83.8	105.6	83.3	88.9	94.4	...
	- Exports	100	...	134.1	...	208.2	211.1	222.5	235.9	242.7	...
	- Imports	100	...	127.2	...	193.1	192.7	212.0	244.3	244.3	...
Clothing	- Production	100	96	90	85	87	79	71	70	...	...
	- Employment	...	...	100	100	100	75.0	106.3	87.5	56.2	...
	- Exports	100	...	120.1	...	181.7	187.1	217.6	246.3	269.5	...
	- Imports	100	...	140.7	...	200.5	255.3	307.0	382.6	387.1	...
Morocco											
Textiles	- Produciton	...	...	...	...	...	...	...	...	...	...
	- Employment	...	...	...	...	...	...	...	...	...	...
	- Exports	100	...	207.9	...	...	456.3	530.6	636.5	846.8	...
	- Imports	100	...	123.5	...	212.5	222.9	294.0	327.1	367.1	...

Annex table III (cont.)

Country	Year	1970	1971[3]	1972	1973[2]	1974	1975	1976	1977	1978	1979
Clothing - Production		...	...	...	...	...	...	...	...	...	...
- Employment		...	...	...	...	...	...	...	...	...	...
- Exports		100	...	254.0	...	...	870.0	1 164.0	1 162.0	1 316.0	...
- Imports		100	...	100	...	125.8	161.2	364.5	396.2	...	...
Colombia											
Textiles - Production		100	111	126	145	133	125	138	...	...	...
- Employment		...	100	111.0	129.3	124.5	125.9	125.5	130.5	...	...
- Exports		100	...	248.8	...	710.2	525.9	719.6	658.2	...	...
- Imports		100	...	124.2	...	515.1	280.3	316.6	450.5	...	...
Clothing - Production[f]		100	100	126	137	116	123	120	...	...	...
- Employment		...	100	117.1	133.8	142.8	140.3	164.9	159.8	...	...
- Exports		100	...	536.3	...	4 763.6	2 645.4	3 609.0	4 527.2	...	...
- Imports		100	...	108.0	...	336.0	384.0	292.0	362.9	...	...
Malaysia											
Textiles - Production[e]		(100)	(107)	(136)	(172)	(123)	(187)	(265)	(275)	...	...
- Employment		100	124.0	188.4	258.1	274.9	...	...	...	...	...
- Exports		100	...	262.2	...	536.0	555.7	849.1	963.9	...	...
- Imports		100	...	113.1	...	328.9	270.1	842.1	925.4	...	...
Clothing - Production		...	...	...	...	...	...	...	...	...	...
- Employment		100	138.1	211.0	238.3	253.5	...	...	...	...	...
- Exports		100	...	200.0	...	545.2	796.2	1 073.5	1 120.7	...	...
- Imports		100	...	52.0	...	156.0	152.0	378.0	332.6	...	...

* Data cover textile and clothing and leather industries. When indexes on employment are between ( ), it means that the series has changed, with a different coverage.

[1] Data concern Belgium and Luxembourg.

[2] Exports for 1973: GATT International Trade 1975-76 (Geneva, 1976), p. 66.

[3] Exports for 1971: GATT International Trade 1973-74 (Geneva, 1974), p. 52.

[4] Imports between ( ): Source: GATT International Trade; (Imports CIF) basis 1970 = 100: Source: GATT International Trade 1971 (Geneva, 1972), pp. 70-71; years 1971-76: Source: GATT International Trade 1973-74 (Geneva, 1974), p. 53; year 1973: Source: GATT International Trade 1975-76 (Geneva, 1976), p. 66; years 1974-76: Source: GATT International Trade 1976-77 (Geneva, 1977), p. 66.

[5] With exception of the European Community, production data for 1979 cover only the first six months.

[6] Austria. Employment - new series in 1973. Before 1973 data cover textiles and clothing.

[a] Quarterly data seasonally adjusted.

[b] Includes made-up textiles.

[c] Three months.

[d] Textile spinning and weaving.

[e] Data between ( ) cover textile and clothing.

[f] Including shoes.

Sources of data: Employment: ILO Year Book of Labour Statistics 1977, pp. 365-436 + indices calculated on the basis of unpublished data provided by the Statistical Department of the ILO. Exports and imports: ICC data. Production: Calculated from "Textiles and clothing: Production, employment and trade statistics, 1973-79", GATT (Com Tex/W/63, Oct. 1979) and GATT (Com Tex/W/63 RW, 1 Dec. 1979); for the European Community: various issues of "Monthly Industrial Short Term Trends" (EUROSTAT).

Source: A.J. Field: Trade and textiles: An analysis of the changing international division of labour in the textile and clothing sector 1963-78 (Quezon City (Philippines), New Day Publishers, forthcoming 1984), table 13.

ANNEX TABLE IV

WESTERN EUROPE: SELECTED EMPLOYMENT-RELATED RATIONALISATION AND RESTRUCTURING MEASURES IN THE PETROCHEMICAL INDUSTRY WITH SPECIAL REFERENCE TO SYNTHETIC FIBRES

1977 - Hoechst reduced its total labour force by 25 per cent in the 1976-77 period and shut down a polyester filament plant in Berlin employing some 700 people.

- ICI closed down several polyester filament plants as part of a cost-cutting exercise that will reduce its total fibres labour force by 30 per cent.

- Akzo's Enka subsidiary closed a number of units in the Federal Republic of Germany and in Holland and abandoned its interest in acrylic fibre production.

- United States-based Monsanto closed its nylon plant in the Federal Republic of Germany and reduced by 25 per cent its labour force at another unit in Luxembourg.

- Montefibre, the fibres arm of Montedison, announced a cut-back of 6,000 jobs.

- United States-based Du Pont (the world's largest fibre producer) closed an acrylic plant in Holland.

1977/ - Akzo phased out 14,000 jobs in the EEC in the three-year
78/79   (1977-79) period.

1979 - The United States-based Monsanto group closed down its nylon operations in Europe which resulted in a loss of 2,300 jobs.

- ICI cuts in firbres production alone resulted in a reduction of 2,800 in its British workforce.

1980 - Akzo's planned wide-scale capacity reductions throughout Western Europe caused the loss of more than 4,000 jobs. This was in addition to the 14,000 jobs already lost as mentioned above.

1980/ - ICI was reported to have reduced its workforce in 1980 by
81   5,000 and to be planning an additional 5,000 reduction in 1981, mostly in the fibres and plastics divisions.

- BP closed 12 petrochemical plants in the 12-month period November 1980-November 1981.

Annex table IV (cont.)

1981   - Courtaulds withdrew altogether from nylon fibre production
        and closed United Kingdom-based plants (located in areas of
        exceptionally high unemployment) with the loss of over
        1,900 jobs.   This brought the total number of jobs shed by
        the company over the preceding two years to some 27,000.

      - Bayer announced the withdrawal from production in 1981 of
        those chemical fibres areas in which no improvement in sales
        could be expected; 700 employees in one fibre plant were to
        be transferred to other production areas.

      - Cuts in artificial-fibres activities by Rhône-Poulenc by the
        end of 1981 were expected to involve the reduction of its
        1980 workforce in France by half, to 4,000.   In 1978,
        13,000 workers were employed by this company.

Source: ILO: General report, Report I, Chemical Industries Committee,
        Ninth Session, Geneva, 1982, pp. 121-122.

ANNEX TABLE V

CHANGES IN DEGREE OF MULTINATIONALITY OF PRODUCTION
OF SAMPLE TEXTILE, APPAREL AND LEATHER GOODS FIRMS

	Number of multinational enterprises		
	Higher	Same	Lower
1972/77[*]	12	2	2
1977/82[**]	5	2	2

[*] Firms were asked whether the sales of their overseas affiliates (excluding finished goods from parent for resale) were higher, the same, or lower as a proportion of the total group sales in the year of reporting (usually 1977) than they had been five years previously.

[**] Firms were asked whether they expected the sales of their overseas affiliates (excluding finished goods from parent for resale) to be higher, same or lower as a proportion of the total group sales five years after the year of reporting (usually 1977) than in that year.

Note: The firms were selected from the Fortune list and surveyed by the authors.

Source: Adapted from J. Dunning and R. Pearce: The world's largest industrial enterprises (Farnborough, Hampshire, Gower, 1981), taken from table 6.25, p. 143 and table 6.21, p. 140.

ANNEX TABLE VI

US RELATED-PARTY IMPORTS AS A PERCENTAGE OF TOTAL IMPORTS OF SELECTED MANUFACTURED PRODUCTS, FROM SELECTED "NEWLY INDUSTRIALISING" DEVELOPING COUNTRIES, 1977

Country	Textiles 65*	Non-electric machinery 71*	Electric machinery 72*	Clothing 84*	Footwear 85*	Scientific instruments 86*	Total mfg.	Total mfg. import value ($ million)
Argentina	0.5	39.1	76.1	2.9	0.8	10.0	9.2	167
Brazil	9.2	59.9	95.3	18.0	0.5	38.4	38.4	755
Colombia	1.5	16.8	3.9	15.7	81.2	87.8	14.1	60
Mexico	9.6	87.8	95.6	68.0	60.9	93.6	71.0	1 798
Hong Kong	4.9	68.5	43.4	3.4	3.6	30.4	18.1	2 618
India	6.1	30.5	58.7	15.8	6.1	16.7	10.1	180
Korea, Rep. of	5.5	64.2	67.3	7.1	1.8	12.1	19.7	2 328
Malaysia	0.2	83.2	97.0	1.9	0.0	91.9	87.9	385
Philippines	28.9	69.7	31.7	53.4	0.0	27.0	47.5	352
Singapore	4.3	90.5	97.0	0.5	0.0	85.3	83.3	630
Haiti	2.9	33.7	36.5	24.8	77.2	97.9	28.4	101

* Standard International Trade Classification (SITC).

Source: G.K. Helleiner and R. Lavergne: "Intra-firm trade and industrial exports to the United States", in Oxford Bulletin of Statistics, Nov. 1979, p. 307, reproduced in ILO: Employment effects of multi-national enterprises in industrialised countries (Geneva, 1981), p. 75.

CHAPTER II

EMPLOYMENT AND MANPOWER POLICIES

The effect of internationalisation of production on employment

The replies received from the respondents to the questionnaire addressed to the tripartite constituents of the ILO (see Appendix III) confirm the general terms noted in the introductory chapter but add a number of interesting details.   They also indicate that employment problems in the sector are not exclusively found in the industrialised countries.

Nine governments responded to the question concerning the effects of internationalisation.   Three, Colombia, Hong Kong and Spain, found that internationalisation has no influence on employment in the three industries of the sector.   Malaysia, Nigeria and the United Kingdom reported that internationalisation of production has negatively affected employment but that they could not measure exactly the number of jobs lost.   Two other countries, India and Sri Lanka, reported that the phenomena has not been studied or was not substantially measurable. One country, the Federal Republic of Germany, pointed out both negative and positive effects of the internationalisation of production.

It was mentioned by Hong Kong that no significant effects of the internationalisation of production in the sector on the employment market could be detected, as the number of persons employed in the textile, clothing and footwear factories known to have overseas interests is only around 26,000 (as of June 1981), which was about 3 per cent of the total number of persons engaged in manufacturing industries (around 890,000 according to March 1981 statistics).   For the Government of Spain the degree of foreign investment in the sector in question is very small and it is therefore said to have no influence on the employment market.

The Government of Colombia felt that the impact of the internationalisation of production in the textile industry is not statistically measurable.   Moreover, as most of the textile enterprises in the country are national enterprises, repercussions of internationalisation were less felt in Colombia than in other countries.

In Malaysia the Government indicated that the country is facing a shortage of female labour.   Retrenchment of workers, if any, as a result of the decline in the international market would not have a significant impact since these workers would secure alternative employment opportunities.

The Nigerian Government felt that the general slump in trade especially in regard to the clothing industry is aggravating the unemployment problem in Nigeria as many workers in the clothing industry are being declared redundant.

In the opinion of the United Kingdom Government, trade in textiles and clothing is truly international with much of the production of basic items being dominated by low-cost suppliers from the Fat East who themselves invest very little in the United Kingdom.   The situation is different for man-made fibres where production tends to be con-centrated in the hands of large-scale multinational chemical-type companies.   The bulk of production in the United Kingdom is con-centrated in five companies, one of which is a subsidiary of a large American multinational and two of which are subsidiaries of large European companies.   The employment in the United Kingdom has suffered because of the increasing competitive strength of the low-cost countries, but it is not possible to assess by how much this is attri-butable to the transfer of resources away from high-cost to low-cost producers.

The Government of India noted that the effect of the inter-nationalisation of production on employment in the sectors concerned cannot be studied in isolation.   Any adverse effects have been offset by the national policies followed to increase employment, particularly in the small-scale sector.   The entire question has to be viewed in the context of the economic goals set by the developing countries. Protectionist measures followed by industrialised countries were bound to adversely affect the export market of developing countries and hence employment.

The Government of the Federal Republic of Germany saw the main reason for the decrease in employment observable in the textile and clothing industries since 1970, in rationalisation measures which became unavoidable as a consequence of the pressure which imports exercise on the local market.   It felt that in the light of competitive advantages, especially of the so-called low-wage countries, inter-nationalisation of production is often the only possibility for multi-national and other enterprises in industrialised countries to stay competitive at the international level.   The Government added, however, that the internationalisation of production contributes to saving jobs in the Federal Republic of Germany.   In particular, more and more producers, especially in the shoe industry, subcontract high-cost work to low-wage countries to remain competitive in the home market.

Employment trends in participating enterprises

The replies of participating enterprises provide further details regarding the developments in the individual multinationals (a description of the participating enterprises can be found in Appendix I). All enterprises reporting except Mölnlycke AB (Sweden) noted a decline of the home workforce, together with an increase of employees abroad. Each tied this phenomenon either directly or indirectly to the changing economic conditions, especially the need to maintain a competitive position.

Asahi Chemical Industry Co. Ltd. (Japan) reports that the work-force of its parent company has been reduced from 18,200 in 1975 to 16,300 in 1976, 15,100 in 1977 and 13,800 in 1978. The number of employees in foreign affiliates (joint ventures) amounted in 1980 to 4,908 plus 45 detached from headquarters.

Out of 45 expatriates referred to in the table II-1 about 40 persons from Asahi headquarters were stationed in 1980, as directors, plant managers, and technical advisers. In the 1970s, the period of establishment and initial operations of overseas joint ventures, more than 100 such persons were stationed abroad. Most of these have been gradually replaced by local citizens as a result of Asahi's programme for employee training and education and their basic policy of encouraging local employees to positions of skill and authority.

Dollfus-Mieg & Cie. (DMC), France, related the drop in the total workforce which is distributed mainly between the Latin American Branch, the thread making branch and the Texunion Branch, in recent years to the oil crisis and overall crises in the textile industry. Employment in France was reduced due to internal restructuring in order to regain a satisfactory competitive position. The workforce of the French enterprises of the group which amounted to 74 per cent of the total workforce in 1977, dropped to 62 per cent in 1979. Between 1979 and 1980, the workforce in France was again reduced by 1,600 employees. Generally, one can observe a drop in the workforce in France and simultaneous increase in the workforce abroad. The DMC group's policy of expansion abroad (Latin America, North and Central Africa, Spain, Portugal and Lebanon) was initiated as far back as 1961. In 1969, the group made significant investments in the Federal Republic of Germany. Accordingly, from 1977 to 1979, the share of the foreign workforce grew from 26 per cent to 38 per cent of the global workforce of the DMC group.

The employment evolution of Enka A.G. (Federal Republic of Germany) - for whom Akzo NV (Netherlands) is the major shareholder - reflects, in the view of the management, the economic development of the whole textile branch and synthetic fibre branch in specific countries. Thus, in middle and northern Europe the decline of synthetic fibre production and employment levels were attributed to increasing imports of finished textile goods. The opposite evolution was noted for south-west Europe and overseas locations of Enka subsidiaries.

Confronted by massive losses, Enka has suppressed more than 14,000 jobs since 1975. After these adjustments the total workforce of the Enka group in Europe was distributed in 1980 as shown in table II-3 below.

Table II-1: Number of Asahi Chemical Industry Co. personnel in host countries (1980)

Company name	Country	Number of employees	
		Total local employment	Detached from head-quarters
P.T. Indonesia Asahi Chemical Industry (INDACI)	Indonesia	910	14
Industrial Acrilicas de Centro America S.A. (ACRICASA)	Guatemala	323	3
Tong Yang Polyester Co. Ltd.	Korea, Rep. of	1,680	3
Paragon Textile Industry Ltd.	Sri Lanka	n.a.	0
The Baroda Rayon Co. Ltd.	India	n.a.	0
Asahi Synthetic Fibres (Ireland) Ltd. (ASF)	Ireland	313	14
Asahi Spinning Ireland Ltd. (ASP)	Ireland	201	2
Asahi Chemical Industry Ireland Ltd. (ACI)	Ireland	n.a.	0
Alliance Spinners Ltd. (ASL)	Mauritius	n.a.	0
Tong Suh Petrochemical Corporation Ltd.	Korea, Rep. of	252	2
Quimica Sol S.A.	Peru	84	3
Other	-	1,145	4
Total		4,908	45

Source: Data supplied by Asahi.

Table II-2: Evolution of employment in the DMC group operations

	World-wide	France	Other countries
1975	25 650	19 450	6 200
1976	22 681	19 111	3 570
1977	21 375	15 849	5 526
1978	20 744	15 034	5 745
1979	22 269	13 929	8 340
1980	20 955	12 313	8 642

Source: Data supplied by DMC.

Table II-3: Enka workforce in Europe 1980

		Per cent
Germany, Federal Republic of	17 180	50
Netherlands	8 930	26
United Kingdom	2 330	7
Spain	4 000	12
Other countries	1 630	5
Total	34 070	100

Source: Data supplied by Enka.

The recovery strategy of Enka aims at a further reduction of around 4,000 jobs from its 30,000 strong workforce in the Federal Republic of Germany, the Netherlands and the United Kingdom between 1981 and 1983. In Antrim, Northern Ireland, the workforce of 2,000 at the beginning of 1981 had already been cut to 800 by September of the same year. In Breda, the Netherlands, 600 jobs had been cut by the end of 1982 with the closure of polyester filament and texturising activities. In the Federal Republic of Germany, 236 jobs had been cut at the group's Wuppertal headquarters during 1982-83 and a further reduction of 100 jobs is planned from administrative and research staff in Obernburg. At the same location, a further 200 manufacturing jobs are to disappear due to the concentration of carpet yarn production.

In 1982, Enka was also planning the gradual closure of steel rod production at Oberbruch (Federal Republic of Germany) with 600 jobs being eliminated, but no time-scale had yet been agreed there.

Enka also plans the closure of the Kassel works (Federal Republic of Germany) and its polyester and polyamide production. In the early 1970s the workforce totalled some 2,200 in Kassel, by January 1981 the remaining jobs were 820. Heavy workforce cuts were effectuated there in 1981-82 and 1983.

Table II-4: Evolution of employment in Enka (Europe)

1977	36 400
1978	35 300
1979	34 700
1980	34 070

Source: Data supplied by Enka.

Kanebo Ltd. (Japan) reported a reduction of 64 per cent in the parent company workforce: between 1975 and 1979 the number dropped from 15,200 to 5,522 employees.

In 1979, the number of employees in the domestic subsidiaries amounted to 23,375 which, together with the employment in the parent company gave a figure of 28,897 employees in Japan. In the main joint ventures abroad (in particular, Brazil, Indonesia, Australia, Malaysia and Hong Kong) employment amounted to 7,968.

Table II-5: Evolution of employment in Kanebo (parent company)

1975	15 200
1976	13 900
1977	6 800
1978	5 500
1979	5 522

Source: Data supplied by Kanebo.

In 1980, about 60 persons dispatched from the Kanebo headquarters were working for the 12 overseas companies as presidents, plant managers, technical advisers, etc. In the 1970s the maximum number of these officers and technicians had amounted to nearly 100, but the number had gradually decreased as positions for technicians responsible

for production have increasingly been occupied by local personnel.
This tendency of replacing headquarters' technicians by local and other
personnel would continue in future, Kanebo stated.

Although Mitsubishi Rayon Co. Ltd. (Japan) also reported a
reduction in the workforce of the parent company of 60 per cent from
1975 to 1980, according to the company's projections employees will
remain at the level of 3,500 to 3,600 in the near future.

Table II-6: Evolution of employment in Mitsubishi Rayon
              (parent company)

1975	8,828
1976	5,486
1977	4,867
1978	4,373
1979	3,464
1980	3,561

Source: Data supplied by Mitsubishi Rayon.

Broken down according to sex the employment distribution was as
follows:

Table II-7: Employment by sex in Mitsubishi Rayon

Year (end March)	Male	Female
1975	6 526	2 302
1976	4 642	844
1977	4 139	728
1978	3 774	599
1979	2 926	538
1980	2 973	588

FISIBA (Mitsubishi's subsidiary in Brazil) has no employees dispatched
from the parent while FISIPE (Mitsubishi's subsidiary in Portugal) has
two employees dispatched from the parent. Their total employment is
513 with no increase of employment being foreseen in the near future.

Mölnlycke AB (Sweden), acquired by the Svenska Cellulosa Aktiebolaget (SCA) Group in 1975 is an exception among the participating MNEs. Its home workforce did not undergo any decline in the reporting period.

Table II-8: Employment evolution in Mölnlycke AB

	Sweden	Abroad	Total
1977	3 202	3 799	7 001
1978	3 221	3 520	6 741
1979	3 081	3 647	6 728
1980	3 430	3 747	7 177
1981	3 483	3 779	7 262

Source: Data supplied by Mölnlycke AB.

In 1981 the total workforce of Mölnlycke's textile sector (sewing thread division and Melka-Tension division) was 1,953 employees, 1,553 of which were employed outside Sweden.

The reduction of the number of workers employed by Rhône-Poulenc Textile (RPT), France - one of the three operating groups of Rhone-Poulenc with world-wide responsibilities - was attributed to the crisis in the chemical and textile industry (21,000 workers in 1971 and 13,400 by 1977). Realising the prolonged nature of that crisis the company decided to rationalise further and to limit its activities to the production of only three products, namely, nylon, polyester and acryl, and to construct for this purpose highly automated plants capable of competing internationally. As a consequence of these rationalisation measures, five plants were shut down in France between 1977 and 1981, and by the end of 1982 only eight of the initial 17 plants which existed in 1977 had survived. This had, of course, considerable effect on employment. The number of workers was reduced to 12,070 in 1978, 10,410 in 1979, 8,520 in 1980 and 7,230 in 1981 (August) with the final objective of reducing to some 3,900 by 1984 which would represent 29 per cent of the workforce in 1977.

Viscosuisse AG (a subsidiary of Rhône-Poulenc located in Switzerland) indicates that employment had dropped from 5,500 in 1973 to 3,600 by 1981. Included in this figure are 270 workers at "Viscosuisse Textured Yarns Ltd." in Cardiff (United Kingdom). This subsidiary was acquired in 1972 and employed 460 people at the time.

Table II-9: Evolution of employment in Rhône-Poulenc Textile (RPT) operations in France

1977	13 400
1978	12 070
1979	10 410
1980	8 520
1981	7 230
1984 (objective)	3 900

Source: Data supplied by RPT.

The takeover of this firm in England and of Hetex Garn SA ("Helanca") in Switzerland were motivated by changing market conditions and technological developments. In the meantime, rayon production in Steckborn had gradually been discontinued. The recession also led to a decrease in production between 1973 and 1978 which was accompanied by a reduction in personnel. However, the enterprise itself feels that it has weathered the crisis better than some of its competitors, and in 1980 the industrial yarn factory in Switzerland (Emmenbrücke) could be expanded and new equipment installed for nylon and polyester. In 1980 some 53,500 tons were produced. Of the 3,330 employees in Switzerland, 823 were women.

Table II-10: Evolution of employment in Viscosuisse

1973	5 500
1977	4 100
1978	3 900
1979	3 803
1980	3 635
1981	3 600

Source: Data supplied by Viscosuisse.

Motives for investing abroad

When planning investment abroad, the headquarters of the enterprises which responded to this study indicated that the decisive factors were as follows:

For Kanebo the decision-making for overseas investment was based upon an overall assessment of the following factors: (1) political situation; (2) economic considerations including growth potential of the markets; and (3) social circumstances. Both Asahi and Sam Hwa Ltd. Republic of Korea indicated a similar order of priorities for investment decisions. Mitsubishi Rayon noted that it considers all the relevant political, economic and social factors together when planning investment abroad. Enka stated that its investment decisions were primarily subject to economic considerations. However, at the implementation stage of projects the specific social and political conditions of a country are also taken into account.

The International Textile, Garment and Leather Workers' Federation (ITGLWF) felt that in the labour-intensive industries of the sector wage cost differentials were a prime motive for multinationals for investing or expanding operations abroad. For example, it had been calculated by the ITGLWF that wages in Indonesia (a host country) were only a fraction of those paid by a major footwear multinational in its North American home base.

It should also be seen from the annual report (1982) of Mölnylcke that the workers in its Portuguese subsidiaries were paid a fifth of the workers in the home country, Sweden. The importance of wage cost for the location of multinationals' production was highlighted in recent research.[2]

Competitive position of participating MNEs

Asahi noted that its joint ventures in southern Asia are highly competitive. This is not the same for its European subsidiaries, for which an unfavourable balance in supply and demand was reported, resulting in a difficult market condition for the enterprise. All Kanebo's overseas operations are said to face severe competition, but there are some which have acquired the top position in the host country and have become the price leader in the industry. Acrylic fibre manufactured by Mitsubishi Rayon is reported to be internationally competitive and is exported to almost all countries of the world. Enka noted that the different branches of the group do not compete with each other as their activities are too specific or limited to the region. Competition in Central and northern European countries is strongest as these constitute fully liberalised markets. Among Asahi's subsidiaries, INDACI (Indonesia) held that its projects are highly competitive in the expanding fibre and textile market of Indonesia. Both ASP and ASF (both in Ireland) reported that market conditions had become quite difficult because of stagnating demand. TPC (Republic of Korea) also noted that market conditions have become difficult because of recent slow-downs in the economies of the Republic of Korea and other countries. For Kanebo's subsidiaries the following observations were made. KTSM (Indonesia) considered that its products were competitive because they were mainly for the domestic market and had outstanding high quality. Lachlan (Australia) indicated that over 90 per cent of its production was exported to Japan, the Republic of Korea, Pakistan, India and the Islamic Republic of Iran.

Among its competitors are top wool manufacturers in Malaysia, as well as in the host country. FISIPE (Mitsubishi Rayon's subsidiaries in Portugal) sells essentially to the domestic market. LSB, Enka's subsidiary in Spain, reported that it occupied a leading position in the Spanish market (covering in 1980 nearly 40 per cent) despite heavy competition. In 1980 its products held the following market shares in Spain:

Table II-11: LSB's market shares in Spain

	Per cent
Polyester fibres	43
Textile polyester filament	21
Polyamid	25
Viscose	82
Viscose for industrial use	98
Polyamid	57
Polyester	47

Exports channelled through the parent enterprise of Viscose for industrial use and Polyester Filament could be increased.

Viscosuisse (Rhône-Poulenc subsidiary in Switzerland) noted that its market position in Switzerland was a good one. Although another producer of synthetic fibres exists in Switzerland (the Emser-Werke AG), the degree of competition between this enterprise and Viscosuisse was low. The destination of Viscosuisse products was as follows: in 1980 (in per cent) Switzerland 14, EFTA 37, EC 25, other European countries and other regions of the world 23.

Characteristics of employment structure and problems encountered in this connection

Female-dominated workforce

The main feature of the employment structure in the sector is the predominance of women. In the clothing industry, the number of women employed is always very high and ranges from 65 per cent to 90 per cent of the total labour force. In the textile sector employment of women is high in developed economies or newly industrialised countries (from 40 per cent to 80 per cent) while it is very low in Africa and in some Asian countries like India, Pakistan and Bangladesh. The leather and footwear sectors also employ a relatively large number of women. In Africa, no women work as manual workers in the shoe and

leather industries.   In the shoe industry in Asia employment of women
varies considerably according to countries: it is relatively large in
places like Malaysia and Singapore, while it is nil in India.[3]

Thus, for example, 93 per cent of the workforce in the Australian
clothing industry is female, according to a study[4] undertaken in
September 1981 by the Clothing and Allied Trades Union of Australia.
The Federation of Korean Trade Unions stated that in the Republic of
Korea the corresponding figure for the sector under study amounted to
70 per cent.   Without giving detailed statistics, a predominance of
women was also reported by the Amalgamated Clothing and Textile Workers'
Union (ACTWU) Canada and the Japanese Federation of Textile, Garment,
Chemical, Distribution and Allied Industry Workers' Union (ZENSEN).

The Irish Transport and General Workers' Union remarked with
reference to the Asahi operation in the country that perhaps because of
traditional attitudes a mainly female workforce is employed in the
enterprise's spinning plant.   The company is quoted to say that this is
connected with the greater dexterity of women at performing the required
work.

The National Confederation of Industrial Workers, Brazil, noted in
the same sense with reference to the Brazilian subsidiary of Kanebo that
women workers play an important role in work which requires special care
and attention in the knotting of yarn and inspection of woven fabrics.

As concerns the age structure, the picture is not uniform for the
various countries on which information has been received.   The Clothing
and Allied Trade Union of Australia stated that according to its aforementioned study in addition to being dominated by females, a significant proportion of the industry workers, some 30 per cent, are young.
There is a fairly even spread of ages within the industry.   A less
homogeneous age structure was reported by the Federation of Korean Trade
Unions: in their country, 43 per cent of the workers in the sector
(textile, clothing and footwear industries) being studied are between
18 and 20, 25 per cent between 21 and 23, and 24 per cent between 24 and
26 years old.   Only 23 per cent are above the age of 27.   While the
French Federation of Textile and Allied Workers indicated that only
7 per cent of the workers of TEXUNION branch of Dollfus-Mieg are below
the age of 25; this is seen related to a specific recruitment freeze.
The Japanese Federation of Textile, Garment, Chemical, Distribution and
Allied Industry Workers' Unions (ZENSEN) stated, too, that the average
worker in the sectors under study belongs to the higher age categories.

As concerns problems related with the specific employment
structure in the sector, the Clothing and Allied Trades Union of
Australia stated that women workers typically experience low and
unequal pay and job segregation and have difficulty participating
equally in the workforce or the trade union.   It also referred to a
lack of freely available and inexpensive child care and the onerous
double burden of domestic work along with paid work.   The Irish

Transport and General Workers' Union observed that wages for women were lower in the male dominated fibre plant of Asahi. This had given rise to equal pay claims which were successful and were conceded by the enterprise without the involvement of an equal pay officer.

Homeworkers, part-time and temporary workers

In their above-mentioned study of 1981 the Clothing and Allied Trades Union of Australia refers to homeworkers as an often forgotten, underprivileged group in the industry. Their significance in numbers is difficult to gauge, although the garment manufacturers' association, which is the employer organisation for markers-up in the industry, has estimated to the Industries Assistance Commission that they could comprise between 5,000 and 15,000 employees in the country.

The significance of the homeworker to the industry is not contested. They are usually composed of women working in their own homes and they are working either for markers-up or manufacturers. Many of these, according to the above study, work illegally and are, therefore, thoroughly exploited. Their pay is usually much less than the award rate for the work, and they are rarely provided with conditions which indoor factory workers have come to regard as their rights.

The Spanish State Federation of Textiles and Furs (UGT), too reported that home work and illegal work proliferates in the country while the Japanese Federation of Textile, Garment, Chemical, Distribution and Allied Industry Workers' Unions (ZENSEN) reported that the number of temporary workers and part-timers are on the increase, while homeworkers have not decreased appreciably. As a result, the workers who are obliged to work long hours at low wages are rising.

On the other hand, several MNEs such as Enka and Viscosuisse confirmed that they did not have home work since the production of synthetic fibres is not suitable for home work.

Migrant workers

Another distinct manpower group employed in the sectors under study would appear to be migrants. Thus, the Clothing and Allied Trades Union of Australia reported in their study of 1981 that for the whole of the sector half of the workers are migrants and that their proportion is even higher in the clothing industry. The study also indicates that migrant workers experience severe difficulties as a result of lack of English language ability associated with cultural alienation. A high percentage of immigrants among the workers in the clothing and textile industries is also reported by the Amalgamated Clothing and Textile Workers' Union, Canada. The French Federation of Textile and Allied Workers observed that immigrants are mainly given

night shift and maintenance jobs.   The ITGLWF notes in this connection
that in Austria 25,000 foreign workers are employed in the clothing,
shoe and leather industries; in the Federal Republic of Germany 21,000
are found in the leather industry, in Belgium 5,000 and the Netherlands
some 9,000 in the textile industry.   By contrast, in the United Kingdom
the number of foreign workers are reported to be a small fraction and
come mainly from Commonwealth countries.[5]

Manpower problems of MNEs at host-country level

Enka made the general remark that given the economic inter-
dependence within the group and despite variations in national
legislation, the effects of production changes are never considered
in the isolated context of one specific country alone but in the light
of the interests of the group as a whole.   This was at least so within
the enterprise's European operations.   Transfers of operations from
the home country had been rare in the case of Enka so that their effects
on employment at home and abroad were insignificant.

Although manpower was felt to be generally abundant in most of the
host countries of the multinational enterprises, several firms report
difficulty in obtaining technically qualified personnel.   This
included the Asahi subsidiaries in Indonesia (INDACI) and Ireland
(ASP and ASF), Enka Spain (LSB) and Kanebo's subsidiaries in
Indonesia (KTSM) and Australia (Lachlan).   Thus, most of these enterprises find it necessary to organise special education and training
courses.   [See also Chapter III of this present report on Training.]
However, Lachlan (Kanebo's subsidiary in Australia) finds it difficult
to institute this type of programme because of different attitudes
towards job tenure and careers in Australia and Japan.   In Australia
the enterprise cannot expect a worker to stay long at one company.
For this reason the enterprise holds that it is hard to train employees
within the company and feels compelled to seek experienced workers from
outside who are, however, in short supply.

To a certain degree this problem was also noted for Kanebo do
Brazil and attributed to the location of the plant in an area of
industrial concentration.   The competition for securing appropriate
labour among enterprises was found to be severe.   Additionally, the
low standard wages prevailing in the local textile industry was considered as another factor affecting the competitive position of Kanebo.
Low productivity and high absenteeism of local staff was listed as a
concern of Enka's subsidiary in Spain (LSB).   However, the major
obstacle to meeting LSB's manpower needs was seen in the strict
regulation by the Spanish Government of manpower mobility.   Thus, the
Government's authorisation to reduce the workforce in order to adjust
the number of workers to the needs of the enterprise is only granted
if the enterprise is in a critical economic situation (e.g. unable to
pay the wages or bankruptcy).   Subsidiary management added that the
same inflexibility existed in case they wanted to hire additional staff

on a temporary basis, if there was, for example, a sudden increase in demand.   Recently, greater flexibility was shown by the authorities though, so that it was possible for the time being to hire additional temporary staff but only for a period of six months.   This needs be justified by the market situation, seasonal requirements or unfilled orders.   It was also noted that recently part-time employment has been introduced (up to two-thirds of the normal working time).

Lotus (Sam Hwa's subsidiary in the Philippines) mentioned a number of problems for the employment of expatriates in the country.

Restructuring of MNEs activities and Employment problems

MNE replies

Rhône-Poulenc Textile (RPT) indicated that in 1980, 1,400 workers were affected by restructuring measures within the group as a whole, 900 of whom were in the RPT home operations.   The policy of the MNE as outlined in their annual report for 1980, aimed at making a special effort to alleviate the employment or income problem of workers caused by restructuring.   Thus the following measures were introduced for the French operations of the company: (i) retiring all workers reaching 55 years of age on full pension;   (ii) transferring some of the redundant workers to other plants of the company;   (iii) finding jobs for redundant workers in other neighbouring firms;   (iv) training workers for employment in other industries where jobs are available;   (v) some outside firms were assisted through low-interest loans, etc., thus inducing them to employ redundant RPT workers.

The management of RPT thinks that only very few workers were not able to benefit from any of these measures.   As a matter of fact, nearly one-third of the redundant workers retired and some two-thirds were found alternative jobs.   As regards re-employment within other sections of Rhône-Poulenc, management noted, however, that the geographical mobility of their workers was rather low.   Also, changes in residence due to a transfer are not foreseen in the collective agreement.   To encourage mobility, special provisions were introduced, such as continuity of contract upon transfer, reclassification at the same salary level as the previous position, special loans to workers, low rent for company housing, etc.   As concerns the RPT management staff, they are by definition supposed to be mobile.   This is one of the conditions of their contract and, if they refuse transfers, they expose themselves to dismissal.   As fixed by the industry-wide collective agreement, the multinational pays transportation or removal costs in such cases.

RPT indicated that during the last five years their activities had experienced a remarkable evolution.   Parallel to an expansion of the pharmaceutical and agro-chemical sector, a strong decline was, on the contrary, observable in the heavy chemicals and especially the textile sector in connection with the general crisis in this industry in Europe and throughout the world since 1975.

The same type of measures to mitigate the negative employment effects of restructuring as reported by RPT, were also mentioned by Dollfus-Mieg & Cie.(DMC) France.   The latter company emphasised, in particular, that with respect to employment cuts, workers' representatives are kept informed at all stages of the plans.

Without making allusion to any specific employment problems, Viscosuisse, Rhône-Poulenc's subsidiary in Switzerland, indicated that the enterprise has been in a systematic and investment-intensive restructuring process for the last 20 years during the course of which the synthetic silk production had been totally replaced by the production of other synthetic fibres.   As there existed a certain workforce shortage in Switzerland, it was only due to intensive rationalisation and automation measures that Switzerland had remained interesting as a location for the synthetic-fibre industry.

Government replies

The Governments of Colombia, Hong Kong and Sri Lanka reported that no social and labour problems existed in their respective countries in connection with the restructuring of MNE activities.   Yet the Government of Colombia added that it had made provisions to prevent such problems from arising: Article 37 of Decree No. 1469 of January 1978 states that any enterprise including MNEs, intending to reduce its workforce or to stop, temporarily or definitely, all or part of its activities, is obliged to ask the Ministry of Labour and Social Security for permission to do so.

The Government of the Federal Republic of Germany reported that in the past the textile and clothing industry had to a large extent been able to cope alone with structural change.   Moreover, negative effects on employment of too rapid structural changes had been mitigated by means of aid programmes within the general framework of regional policies and by specific labour market measures, such as, in particular, the adaptation of qualifications of those affected to new job requirements.

The Government of Ireland indicated that Asahi Synthetic Fibres (Ireland) Limited and Asahi Spinning (Ireland) which employed 475 people over the coming months in order to achieve productivity increases. When establishing new enterprises in Ireland, a manpower forecast is included in the required documentation.   This is monitored in association with the training provided.

The Government also noted that information and consultation of workers regarding employers' decisions affecting them are primarily a matter for free negotiation and collective bargaining. However, there is provision in a number of statutes for mandatory consultation with employees, e.g. (i) the Protection of Employment Act 1977 which requires that employees be informed and consulted regarding proposed redundancies, and (ii) the Safeguarding of Employees Rights on Transfer of the Under- taking - European Communities Regulations, 1980 - which requires that the workers be informed and consulted regarding transfer of ownership of undertakings, business or parts of business, which entails a change of employer.

The Government of Japan stated that under the severe economic situations after the first oil crisis in the 1970s, the textile industry in Japan was confronted with excessive production capacity, as a result of a rapid decrease in domestic demand, the increase of imports from developing countries, and fierce competition in the export markets. Therefore, the enterprises concerned had to rationalise their production systems, including the scrapping of excessive production equipment as well as business reconversion. The Government took the following two types of measures to cope with employment instability in the process of these changes: (a) promotion of business reconversion in such a manner as not to produce unemployment; and (b) promotion of the re-entry of those unemployed to employment and the extension of the entitlement period for unemployment insurance benefits, as well as other payments in those trades where a considerable number of workers lost their jobs. The number of workers in the textile industry decreased by more than 20 per cent during the period from 1972 to 1979.

As concerns the situation in host countries of Japanese multi- nationals, the Government of Japan indicated that in view of the remarkable increase of direct overseas investment by Japanese companies, it has conducted a survey (starting from 1979) on the effects of Japanese foreign direct investment on domestic employment including employment in the textile, clothing and footwear industries.[6] It is expected that these surveys will continue on a triennial basis.

The Government of Malaysia explained that most of the multinational textile companies in the country export at least 80 per cent of their products. They were therefore affected by the cyclical change in world demand for textile products which in turn adversely affected the companies' profitability. With the decline in profitability, the companies find it difficult to meet the wage demands of the active textile workers' union.

The Government of Mexico drew attention to the fact that the unions are fully autonomous vis-à-vis the government in defining and working out strategies for the protection of their rights in labour matters in accordance with existing legislation. Moreover, article 439 of the federal labour law foresees, for instance, that in case of work- force reductions due to the installation of machines or the introduction of new technology, and if no agreement can be reached, the employer has to obtain the permission of a conciliation and arbitration commission (article 782 and following).   Dismissed workers are entitled to four months' salary plus 20 days' salary for each year of service or the corresponding sum fixed in the work contract and a seniority premium (as foreseen in article 162) both in multinational and other companies.

The Government of Nigeria reported that changes in operation including mergers, take-overs or transfers of production are governed by the provisions of the Companies Act and the Nigerian Enterprises Promotion Act with which national and multinational enterprises comply.

The Government of the United Kingdom stated that as far as social and labour problems in connection with restructuring are concerned, Northern Ireland, in particular, has suffered substantially from reductions and closures by all the major man-made fibre producers which have cut back their capacity by over 70 per cent since 1979.   These enterprises were initially attracted by Government grants, but, as the recession has taken its effect, there was increasing difficulty in maintaining operations.   However, as employment problems were a serious concern throughout the whole textile industry, fibre producing firms received no different treatment from other firms in the industry. However, the United Kingdom, like India and Spain, reported that no special government policies had been formulated regarding the restructuring of activities in the sector covered by the present report.

The Government of the United States indicated that it did not view the unemployment and other problems which may exist in the textile, clothing and footwear industries to be particularly related to or a function of the national or multinational character of enterprises. Such problems were attributable to economic factors like production costs, industry structure, automation and others, as well as to the trade practices of some countries, which may affect the competitiveness of companies operating in the United States.   It was likewise noted that in conjunction with the parties concerned, that measures against unemployment, trade adjustment and other policies, had been introduced to assist affected individuals and firms.   For example, the trade adjustment assistance programme has provided, since 1962, federal financial and technical aid to enterprises and workers adversely affected by rising imports.   Current emphasis is given, however, to worker retraining.   Moreover, some collective bargaining agreements contain provisions aimed, inter alia, at mitigating the adverse effects of workforce reductions and restructuring whatever their origin is.

Trade Union replies

The French Federation of Textile and Allied Workers indicated that employment problems due to restructuring - caused in particular by a decline in activities and transfers abroad - had been numerous.   To illustrate the downward trend in employment as a direct effect of these

measures, the trade union refers to the declining employment in all
of the enterprises participating in the present study. According to
the union, Dollfus-Mieg (DMC) employed in 1975 a total of 25,506
workers (81 per cent in France, 19 per cent abroad), this figure has
dropped to 21,318 in 1980 (58 per cent in France, 42 per cent abroad),
meaning a decrease of 16.5 per cent for the company as a whole and of
41 per cent in the home country, France (see also the similar data
above provided by the company).

The Irish Transport and General Workers' Union referred to a
problem in relation to restructuring of Asahi, one of the enterprises
participating in the study: Asahi changed the shift system in its
spinning plant. Originally, the multinational had rotating second
and third shift operations, but the company wished, for financial
reasons, to introduce fixed working hours for the shifts. This,
according to the union, meant a loss of earnings and confined many
workers to the disagreeable 4.30 p.m. to midnight shift.

The Japanese Federation of Textile, Garment, Chemical, Distribution
and Allied Industry Workers' Union (ZENSEN) noted that the consultation
system in existence had avoided labour disputes in the case of employment adjustments.

Employment policy concerning the textile industry in general, production adjustment at various levels of the industry, or adjustment in
the amount of equipment are discussed between ZENSEN and the industrial
organisations concerned, and an agreed solution is sought there. In
many cases past consultations included the Government and thus had
become tripartite.

Additionally, solutions are sought through prior consultation
meetings between labour and management at the enterprise level is to
individual and concrete employment problems. If, after resorting to
this measure, unemployment is still to occur, ZENSEN guides the local
union in requesting acceptable compensation for the displaced workers
and reserves its right to approve the final solution at the enterprise
level.

The Trades Union Congress (United Kingdom) indicated that each of
the industries - clothing, textiles and footwear - had suffered an unprecedented decline from 1977 to 1980, during which time over 200,000
jobs had been lost. This has created intense problems of adjustment
for companies within these sectors. In several cases, enterprises have
attempted to solve these problems by relocating related production to
their overseas operations. The union noted in this connection that
since the abolition of exchange controls in the United Kingdom in 1979,
there had been a marked increase in overseas investment by companies
in these industries.

The Clothing and Allied Trade Unions of Australia stated that the
structural change in Australian industry is having a profound effect on
clothing industry employment. Along with competition through imports

from cheap labour countries, restructuring has meant a significant decline in employment in the industry, which declined between 1967 and 1976 from 140,000 to 99,000 workers (a drop of 30 per cent).

The union noted that modification of production has had a relatively small effect on employment, deskilling some employees and increasing the skills of others in areas of technological change where fewer people are required to produce the same output. However, the results of technological change were potentially very serious although, for the time being, few employers had dismissed employees specifically for this reason. Redistribution of production facilities, or rationalisation, working hand in hand with structural change had, however, a detrimental effect on employment. Even where a firm's total number of employees were not altered, due to geographic immobility, displaced employees experienced hardship.

Changes in demand were significant when considered in the light of competition from imports. As demand for the products of the industry is not increasing rapidly, this can be expected to aggravate other causes of employment decline such as the internationalisation of the sector due to wage cost differentials and free trade.

Indirect employment effects of multinationals
in the sector (including those of subsidiary
operations on home country employment,
subcontracting, etc.)

The Asahi subsidiaries in Indonesia (INDACI), Ireland (ASP and ASF) and the Republic of Korea (TPC) indicated that in addition to direct employment they also provided substantial indirect employment through procurement of material, oil and utilities, factory maintenance and transportation. INDACI noted that its influence on industry and business in Indonesia was wholly positive, since the company was opening up a new market₇and was not in competition with previously existing textile plants.[7] Enka observed in the same context that indirect employment effects depended, in particular, on the extent of investment and the importance of each plant for a country or a region. Thus, indirect employment effects were high in countries where the chemical fibre sector was still expanding. The operation of Enka subsidiaries abroad were felt to have practically no effect on production or employment in the home country operation.

Lotus, Sam Hwa's subsidiary in the Philippines, is of the opinion that its operations had both advantageous and disadvantageous effects on employment at the home country level, but on an average the effects were assessed to be neutral.

Several employers' organisations noted that the direct and indirect employment effects of MNEs are not of a different nature than those of other enterprises. Thus the National Association of Industrialists in Colombia indicated that generally it can be said that foreign multinational enterprises have no specific impact on social and labour practices in the textile, clothing and footwear industries as distinct from other enterprises.

Similarily, the Confederation of German Employers' Associations felt that in the Federal Republic of Germany, MNEs did not have an effect on the employment market in the clothing industry. As in other European countries the chemical fibre industry in the Federal Republic of Germany had to overcome structural economic difficulties. Owing to this situation, employment had been receding for years, and an aggravation of this tendency had to be expected. There were no major direct or indirect employment effects of MNEs observable in the shoe industry, either. For many years the sector has undergone structural changes aggravated from time to time by economic difficulties. This led to a certain loss in employment, especially in the first half of the 1970s. Since 1975, the situation had stabilised, although, for the future, a further slight decrease in employment had to be expected.

The Central Union of Swiss Employers' Associations felt that there was neither a special direct nor indirect effect of MNEs on the Swiss textile sector.

The presence of multinational enterprises was seen by the Confederation of Australian Industry as an integral part of the development of the textile and clothing industries in the countries concerned. This had, in certain instances, opened up opportunities for employment in operations established as a consequence of new and improved techniques applied by multinational enterprises. Due largely to changing patterns of international trade, the level of employment in these industries had fluctuated in recent years tending towards permanent decline. This situation has affected both national and multinational enterprises. However, the level of resources and technical ability available to multinational enterprises had enabled them to adopt more readily than national enterprises to these changed circumstances.

According to the Japan Federation of Employers' Associations, out of a total of 770,000 employees abroad, workers in the textile industry accounted for 175,275 (or 22.8 per cent). This means that the Japanese textile MNEs employ the greatest number of people overseas. A major cause of the textile manufacturers' venturing into overseas operations was apparently to seek comparative advantages with cheap labour markets, but they were at the same time contributing directly and indirectly to creating employment opportunities in the host countries.

The Malaysian Employers Federation noted that multinationals in the sector undertake semi-skilled assembly and/or processing activities in the country. The clothing and footwear trades cater largely for the domestic market with products within the reach of the lower income earners.

Several enterprises mentioned subcontracting to local suppliers and purchases on local markets as an important aspect of indirect employment provided by them while others have not developed such purchases.

Enka noted that they do not use subcontracting. As concerns the acquisition at the local level of investment goods, raw materials or other material needed for production, this is purchased where it is the cheapest and of the best quality, which would be mostly the case on the host country market. KTSM (Kanebo's subsidiary in Indonesia) indicated that they have commission weavers under contract who are paid on the basis of the length of finished fabric they deliver to the multinational. KTSM claims that it thus ensures employment for about 100 people who produce together some 500,000 yards of fabric per month.

Lotus, Sam Hwa's subsidiary in the Philippines, on the other hand, stated that all goods are produced in their own plant excluding any kind of subcontracting. With a view to the purchase of material they reported that about 10 per cent of it is purchased on the local market in the form of finished goods. Mitsubishi Rayon indicated that their affiliates in Brazil and Portugal do not practise subcontracting. As concerns the purchase of raw materials, their Brazilian affiliates buy them from local manufacturers, while their subsidiary in Portugal (FISIPE) imports their main raw materials.

The French Federation of Textile and Allied Workers holds that Dollfus-Mieg & Cie. (DMC) practises subcontracting rather widely. According to the Union, the plants normally produce 70 to 80 per cent of the end product while the remaining 20 to 30 per cent is produced by subcontractors which are very dependent on the multinational. In times of crisis the plants of the MNE are not affected as long as production does not decrease by more than 20 to 30 per cent, says the Union; this means that it is essentially the subcontractors who are affected by production slow-downs, unemployment, dismissal and even closure. DMC also practises subcontracting in the case of marginal products of their main production line or products of small quantity but, none the less, indispensable to their production programme. The Union notes that there exist agreements with subcontractors on important markets and the sectors are split up as to the different stages of production such as spinning, weaving, dyeing, manufacturing of garments; all these various aspects of subcontracting have an important impact on the employment structure, on transfer of production, etc., of the multi-national. Subcontracting as above, can be found in France or abroad. The textile union holds that unions and workers' representatives are insufficiently informed about these practices.

The Federation of Korean Trade Unions noted that workers employed through subcontracted work by multinational enterprises are mostly concerned with sewing, sweaters, wigs and leather-related activities.

Transfer of technologies, and location
of research and development facilities

In describing differences in the type of production facilities at
home and abroad, Asahi indicated that the plant and equipment of their
overseas joint ventures are always designed and constructed by utilising
the same highly advanced technology that is used by the parent company
in Japan.   Its subsidiaries in Indonesia (INDACI), Ireland (ASP and
ASF) and the Republic of Korea (TPC) stated that in the same context
they had been equipped with the latest type of production facilities
since their operations began.   Kanebo reported no major differences in
the type of production facilities at home and abroad.   The research
and development activities (R and D) are conducted at each overseas
affiliate independently.   The Kanebo's subsidiary in Indonesia (KTSM)
confirmed that no difference is intentionally made in the type of production facilities at home and abroad.   Lachlan, Kanebo's subsidiary
in Australia, indicated even that more modernised production equipment
was installed in that subsidiary than at the parent company.   The
productivity of an individual machine was two to three times higher than
that in the parent company.   With a view to the location of R and
D facilities, Lachlan added that in Australia research and development
is now not active and that all manufacturers largely relied on foreign
companies for these activities.   Mitsubishi Rayon noted that research
and development activities are only carried out at the parent company.
Approximately ten researchers are employed for research on acrylic
fibres.   FISIBA and FISIPE (Mitsubishi Rayon's subsidiaries in Brazil
and Portugal respectively) do not have research facilities.

Enka indicated that there are no major technological differences
in the production facilities at home and abroad.   Especially the
latter generally correspond to the latest technical standards.   Due
to limited markets there are no extensive basic research and development
programmes at the host-country level.   Although research at the
subsidiary level exists, it is oriented towards the specific requirements of the local market.   LSB, Enka's subsidiary in Spain, reported
in this context that they have two pilot plants, one in Alcalá de
Henares and the other in El Prat, the latter being the location
of the central research laboratories of the MNE comprising textile-
chemical-equipment and dyeing laboratories, a spinning control installation and the "Centro Enka" specialising in textile development
research.   The research center also has a documentation section
and a patent service.   LSB's main objective in the field of research
and development is the promotion of production and sales with particular
emphasis on the development of existing or the creation of new types
of yarns and fibres.   Of equal importance is the search for new
markets for their existing products and the development of regular
contacts with their customers.   The research activities of LSB do
not include basic and applied research as the costs involved -
acquisition of machines and raw material - would be too high.   LSB
employs 92 persons in the research sector, 22 of whom are middle- or
high-level staff.

Employment-generating technology choice

In response to the question designed to indicate if the multinationals in the sector were transferring to developing countries
technology that would generate employment in the host country, or
if the development of appropriate technology was being pursued,
no uniform trend appeared from the replies received. Each MNE
responding, seemed to be pursuing company policy, although no respondent ignored the problem of capital-intensive technology in a labour-
intensive society. However, none of the MNEs covered actively pursued
a policy of adapting technology. This can already be implied from
answers to the previous section from which it appeared that the
most modern technologies were generally applied in the host countries.

A number of respondents noted, however, that indirectly, technology
choices made by MNEs in the host country were generating employment,
or were maintaining the present employment level. This was true
especially for the aspect of subcontracting to local suppliers or
by familiarising local workers with relevant technologies. Some
enterprises co-operate in the local development of technologies.

Kanebo's subsidiary in Indonesia (KTSM) realised that expansion
of employment was an urgent necessity in Indonesia. One enterprise
is, therefore, trying to keep the level of automation and labour-
saving moderate, but at the same time appropriate in order to be
cost-competitive. KTSM does not participate directly in the technology
development in Indonesia, but it provides technical training for
smaller local companies, students or sometimes for employees of
government enterprises.

Mitsubishi Rayon indicated that their subsidiaries in Portugal
(FISIPE) and Brazil (FISIBA) requested headquarters to grant them
licences for new technologies, which Mitsubishi Rayon then did.
Some of these technologies are considered employment-generating by
the company.

Viscosuisse, a subsidiary of Rhône-Poulenc in Switzerland,
indicated that this aspect was less important in Switzerland as
the creation of additional workplaces (for untrained workers, for
example) was not foreseen by the employment policy of the country.

As concerns work- or capital-intensive technologies, Enka remarked
that this choice is in general subject to economic considerations.
This means that the replacing of workers by capital-intensive
technologies is more frequent in sectors with high wage levels.
This problematic aspect is less important though, in the synthetic
fibre sector, as it is typical for the production processes there
to be highly automated and, therefore, work-intensive production
processes disappear more and more, Enka operations making no
exceptions.

The Malaysian Government stated that the government policy
requires all manufacturing projects licensed by the Ministry of
Trade and Industry to obtain the prior written approval of the
Ministry before entering into any agreement involving foreign
partners.   This is done to ensure that: (i) the agreement will not
impose serious and unjustifiable technological handicaps on the
local party; (ii) the agreement will not be prejudicial to the
national commensurate with the level of technology to be transferred
to the country.[8]

The United States Government noted that competition from enterprises located in other countries in the textile, clothing and footwear
industries has contributed to the unemployment and economic difficulties
of these industries experienced in the United States.   While this
problem was not specifically related to multinational enterprises,
in some industries concerned, particularly the textile industry,
multinational as well as national enterprises operating in the
United States have maintained or enhanced their competitiveness
vis-à-vis foreign producers by introducing new, cost-reducing
technologies and management techniques.   Moreover, such enterprises
have improved their marketing and sales by operating in foreign
markets.   While the necessary introduction of new technologies probably
has tended to increase unemployment in such industries, the resulting
increased sales abroad have likewise tended to promote employment.

A recent ILO study[9] suggests that there are close linkages between
the technology choices made by MNE subsidiaries abroad and the volume
of employment directly and indirectly generated by these subsidiaries
in the host countries.   It also points to close linkages between
government policies on the one hand and the technology choices and
employment-generating effects of MNE subsidiaries on the other.
However, these two sets of linkages appear to be, contrary to what is
often expected, essentially indirect.

The most important determinants of technology choice in MNE
subsidiaries in developing countries appear to be (a) the economic
constraints facing the firm, (b) the technical specifications and
quality standards set by the parent company, and (c) the firm's
internal innovative drive.   If, in the framework of these
co-ordinates, labour-intensive technologies are competitive - and
as a rule this is the case when the local market is small, or investment resources are limited - the enterprises are likely to use them.
To encourage or to force foreign subsidiaries to use these technologies
when they are not economically viable is, however, likely to affect
the subsidiary's rate of growth and reduce its capacity to generate
new jobs in the long term.

While none of the enterprises surveyed in the above-mentioned
ILO study made a deliberate effort to use labour-intensive

technologies - irrespective of the sector involved - it emerged that
their technology choices do have an important direct and indirect
impact on local employment opportunities, i.e. not only on those
within the enterprise itself but also in a broader sense on employment
generation throughout the economy of the host country. It was found
at the same time that subsidiaries were usually more labour-intensive
than the parent enterprises as a result of the scaling-down of
production to hit the smaller local markets.

As regards the generation of direct employment in the subsidiaries
themselves, the study shows that its volume depends on the subsidiaries'
success in the market, which in its turn, is essentially determined by
the enterprises' ability to make the "right" technological decisions
over a long period of time. Hence, enterprises likely to contribute
the most in terms of direct employment generation are those able to
choose technologies that are not necessarily the ones which create
the largest number of jobs instantly, but rather the techniques that
harbour the greatest evolutionary capacity, thereby allowing the
enterprise to grow and create new jobs in the process.

The ILO study also brings to light the considerable importance
of a foreign subsidiary's indirect employment-generating effects in
the host country: the number of new jobs indirectly generated is often
several times higher than the number of new jobs directly employed
within the enterprise itself.

The study shows that the process of indirect job generation in
the host country is closely linked with the MNE subsidiary's technology
choices and technological decisions. One of the key variables in this
process is the subsidiary's technological capability and experience.
If the subsidiary operates as an industrial enclave in the host
country, importing all its machinery and raw materials and remaining
a mere assembler of foreign-made parts and components which exports
finished products to the world market, its indirect job-generating
effects are likely to be very small.

If, by contrast, it gradually builds up its local purchases of
raw materials, parts and components, and eventually machinery,
develops its distribution network in the host country, and stimulates
local competitors without overwhelming them, the indirect job-generating
effects can be very large indeed. The problem facing national policy-
makers is that this process of gradual integration of MNEs into the
local economy does not necessarily take place in an automatic way, and
depends to some extent on factors over which the host government has
little, if any, control. The study suggests very clearly that this
process of integration, with all its positive effects on local employment, can be directly and effectively stimulated by appropriate
policies and incentives on the part of the host country, even in the
presence of such structural obstacles as the low technical level of
local suppliers. In fact, one of the main conclusions of the ILO
project is that this process of integration of foreign subsidiaries

into the host country's economy has much more far-reaching effects on
employment generation than the specific technology choices as such
made by these subsidiaries at any point in time.

Harmonisation of the manpower policies of MNEs
with national social development policies

Three Governments, i.e. those of Hong Kong, the Republic of Korea
and the United Kingdom, noted that multinationals were under no legal
obligation to harmonise manpower policies, while one, Spain, referred
to conflicting policy objectives. The United States Government found
the question on this subject-matter not to be applicable due to the
existence of a legislatively prescribed minimum wage for all
manufacturing industries.

According to the Government of Colombia, the manpower policy of
the multinationals in the textile sector and, in general, in all
sectors of industry, are supposed to be in harmony with the national
social development policies. The enterprises are, in particular,
requested to fulfil their obligations in relation to the clauses they
signed upon receipt of the investment authorisation, as otherwise
they lose the advantages provided for in the recent more liberalised
programme set up under the Carthagena Agreement.

In India, MNEs in all industries are expected to harmonise their
manpower policies with the national social development policies,
according to the Government.

In Ireland, in assessing a textile project for a particular
location the country's Industrial Development Authority takes account
of national social development policies as well as of the existing
textile sector.

In Malaysia, all manufacturing companies which have more than
250,000 Malaysian dollars of paid-up capital or which employ more than
25 full-time employees are required to apply for a manufacturing
licence under the Industrial Co-ordination Act 1975, before establishing a plant. One of the conditions of the manufacturing licence
stipulates that a company shall, as far as possible, employ and train
Malaysian citizens to reflect, at the earliest possible opportunity,
the multiracial composition of the country's population in all grades
up to the managerial level. All manufacturing companies including
textile companies should strive to comply with these conditions imposed
by the Government.

In Mauritius the main priorities of development plans have been
the creation of gainful employment and increases in productivity. The
MNEs provide gainful employment and training, while abiding by the
minimum wage legislation. No conflict with their manpower policy has
been experienced, the Government says.

In the Netherlands the normal tripartite structures of information/
consultation in the country provide for the harmonisation of manpower
plans between major enterprises and the Government.

In Nigeria the manpower policy objectives of the federal Government
are: (a) the expansion of employment opportunities through implementation of employment-oriented programmes and the removal of constraints
on the growth of employment in various sectors of the economy;
(b) provision of industrial attachment programmes, occupational
guidance and similar schemes which are aimed at bridging the gap between
education and training and the world of work; and (c) strengthening
of existing educational and training facilities and establishment of
additional ones in identified areas of need.

According to the Nigerian Government, multinational enterprises
in the clothing, textile and footwear industries contribute to the
achievement of the above goals by: (i) participating in the Industrial
Training Fund (a government establishment which finances industrial
training of Nigerians through funds provided by the Government and
industrial establishments); and (ii) establishing training centres
and workshops for the training of their employees.

Spain stated similarly that in the current economic situation the
trend in industry is towards reorganisation involving reductions in
the workforce, a policy also adopted by multinationals operating in
Spain. It cannot be said, therefore, that their activities are
harmonised with the Government's policy, which is to create the
greatest possible number of jobs.

In Sri Lanka manpower policies of Greater Colombo Economic
Commission (GCEC) enterprises have not been found to be in conflict
with the Government's objectives.

In the United Kingdom there is no systematic and organised linking
of national and company policies or plans. There used to be some
limited co-operation in training via Industrial Training Boards, but
those relating to textiles are among the brands being abolished.
There are also industry-level consultations via Economic Development
Councils. These are purely consultative, however, with no effective
leverage over companies in the industries concerned. At the same
time, there is an obligation for advanced notification of substantial
redundancies which provides a framework for faciliating consultations.
It is noted in the Government's report that a great deal depends on
a good working liaison between individual companies and the appropriate
existing government service agencies to obtain harmonisation of plans
at the respective levels.

Some MNEs participating in the study reported that consultation
and collaboration existed between them and public authorities and
national employers' and workers' organisations on employment issues
in accordance with the legislation and traditions of the various host

countries while other MNEs indicated that such practices were not yet
established nor legally required in the majority of the countries
where they operated.[10]

The French Textile Employers' Association noted that the MNEs
do not have a leading position in social matters.   The numerous
restructurings have been detrimental to the development of a social
policy at the enterprise level.   Moreover, few initiatives are taken
to implement social strategies in periods of economic difficulties.

Government policies towards multinationals
in the sector

It seems that policies specifically designed for multinational
enterprises in the textile, clothing and footwear industries do not
exist in any of the countries which replied to this part of the
questionnaire.   A number of governments have policies and legislation
equally applicable to all enterprises, regardless of their national
or multinational character (Hong Kong, Malaysia, Nigeria, United States).
And various governments have introduced measures to help adjust the
sector industries.   For example, the Government of the Federal Republic
of Germany notes that as MNEs are of lesser importance in the textile
and clothing sectors, development of a specific policy within this
group of enterprises is not necessary.

Several governments reported on their general policies as regards
MNEs:

The Australian Government established the Foreign Investment
Review Board in 1976 to provide advice on foreign investment proposals
and to foster an awareness and understanding of government policy.
The Board, which includes members of the business community, also has
a responsibility to assist foreign investors to frame their proposals
in a manner which is consistent with the objectives of governmental
policy.

Generally speaking, the basic approach to particular foreign
investment proposals is to ensure that they are harmonised with
Australia's interests.   Apart from certain limited areas of the
economy where overseas investment is restricted, particular
proposals - new projects and take-overs - are considered against broad
criteria that take into account economic, social and other national
interest considerations.   Full details of the Government's foreign
investment policies are set out in a booklet prepared by the Department
of the Treasury.[11]

However, there are no sectoral policies of special restrictions
relating in particular to the operations of multinational enterprises
in the textile, clothing and footwear industries.   In fact, some of

the larger Australian firms in this sector are partly or totally controlled by foreign multinational interests. The most recently available statistics on the textile industry, for example, indicate that approximately 10 per cent of these companies are fully foreign controlled and that 40 per cent of fixed capital assets in the industry are foreign owned. This is approximately equivalent to the average for the Australian manufacturing industry in general.

While there are no specific policies covering the activities of multinationals in these industries, there are policies for the textile, clothing and footwear industries as a whole. In August 1980, the Ministers for Industry and Commerce, and Business and Consumer Affairs respectively, announced the Government's decision on a new programme of assistance for these industries for a period of seven years commencing on 1 January 1982.[12]

The Government of Colombia reported that their general policy with regard to MNEs is determined by the provisions of the Carthagena Pact. Thus, in accordance with its Article 3, Decision 24, Chapter II, MNEs in the textile sector, for example, are permitted to operate in the country only if the national enterprises in the sector cannot furnish the required supplies.

The Government of India pointed out that in so far as industries in general are concerned, the activities of the MNEs are sought to be regulated by certain specific legal provisions, such as the Foreign Exchange Regulations Act, the Companies Act, and the Monopolistic and Restrictive Trade Practices Act. They also referred to their report on the implementation of the ILO Tripartite Declaration of Principles concerning Multinational Enterprises and Social Policy.[13]

The general policy of the Irish Government is to encourage the establishment of suitable new companies and the training of Irish people in new skills related to viable industry. There is no special policy exclusive to multinational enterprises and even less to multinationals in the textiles, clothing and footwear industries as far as employment and training is concerned. The policies are the same as those applying to all new companies. The textile industry is eligible for the same range of incentives under the programme of the Industrial Development Authority as any other industry.

Without making specific reference to MNEs in the textile, clothing and footwear industries, the Government of Mauritius reported that their general policy is to encourage foreign investment to promote industrial development. The various schemes to meet this objective are as follows: (i) the Development Incentives Act No. 50 of 1974; (ii) the Export Processing Zones Act No. 51 of 1971; and (iii) the Export Service Zones Act No. 8 of 1981.

The Government of Spain indicated that the Legislative Decree of 27 July 1959 facilitated the entry of foreign capital by abolishing

previous prohibitive regulations.   It provided that foreign investors
were free to hold up to 50 per cent of a company's share capital; any
percentage beyond that amount was subject to government authorisation.
The Decree of 18 April 1963 provided for exceptions to the 50 per cent
limit, thus facilitating the direct penetration of foreign capital in
a number of sectors, including the textile, leather and footwear
industries, on which no restrictions were placed.   The Decree of
18 April 1963 was repealed by Decree No. 2495/1973, which made the
excepted sectors subject again to the general authorisation required
for foreign investment exceeding 50 per cent of a company's share
capital, in accordance with the provisions of section 5 of the
Legislative Decree of 1959.   The Government pointed out that the
amount of direct foreign investment in the textile and other
manufacturing sectors is small - about 4 per cent of the share capital
of the undertakings among the 500 largest industrial undertakings.
Of these, there are only three textile undertakings where direct
holdings amount to 50 per cent or more of the share capital and only
four where they amount to less than 50 per cent.

The Government of the United Kingdom observes, likewise, that
there are no special governmental policies regarding MNEs in the
textile, clothing and footwear industries.   The policies for the sector
concerned are not different from policies towards MNEs in general, i.e.
there is no discrimination either in favour of, or against textile and
clothing MNEs.   The Government adds that MNEs are expected to observe
the guide-lines laid down by the Organisation of Economic Co-operation
and Development (OECD) as well as the ILO's Tripartite Declaration of
Principles concerning Multinational Enterprises and Social Policy.

The Portuguese Textile Trade Union, SINDETEX (UGT) holds that
the Government stimulates foreign investment in the sector and in other
sectors "at any price", i.e. for economic purposes only.

Employment security

National legislation concerning employment security seems to make
little or no distinction between multinationals and other enterprises,
as reported by the Governments of Australia, Colombia, the Republic
of Korea, Nigeria, Spain, the United Kingdom, and the United States.
Only the Government of India mentioned MNEs specifically, saying that
it takes into account all aspects, including the employment aspects,
before approval is given to the MNEs to operate in the country.
Nevertheless, employment guarantees are neither required nor provided
in India.   This seems to be the case in most other countries.   In
the United States, the Government opposes the imposition of performance
requirements as a matter of general policy, including those related
to employment and social practices.

The Government of Australia indicated that multinational enterprises and their Australian subsidiaries are generally regulated by

those government policies and legal and administrative provisions
which govern the operation of all companies in Australia.   With
this remark in mind it is understood that there are generally no
guarantees given by companies in the industries under study of
continuity of employment for their employees or in any other
industries.

Employees in the textile, clothing and footwear industries are
covered, as other industries, by the terms and conditions of either
federal or state awards or agreements.   The provisions in these
awards and agreements regulate the conditions of employment and
generally contain a contract of employment clause which sets out
the terms of engagements and termination.   This is the case, for
example, for the Textile Industry Award 1976 to which Lachlan is
a respondent.[14]

The Government of Spain indicated that the employment guarantees
offered by multinational enterprises are the same as those offered
by other enterprises since all are subject to the same labour legislation which establishes the grounds for termination of employment
in sections 49 to 56 of the Worker's Charter.

The Government of the United Kingdom reported that as regards
employment security there is, on the whole, no significant difference
between multinationals and other enterprises in any industry,
including those in the sector studied.   The Employment Protection
Act (1974) applies equally to multinational and domestic enterprises.
The Act requires an employer to discuss impending redundancies with
the trade union concerned at least 30 days before the first dismissal
is to take place.   Where 10 to 99 workers are to be made redundant
at one establishment over a period of one month, or 90 days in advance
where 100 or more workers are to be made redundant over a period
of three months, the employer is required to inform the trade unions
and to consider complaints made by workers.   Workers of all enterprises are protected by law from arbitrary dismissal.

The French Textile Employers' Association felt that safeguarding
the employment level is not a priority in determining the policy
of the enterprises.   However, more than other enterprises, the large
groups have tried to find solutions in the event of redundancies.

The Irish Transport and General Workers' Union indicated that
job and income security depends on the viability of the enterprise
on an ongoing basis.   There is no collective agreement to the contrary.
If the market price and competitive position is unsatisfactory, the
enterprise would be at risk and also the jobs and income security,
whatever statements or voluntary guarantees an enterprise may give.
It is also mentioned that the experience with one enterprise taking
part in the present study (Asahi) is positive as regards employment
security.   The enterprise is said to have shown a commitment to
stay in the country despite short-term losses incurred and to provide
ongoing employment.

The Japanese Federation of Textile, Garment, Chemical, Distribution and Allied Industry Workers' Unions (ZENSEN) noted that there is no specific legislation on guarantee of employment in Japan and that practically none of the labour agreements touches on this point. The long-rooted Japanese practice of a lifelong employment system restricts management to a considerable extent to discharge workers.

The Federation of Korean Trade Unions mentioned the following national laws existing in the field of job security: (a) Labour Standard Law; (b) Employment Security Law; and (c) Basic Law for Vocational Training. They apply to multinational as well as other enterprises.

Among the laws and agreements mentioned by the Swedish Trade Union Confederation in relation with job security, two are of particular importance, viz: (i) the Law for the Protection of Employment which entered into force in 1974 and which lays down certain requirements for the way in which dismissal can take place thus limiting the employer's influence and giving the employee protection against unjustified dismissal; and (ii) the Law for the Promotion of Employment which entered also into force in 1974 as a complement to the Law for the Protection of Employment. Its objective is to encourage possibilities of employment for persons with some kind of impediment to work. In this Law such impediments are interpreted in a wide sense. Apart from physical or mental and psychological handicaps it can also cover persons who are regarded as too old. These are the people who have the greatest problems with regard to employment. This problem is particularly acute in the case of closure or curtailment of production. The law specifies that an employer considering production cutbacks or lay-offs must notify the County Labour Board of this at least one month beforehand if at least five employees are likely to be affected. If short-term work can lead to dismissals, the period of notice to be given is from two to six months, depending on how many are likely to be affected. When notice of cuts in production is given, a consultative group has to be set up with representatives of the firm, the union, the County Labour Board and the local authority. During the notice period the consultative group plans measures to improve the situation of those likely to be affected. These cases apply normally to all industries. The Swedish Textile, Garment and Leather Trades Union notes that despite these measures, its main concern is the transfer of operations of Swedish multinationals to other European countries. The main locations of Swedish multinationals, according to the union, are in Finland (3,000 employees), Portugal (2,500), Malta and the United Kingdom (500 each). Smaller locations are in Norway, Ireland, Austria, the Netherlands and Switzerland.

The industries in the sector under consideration have been, in several industrialised countries, among those for which collective agreements exist on the protection of workers in the case of rationalisation and technological changes.[15] While these have been

developed over the years, their effect has been more to safeguard
workers' rights to assist them in adjustments to change, to provide
relocation subsidies or compensation rather than to actually safeguard
jobs.   The social importance of such special agreements as well as
of improved protective legislation has been considerable.   However,
in view of the heavy reduction over the past decades of employment
in the textile, clothing and footwear industries in the developed
market economy countries, it is obvious that legislation and collective
agreements have not slowed down restructuring of the sector.

Notes

[1] K. Done: Financial Times (London), 22 Oct. 1981.

[2] See, in this connection, R. Maex: Employment and multinationals
in Asian export processing zones, Multinational Enterprises Programme
working paper No. 26 (Geneva, ILO, 1983);   and C. Ford: "Value added?
Free trade zones in Sri Lanka", in Free Labour World (ICFTU) 1981,
No. 4.   See also ITGLWF: Multinational corporations and trade unions
(Djakarta, Indonesia, 1974; mimeographed), p. 30; and G. McCredie:
"Uncle Sam's jobs south of the border (A special report on Mexico
and the Philippines)", in Guardian Third World Review, 19 Mar. 1982.
With respect to the location of subsidiaries in the Mexican border
region it noted that "... United States companies come in search
of cheap labour.   Ninety per cent of the workers receive the official
minimum wage: with all fringe benefits paid it costs the companies
$2.10 per worker, per hour.   In the United States the basic hourly
wage is $3.55 ...".

[3] ITGLWF: Employment of women, Third World Congress, Vienna,
6-10 Oct. 1980, Annex tables provides further data.

[4] Clothing and Allied Trades Union of Australia: A current
profile of the clothing industry (Sep. 1981; mimeographed).

[5] ITGLWF: The organisation of migrant workers in the textile,
garment and leather sectors (London, 1972), p. 2.

[6] The conclusion of the study held that a remarkable effect
had not yet been revealed; in the case of the textile industry;
however, the volume of domestic employment decreased rather drastically.
See K. Koshiro: "Impact of direct foreign investment on domestic
employment", in Japan Labor Bulletin, 1 Oct. 1982, p. 7.

[7] In this context, however, the ITGLWF estimated that some 250,000 textile workers were out of work or had switched to other sectors of employment because of the closing down of domestic labour-intensive textile plants as a result of the influx of MNEs. They further projected the net employment displacement in Indonesia at 180,000 (with only 70,000 gains).   In their view the situation was probably much the same elsewhere; it was only because not enough empirical studies had been done that data were lacking to demonstrate the point.   International Textile, Garment and Leather Workers' Federation (ITGLWF): Multinational corporations and trade unions, op. cit., pp. 43 and 84.   For a general discussion of job-displacement by MNEs, see ILO: Employment effects of multinational enterprises in developing countries (Geneva, 1981), pp. 69-71.

[8] See also, in this context, Investment in Malaysia: Policies and procedures, which was attached to the Government's reply.

[9] ILO: Technology choice and employment generation by multi-national enterprises in developing countries (Geneva, 1984).

[10] For more details on information/consultation arrangements between multinationals and governments, see idem: Information and consultation practices of multinationals concerning their manpower plans, Chapter I (Geneva, forthcoming 1984).

[11] Your investment in Australia: A guide for investors, 1981.

[12] Details of the programme are described in Industry and Commerce - Press release, 15 Aug. 1980.

[13] Doc. GB.224/MNE/1/1/D.1, 1983.

[14] This clause reads: "Contract of Employment: (a) Employment in the industry covered by this award shall be by the week, except in the case of part-time workers.   (b) An employee to become entitled to payment under this award shall be ready, willing and available for work at the times and during the hours usually worked by him. Provided that any employee starting work shall be entitled to at least one half day's pay and any pieceworker to one half day's work. Termination of Employment - Weekly and Part-time Employees: (c) (i) Employment shall be terminated by one week's notice on either side given at any time during the working week or by the payment or forfeiture of one week's wages, as the case may be.   (d) Notwithstanding anything elsewhere contained in this clause, the employer shall have the right to dismiss an employee without notice for inefficiency, neglect of duty, malingering, misconduct, or non-observance of company safety provisions, in which case wages shall

be paid up to the time of dismissal only, or to deduct payment for
any time the employee cannot be usefully employed because of any
strike or through any breakdown of machinery or any stoppage of work
by any cause for which the employer cannot reasonably be held
responsible, or for a stand-down of employees at any time when no
work is offering ...".

[15] See the article by Y. Delamotte: "British productivity
agreements, German rationalisation agreements and French employment
security agreements", in International Institute for Labour Studies,
Bulletin No. 9 (Geneva, 1972), pp. 30-51.

CHAPTER III

TRAINING

Training in the home country

Three MNEs participating in the study supplied information on their
training at headquarters. Rhône-Poulenc Textile (RPT), for example,
reported that since 1978 their expenditures on training activities
largely exceeded the legally prescribed minimum (i.e. as of 1978
1.1 per cent of the total wages/salaries paid). In 1978, the enterprise spent 1.5 per cent; in 1979 2.9 per cent; and in 1980 3.9 per
cent on training and in 1981 2 per cent. While RPT's total number of
wage earners decreased from 12,070 to 8,520 between 1978 and 1980, the
number of training fellowships increased from 1,796 to 2,816 for the
same period, with an average of 36.9 paid training hours per fellow in
1980 against 8.9 hours in 1978. RPT pointed out that their ratio of
fellows, being trained for semi-skilled, skilled and administrative jobs,
as well as in technical engineering, was higher than the national
average in the French textile sector, while the provision of management
training and the training of unskilled workers was lower. Dollfuss-
Mieg & Cie. (DMC) indicated that although the average sum invested in
training activities for the whole of their French subsidiaries (1.13 per
cent of the total salaries paid in 1980) is only slightly above the
legal national minimum, in some of their French enterprises, such as
the thread-making branch ("Filteries DMC") training funds largely
exceed the minimum with the funds being mainly used for the retraining
of otherwise redundant workers. For all of the French subsidiaries,
DMC spent 1.35 per cent (or Fr.7.7 million) in 1977 of their total
wages/salaries paid, on training activities; 1.21 per cent (or
Fr.7.3 million) in 1978 and 1.19 per cent (or Fr.7.3 million) in 1979.
In 1979 the total number of training hours per fellow amounted to 60.
DMC's cuts in training funds during the last few years were due to
economy measures as a consequence of the recession. At the same time,
the enterprise reduced the number of trainees (from 23.5 per cent of
DMC's total wage earners in 1976 to 14.5 per cent in 1979). Special
emphasis was given during that period to the training of technicians
and management staff. However, DMC also organised retraining courses
for workers affected by the reduction in or reorganisation of activities.
Other courses related to the acquisition of new skills and changed
technologies as well as to safety and health. Moreover, upon the
request of the staff, training was organised in marketing, human
relations and languages and, for members of the works committees, in
economics and administration. Besides in-company training, DMC staff
also participated in courses organised by the Training Institution of
the Employers Union of Textile Industries. DMC like any other enterprise pays a contribution to the public programme in favour of the
unemployed youth.

In view of Mölnlycke AB adequate personnel manning requires
opportunities for the employees to develop themselves within the company
through training efforts enhancing competence and experience.   Mölnlycke
has gradually built up an internal company programme for personnel
development and education covering, inter alia, management development
courses with individual planning discussions, languages and computer
training, and machine education for production groups, etc.   Each
division - and local division manager - has the responsibility to
evaluate the extent of training requirement among the personnel and
the corresponding participation in the various educational activities
offered by the company.   In 1982 the company organised a five-day
"Mölnlycke Course" for new qualified employees who have been with the
company for six months to a year and who are working in the areas of
marketing, economics, administration and production development.   The
objective of the course is to make participants familiar with the
Mölnlycke group's strategy and philosophy, as well as with its administrative and economic structure.   The course is also open to employees
in Mölnlycke's overseas subsidiaries.   Courses are also given on the
work environment and on ergonomics for safety officers, foremen,
production engineers, factory managers and designers.

According to the Confederation of German Employers' Associations,
vocational training in the clothing industry in the Federal Republic
of Germany is, to a large extent, co-subsidised by the larger enterprises, including MNEs.   The same is true for the synthetic fibre
sector.   In this connection it is significant to note that the
chairman of the training committee of the Federal Employer's Association
of the Chemical Industries comes from an enterprise which produces
synthetic fibres.

The Textile Employers' Association reported that the large French
groups have significant training facilities and spend more than what
is prescribed by law.   These possibilities for training have often
been taken into account when restructuring.

The Japan Federation of Employers' Associations mentioned that in
the area of home country training, many of the multinationals have
local staff training programmes for non-supervisory employees.   For
example, the biggest textile multinational, Toray Industries Inc.,
trained 200 local employees from 1974 to 1980, awarding them
scholarships.   With respect to supervisory and management positions,
Toray has provided, among other activities, a programme for "Cross
Culture Management Courses" which is believed to have been effective
for personnel posted to its foreign operations.   The association
noted, however, that certain in-training service systems are risky:
if they are successful, they are likely to increase the rate of trained
labour force turnover and may end up in the dissemination of proprietary
technical know-how to competitors.

The Central Union of Swiss Employers' Associations holds that the
Swiss textile industry and the multinationals therein pay particular
attention to the vocational training of their personnel.   The majority

of textile workers in Switzerland, being migrants on unskilled jobs, receive on-the-job training. Formal training courses are mainly organised for the higher occupational categories such as foremen, management staff, engineers and chemists. Furthermore, thorough apprenticeship programmes are offered for textile and fashion designers, and other textile specialists. The association also organises training courses at the level of maîtrise (master craftsman) at a special textile school in Wattwill, located in a typically textile-oriented region of Switzerland. Moreover, the secretariat of the Swiss Textile Association has the administrative supervision of a training institution specialising in management training courses which are open to all management staff of the Swiss industry. The institution is co-sponsored by the Central Union of Swiss Employers' Associations.

The French Confederation of Christian Workers reported that training and retraining in the sector concerned and the multinationals found therein, is provided usually in accordance with existing legal provisions. However, sometimes workers have to wait for more than a year to participate in vocational training courses or before being awarded a fellowship.

The Japanese Federation of Textile, Garment, Chemical, Distribution and Allied Industry Workers' Unions (ZENSEN) noted that usually, both on-the-job training and formal training are carried out within the enterprises of the sector located in Japan.

Training in the host country

As concerns the situation in host countries, the large majority of multinational enterprise subsidiaries covered by the study reported that they train and/or retrain their personnel as a regular activity. The Asahi subsidiaries in Indonesia (INDACI) and Ireland (ASP and ASF) as well as Kanebo's subsidiary in Indonesia (KTSM) pointed out that special education and training of the staff was a necessity as it was difficult to find technically-trained personnel at the local level although manpower is abundant. The types and extent of training activities vary. All Asahi subsidiaries, INDACI in Indonesia, ASP and ASF in Ireland and TPC in the Republic of Korea reported, for example, that they provide both technical and management training. The managers of Asahi subsidiaries receive three months of training in Japan in languages, management skills and factory operations. Some of the seminars and training programmes in question are sponsored by the Japanese Ministry of International Trade and Industry. Employees are, furthermore, given complete on-the-job training as necessary, as a prerequisite of their work experience and their occupational development. Continuous training is effected also through the use of operation manuals, meetings and discussion on workplace operations, review and planning.

Sam Hwa stated that they have made particular efforts to train as many local people as possible to ensure the functioning of its operation in the Philippines.   An assessment of the effectiveness of these skill development efforts does not exist as yet.

Kanebo's subsidiary in Indonesia (KTSM) reported that it organises one to six month training courses in Japan for managers of the subsidiary for subdivision up to departmental level managers.   This programme includes language training at a public language centre for the first month and practical managerial training at the parent company for the remaining period.   Subdivision managers and section managers attend lecture classes in basic technical education organised by the Indonesian "Institut Teknologi Tekstil" (Technological Institutefor Textiles) and the "Institut Teknologi Bandung" (Technological Institute of Bandung). In addition to these training programmes, the parent company dispatches from time to time specialists in order to identify particular technical problems in the subsidiaries and to conduct related on-the-job training. The technical director and the plant manager of the subsidiary (both Japanese) are actively involved in these programmes.   KTSM also organises language courses in English and Japanese.   Lachlan, Kanebo's subsidiary in Australia encourages the local management personnel to attend various seminars in the country so that they broaden their knowledge and experience and Kanebo do Brasil reported that local management officials are sent to the parent company for overall management training.

In the same vein, Mitsubishi Rayon reported that they organise periodically training courses at headquarters for personnel in their Brazilian and Portuguese affiliates (FISIBA and FISIPE respectively). Most of the top engineers of FISIBA and FISIPE were trained in this way.   Sometimes Japanese engineers from headquarters visit the company's subsidiaries abroad to provide technical guidance as required.

FISIPE indicated that its technical staff is permanently kept up to date with the technical developments of the parent company thus assuring the proper transfer of technical know-how.   For this purpose, joint training programmes are organised with the parent company and the equipment suppliers.   Part of the training is done in Japan.   In addition, FISIPE has a generic training programme for management staff.

Sam Hwa's subsidiary, Lotus, reported that it does not conduct formal training programmes for its local employees.   They acquire the necessary skills and techniques mostly through the usual on-the-job training.

With a view to their subsidiaries abroad, Enka, indicated that the company takes the following factors into account when devising training programmes: the specific needs of the subsidiaries; the vocational requirements of each job; national training legislation and the vocational needs of the host country.   As concerns Enka's subsidiary managers, they are continuously kept informed of technical developments in other countries of the group.   Managers may also be invited to training courses organised at headquarters and sometimes transfers of managers from subsidiaries to the home operation and vice versa take place.   Enka considers that as a by-project it promotes technical knowledge in the host countries, especially in the synthetic fibre sector, which is a rather new branch of industry for developing countries.

Enka's subsidiary in Spain, LSB, reported that through vocational training programmes set up by public or private institutions in Spain, it is possible to acquire certain manual and administrative skills required for the company.   No official programmes exists, though, for continuous vocational training which is generally done at the level of the individual plant, sometimes in co-operation with private or public institutions.   In 1979 and 1980, LSB organised, for instance, courses in general education, languages, administration and management, human relations and safety and health and provided training in specific technical skills.   Some 1,200 persons from all categories of LSB's personnel participated in the courses, with the highest numbers being recorded for management training courses (354 persons), specialised technical courses (254) and safety and health education (254).   The lowest numbers were found in administration and in general education courses (both 79 participants).

In the case of Dollfus-Mieg the direct training impact of the headquarters at the subsidiary level was limited to the training of some management staff, technicians and supervisors.   Owing to the distances involved more extensive systematic training by headquarters was regarded too expensive and, moreover, training needs varied at home and abroad. For that reason   the Dollfus-Mieg subsidiaries had developed their own training   programmes independent of headquarters.

Rhône-Poulenc Textile replied that the enterprise had no uniform training policy for headquarters and abroad;   in each host country the enterprise conformed to national practices.   No systematic exchange of staff between headquarters and the subsidiaries was practised for training purposes.   Sometimes, though, management staff and technicians of a subsidiary may be chosen, on an individual basis, to participate in training courses at headquarters.

Viscosuisse, the Swiss-located subsidiary of Rhône-Poulenc, reported the following types of in-company training activities in 1980: (1) in accordance with national legislation, training of (about 100) technical and commercial apprentices;   (2) training and retraining regarding new work methods and technologies;   (3) vocational training in specialised technical skills;   (4) vocational training of textile specialists and administrative staff;   (5) language courses for Swiss nationals and foreigners;   (6) courses for middle and lower management staff.   In addition, company staff had the possibility of participating in a large variety of training courses offered at the inter-industry level for nearly all professional categories.

The Government of Australia noted that there are no special legislative or administrative provisions concerning training by private

undertakings in Australia. However, provisions for these issues in all
sectors of industry are made in a number of manpower programmes administered by the Department of Employment and Youth Affairs. These include
training in industry and commerce programmes, apprenticeship support
programmes, and the labour market training system. Thus, dissemination
of information and consultation procedures with private enterprises
regarding employment, training and related issues are conducted through
a network of Industry Training Committees which have been established
throughout Australia on a national and state basis. These committees,
including one committee each on clothing, textile and footwear manufacturing, operate under the auspices of the National Training Council.
The Government's training programmes are formulated to apply to all
commercial enterprises, national and multinational, in all areas of
industrial activity.

The Government of Ireland reported that newly established or
existing firms, including multinationals, seeking certain public grants
are required to formulate training programmes. Such programmes are
agreed with the Irish Industrial Training Authority and form the basis
for a training grant recommendation. The conditions for grant-worthy
training activities are as follows: (i) that the principles of systematic training be applied in the preparation and implementation of the
programme; (ii) that a training manager qualified to a level acceptable
to the Industrial Training Authority be responsible for all aspects of
the operation of the programme; (iii) that all training be carried out
by instructors qualified to a level acceptable to the said Authority;
(iv) the basic training manuals be produced and used for the training of
all relevant jobs; (v) that records in a format approved by the
Industrial Training Authority be maintained for each trainee and must be
available for inspection by the Authority or European Social Fund
officers. The training of individual enterprises is monitored by the
Industrial Training Authority on an ongoing basis and all grants
validated. In this connection, the Industrial Development Authority
maintains regular liaison also with Asahi subsidiary management to
monitor its performance.

The Government of the Republic of Korea noted that in addition to
the country's vocational training law, agreements and arrangements
existed in practice for information and consultation with MNEs on
training matters.

The Malaysian Government reported that one of the conditions of the
manufacturing licence stipulates that the companies shall, as far as
possible, employ and train Malaysian citizens to reflect, at the earliest
possible opportunity, the multiracial composition of the country's
population in all grades of appointment up to managerial level. Its
relevant administrative provisions, applicable to all enterprises but
specifically relevant to multinationals, specify that for executive
posts expatriates may be employed up to a maximum period of ten years
subject to the condition that Malaysians are trained to eventually take
over the post. For non-executive posts expatriates may be employed up
to a maximum period of five years subject to the same training conditions.

According to the Confederation of Australian Industry, broadly
speaking, the approach of multinational enterprises in training
practices correspond with that of national enterprises in the industries
concerned.   Multinationals' training efforts were primarily geared
towards the efficient operation of the enterprises' manufacturing
activities.   These practices include, where appropriate, the training
of junior workers to recognised tradesman level with assistance from
established technical training institutions.   Where outside technical
training sources do not exist, many multinationals have established
their own in-plant facilities.   Traditionally, industry in Australia
has provided training facilities for workers other than trades
employees in the establishment.

The Clothing and Allied Trades Union of Australia reported that
training of both new and existing employees takes place under a scheme
sponsored by a National Clothing Industry Training Committee.   It
provides on-the-job and technical college training.

The National Association of Industrialists, Colombia, noted that
multinational enterprises in developing countries are mainly involved
in the training of technical staff of both the parent company and the
subsidiaries to train technical staff for enterprises in the developing
countries.

The Federated Union of Employers, Ireland, reported that of multinational enterprises involved in the Irish textile industry, it was safe
to say that the extent of training provided by foreign textile multinationals compares very favourably with other good employers.   Furthermore, all but one of the companies they had surveyed in this connection
allow time off to their employees to attend training and/or academic
courses outside the enterprise.

The Japan Federation of Employers' Associations indicated that
most MNEs in the sector emphasised on-the-job training.   In addition,
MNE employees participate in various training programmes provided by
public, local and private institutions in the host countries.

The Korea Employers' Federation pointed out that the advanced
training practices found in the MNEs in the Republic of Korea were
expected to exert a positive influence on the training practices in
local enterprises as well.

The Malaysian Employers' Federation has surveyed the training
practices of three multinational enterprises in the textile and footwear
industries.   Company No. 1 (textiles) provided initial training to new
female operators in training rooms specially established for this
purpose.   The training lasts for about two weeks, depending on the
operator's ability.   Thereafter, they are given on-the-job training.
Male employees are given exclusively on-the-job training where they are
expected to learn from their more experienced colleagues and senior
staff.

Company No. 2 (textiles) provides induction training to newly appointed employees on reporting for duty. Production operators are given on-the-job training and financial assistance is given to employees to enable them to attend relevant external courses. Additionally, staff members are sent for overseas training, as required. There are periodic visits of company advisers from headquarters, involved in the training of Malaysian staff.

Company No. 3 (footwear) provides in-plant training for operators and organises overseas study visits and training courses for managerial staff. It also gives employees the possibility to attend courses at relevant local institutions.

The Mauritius Employers' Federation stated that the parent companies of various multinationals organise training courses in different countries both for staff and certain groups of workers.

The Swedish Employers' Confederation added that the training efforts of Swedish-owned textile and clothing companies in most of the poorer countries in which they operate are well respected. These activities are felt to contribute considerably to increased technological standards and labour skills in the host countries.

Collaboration with national institutions and assistance by governments

As concerns joint training efforts with national institutions, Kanebo do Brasil trains six fellows every year in co-operation with SENAI, the industrial training fund. In the case of Kanebo's subsidiary in Indonesia (KTSM), the Ministry of Industries sponsored seminars, and study-abroad programmes to Japan and other countries are widely used. Kanebo's subsidiary in Australia (Lachlan) indicated that a two-year apprentice programme is carried out by the State Department of Technical Education. During the two-year apprenticeship period the trainees, including those from Kanebo, study at a technical college and receive a grant from the Government.

In Mitsubishi Rayon's subsidiary in Portugal (FISIPE) where the local shareholder is the Government, all management staff is exclusively national. Co-operation has recently been initiated in training matters with the Government Office of Professional Training. The implementation by the Government of a training support structure was under way. Mitsubishi Rayon pointed out that the company co-operates with national training programmes wherever such a request is made by their affiliates.

In the case of Viscosuisse, Rhône-Poulenc's subsidiary in Switzerland, vocational training of apprentices is done in close co-operation with the official vocational training schools in Switzerland. Mölnlycke reported that, although its affiliates in the different countries carry out their own training programmes, they also consult with local training institutions. However, government instructors do not take part in the training of local personnel of the company.

Enka's subsidiary in Spain (LSB) indicated that the Government may assist in the implementation of in-company training programmes by permitting access to public training courses partly financed by the Government or by granting tax reductions if a company has its own training facilities. ASP and ASF, Asahi's subsidiaries in Ireland, reported that special government aid is given to the employees who receive training in Japan.

Lotus, Sam Hwa's subsidiary in the Philippines, indicated that their training programmes are not directly linked with any national training programmes.

Several governments of MNE host countries indicated that they have no special agreements or arrangements for information and consultation with MNEs with respect to training programmes.

The United Kingdom stated that there are several government programmes which companies, multinational or not, can use if they wish but they are more likely to be guided by the desires of their share-holders. There used to be some limited co-operation in training between the government and enterprises via the Industrial Training Boards. However, those relating to the textile industry are among those which have been abolished.

On the other hand, several governments mentioned the existence of advisory training services to enterprises, whether multinational or national, and of national apprenticeship schemes.

The Labour Department, Hong Kong, offers advice on employment, training and other questions to any enterprise, national or multi-national who requests it. Moreover, there is detailed legislation for vocational training and various public training institutions, relevant also for the clothing industry.[1]

The Government of India indicated that under the Apprentices Act, 1961, which is equally applicable to MNEs and national enterprises, it is obligatory for all employers in the specified industries to engage apprentices as per the prescribed ratio in specifically designated trades. Certain textile trades groups and leather craft trades are among the designated trades.

The Government of Malaysia reported that a National Apprenticeship Scheme has been in existence for over 20 years. This provides for voluntary programmes for enterprises. Employers sponsor would-be apprentices (who enter into agreement with sponsors) to undertake apprenticeship training usually over a period of four years sandwiched between periods of training at the Industrial Training Institute and the work place. Also, a considerable number of other types of skill upgrading and skill preparation courses exist at various public institutions, all of which are available to employers at nominal cost. Furthermore, the Manpower Department provides an advisory training service to industry to analyse training problems and requirements and to arrange for satisfactory solutions.

In Nigeria, the Federal Government, through the National Labour Advisory Council (NLAC) and other bodies, holds regular consultations with employers' and workers' representatives from all industries before laws or policies affecting employment, training and other relevant matters are formulated. Multinational enterprises contribute, it is said, to the achievement of the manpower objectives by participating in the Industrial Training Fund (a government establishment which finances industrial training of Nigerians through funds provided by government and industrial establishments) and by establishing training centres and organising workshops for the training of their employees.

Retraining of personnel

The information received from MNEs on the retraining of personnel in case of restructuring or closure of enterprises is scarce and, where given, not very detailed.

With a view to their subsidiaries in developing countries, Enka reported that restructuring exercises or closures had not proven necessary thus far, so that connected retraining or transfer of staff was rarely necessary. As concerns the situation in industrialised countries where Enka had subsidiaries, retraining or transfer of staff was done each time it proved necessary and economically advisable. Enka's subsidiary in Spain, (LSB), reported that it was especially the "Instituto nacional de Empleo", which invested a considerable part of their training funds in the retraining of workers who had lost their jobs due to restructuring measures or suspension. There exists, however, no systematic and direct co-operation between private enterprises and public institutions for this purpose. A new law is presently being prepared in the country concerning the restructuring of branches in economic difficulty which will include provisions for retraining measures. Viscosuisse reported that, in their case, no dismissals due to restructuring had occurred thus far. It added that reintegration of affected workers into existing or new company activities was one of the fundamental principles of the enterprise. Lotus, Sam Hwa's subsidiary in the Philippines, reported that immediately after Sam Hwa took it over all the 115 local workers were retrained for a certain period and then re-hired by the new company. Since then, however, there has been no restructuring, closure or suspension. Mölnlycke reported that it provided retraining to workers and salaried employees in the case of individuals requiring such measures. Dollfuss-Mieg noted that it had organised retraining courses for workers affected by the reduction in, or reorganisation of, the company's activities. These courses aimed at the acquisition of new skills and the mastering of new technologies, but covered also related safety and health matters.

Trade union opinions on the question of retraining are not uniform. The Clothing and Allied Trades Union of Australia reported that retraining for displaced employees was a general feature of Australian work life during the years of the Labour Government. Since that time, in its view, retraining has been virtually eliminated under the succeeding governments.

The Irish Transport and General Workers' Union indicated that they did not know of any large-scale training or retraining projects within multinationals and the French Federation of Textile and Allied Workers was of the opinion that very little is done by the enterprises in the field of retraining. Likewise, the Trades Union Congress (TUC) felt that training and retraining facilities in the United Kingdom provided by multinationals in the textile, clothing and footwear sectors are rudimentary and not noticeably better than those provided by smaller companies. Overall, in the experience of the TUC, industries are cutting back on their training and retraining expenditure.

The Amalgamated Clothing and Textile Workers Union (ACTWU), Canada, informed that most collective agreements contain provisions for training and retraining of workers within a particular shop.

The Japanese Federation of Textile, Garment, Chemical, Distribution and Allied Industry Workers' Unions (ZENSEN) reported that retraining and transfers of workers take place in the country after prior consultation between labour and management. As required, special training programmes were prepared for workers transferred to new jobs. Most of this training is planned and implemented within the enterprise itself.

The Federation of Korean Trade Unions reported that the Republic of Korea's Training Law provides for training and retraining and that the latter is partially conducted within the enterprises themselves.

The Swedish Trade Union Confederation noted that training and retraining possibilities are supplied by the Government to all persons who are unemployed or in danger of becoming unemployed.

The Government of the Netherlands reported that, in the case of restructuring, a broad approach was applied in the textile industry by putting into effect a so-called transfer system, providing for social measures, directed to remedy the negative effects of the workers employed, by helping to provide new jobs and training programmes. Moreover, special training programmes were put into effect and monitored by the Ministry of Social Affairs.

The United States Government stated that in conjunction with the parties concerned, it has developed unemployment assistance, trade adjustment and other policies to assist affected individuals and firms, whatever the sector, and that current emphasis is given to workers' retraining in all such cases.

Workers' participation in formulation and implementation of training programmes

KTSM, Kanebo's subsidiary in Indonesia, reported that their training programmes are designed by department managers and then approved by the board of directors before being carried out. In the case of Mitsubishi Rayon's subsidiary in Portugal (FISIPE), the company's technical staff is involved in the formulation and implementation of training programmes.

LSB, Enka's subsidiary in Spain, indicated that while the collective agreement, in principle, provides for workers' participation in planning activities, i.e. existence of a joint training committee, active workers' participation is, in reality, rather rare both in the formulation and implementation of training programmes. Viscosuisse, the subsidiary of Rhône-Poulenc in Switzerland is also of the opinion that workers' participation at the level of the enterprise has been rather low so far as regards the formulation and implementation of programmes. There exists, however, in Switzerland an industry-wide vocational training programme in the textile sector which is jointly organised by the respective workers' and employers' organisations.

Mitsubishi Rayon indicated that its employees in the home country participate actively in the formulation of training programmes including those for engineers in their subsidiaries FISIPE (Portugal) and FISIBA (Brazil). Lotus, Sam Hwa's subsidiary in the Philippines, noted that local workers are actively participating in formulating and implementing on-the-job training programmes.

The Clothing and Allied Trades Union of Australia reported that it is a member of the National Clothing Industry Training Committee in which capacity it represents employees in the formulation and carrying out of training programmes.

The Japanese Federation of Textile, Garment, Chemical, Distribution and Allied Industry Workers' Unions (ZENSEN) stated that the degree of workers' participation in training varies, depending on the labour relations situation existing in the respective multinational enterprise. In some cases workers and management collaborate in the formulation of training programmes, in others, only if special problems arise.

The Federation of Korean Trade Unions noted that workers in the Republic of Korea participate generally in formulating and carrying out training programmes through the Labour Management Councils.

The Portuguese Textile Trade Union (SINDETEX) mentioned that in the manufacture of ready-made clothing, a joint training programme was implemented recently by the Employment State Office and the Employers' Association without any kind of participation requested from the trade union. The Irish Transport and General Workers' Union reported, too, that there is no involvement of workers or unions in the area.

The Trades Union Congress stated that over the last year, six government-backed Industrial Training Boards (ITBs) serving the sector being studied have folded up in the United Kingdom. No suitable alternative arrangements have been established. Trade union representatives previously had a role in formulating the policy of the various ITBs. With the abolition of ITBs, trade union influence in the formulation and implementation of training programmes has greatly diminished.

The French Federation of Textile and Allied Workers reported that training is regulated by an industry-wide collective agreement, the application of which is supervised by the works committee. It is pointed out, though, that other than the training programmes proposed by management - which mainly aim at increasing production and productivity rates by adapting, for example, skills to new technologies - workers have little choice in obtaining training in more general subjects. Thus, study leave would almost be the only possibility for a worker who wants to improve his general education level. The Federation underlined, furthermore, that a successful participation in training programmes has, in general, no positive effect on the wage levels or professional reclassification of the workers afterwards.

The Government of Mexico reported that in accordance with article 153-N of the Federal Labour Law, all enterprises, both national and multinational, are required to submit to the Secretariat of Labour and Social Providence training outlines or programmes set up in agreement with the workers. The same Law also stipulates the conditions governing the training programmes.

In Nigeria, it is reported that workers' organisations or in-plant workers representatives participate in discussions on the implementation of training programmes.[2]

Notes

[1] (a) The Hong Kong Training Council is responsible for advising the Governor on measures necessary to ensure that there is a comprehensive system of industrial training geared to the developing needs of Hong Kong; (b) the Apprenticeship Ordinance provides a legal framework for training at craft and technician levels; and (c) there are two industry-wide training schemes: one set up under the Industrial Training (Construction Industry), Ordinance to provide technician and craft training for the construction industry, and the other under the Industrial Training (Clothing Industry) Ordinance to provide technician and craft training for the clothing industry.

[2] For further information on the subject of training see ILO: Multinationals' training practices and development (Geneva, 1981).

CHAPTER IV

WAGES AND CONDITIONS OF WORK

General aspects

The replies received from MNEs on this issue concentrate mainly on policies for determining their wages and conditions of work in the host countries. The majority of these replies pointed out that the enterprises conform, in principle, to the existing national practices laid down in legislation and/or collective agreements, although benefits are usually said to be higher than in the respective industries as a whole or in local enterprises. Some other MNEs reported that while part of their wage fixing was done locally, certain wage categories were determined at headquarters. Others indicated that they follow an individualised, totally independent wage policy. Various trade union and government replies round off this picture.

The ITGLWF noted that in its experience MNEs in the sector concerned conformed to the statutory wage regulations, in particular, minimum wage legislation of the host country where it exists. This was particularly true for the wages of ordinary workers, while the enterprises paid more in the case of higher still categories, such as technicians, which are normally in short supply. The policy of a minimum wage amounted often in practice to a wage freeze by the government which benefited the enterprises; and minimum wages in some countries were far below subsistence level.[1]

The variety of the approaches followed by the companies can be illustrated by the following examples: Asahi and its five foreign subsidiaries reported that the basic company policy was to conform, in principle, to the wage standards and labour conditions that were prevailing in the countries where their joint ventures operated and that they faithfully followed the existing relevant statutory or collectively agreed stipulations. Kanebo stated similarly that the company conforms to the standards and practices in the host countries in determining wages and conditions of work in international operations. FISIPE, the subsidiary of Mitsubishi Rayon in Portugal, as well as Enka stressed likewise that their whole policy of wages and conditions of work was locally fixed and conditioned to the collective agreements and to the labour legislation in force. Sam Hwa's subsidiary, Lotus, indicated that their wages are determined in line with the relevant Presidential Decree in the Philippines. In its reply, the Government of the Philippines noted in this connection that the country's general policy on wages and conditions of work for multinational enterprises is the same as those applied to domestic enterprises.

According to Dollfus-Mieg & Cie. (DMC), wages in the textile industry are negotiated in France at the national level. The margin

for an individualised company policy is therefore limited.   DMC conforms
to the general wage policy as laid down in collective agreements for the
textile industry which was also pointed out by the Textile Employers'
Association.   With regard to DMC's foreign subsidiaries, wage fixing
for the local manual and management staff is done at the local level;
the emoluments for the directors of subsidiaries and expatriates are,
on the contrary, fixed at the group level.

Rhône-Poulenc Textile (RPT) reported that it has no homogeneous
wage policy for the whole of the group and that each subsidiary follows
an individualised, independent wage policy reflecting the economic
situation of the respective subsidiary.

Factors determining wages and labour conditions in host countries

Against this general background some details can be presented on
the major factors affecting the determination of wage rates/earnings
and conditions of work in host countries.

The replies showed that there was a good deal of variety in the
factors taken into account when determining host country wages and
conditions of work.   Thus, at the Asahi subsidiaries in Indonesia
(INDACI), Ireland (ASP and ASF) and the Republic of Korea (TPC), for
example, the wage and salary levels were, in general, determined by:
(a) the average level of payment in the fibre and textile industry;
(b) the financial and economic conditions of the subsidiary; (c) the
cost of living and consumer prices in the host country; and (d) the
position and performance of the workers.   In addition to regular wages,
annual bonuses paid in these host country operations were equivalent to
approximately one month's wages.   These were provided to the employees
if the circumstances permitted.

Similarly, the criteria taken into consideration for wages and
working conditions by KTSM, the Indonesian subsidiary of Kanebo, were
stated to be: (a) the company's ability to pay; (b) the evolution of
consumer prices; and (c) the locally prevailing wage level.   In
Kanebo's subsidiary in Australia, Lachlan, the rates of wage increase
are determined in accordance with the Arbitration and Conciliation
Commission.   Wages are revised twice a year in the light of the rise
of consumer prices.   For Kanebo do Brasil it was stated that wage
levels and working conditions were mostly determined by the social,
economic and labour policies of the Government, including wage legislation.

Enka's subsidiary in Spain (LSB) indicated that their wages and
salaries, as well as their working conditions and other social achieve-
ments, were the result of collective bargaining.   The following factors
served as a basis when bargaining: cost of living, financial and
economic situation of the enterprise, and wage level of competitors and

other firms established in the region.   Moreover, recommendations by
and agreements with the Government and the leading employers' and
workers' organisations were taken into account if they existed.   Until
recently, it had been possible to seek a binding decision from the
labour authorities in cases of disagreement.   However, this type of
arbitration was no longer existing, and an outside arbitrator - who can
be anyone both parties have agreed to - is appointed.

Viscosuisse (subsidiary of Rhône-Poulenc located in Switzerland)
underlined that their wages and salaries are eventually determined by
the demand situation of the market and generally keep pace with infla-
tion.   The recession from 1975 to 1978 had not resulted in any wage
decrease.

For Lotus, the Philippine subsidiary of Sam Hwa, the following
elements are decisive for wage determination: (a) labour legislation
including wages regulation; (b) situation of labour market; and
(c) educational level of employees.   As to FISIPE, Mitsubishi Rayon's
subsidiary in Portugal, the conditioning factors have been up to now
the collective agreement and the labour market situation.

DMC takes two factors into account when determining the earnings
of the directors at the subsidiaries: a fixed one (not further
described) and a variable factor which is related to productivity.

Factors determining wages and labour conditions in home countries

Only three enterprises commented specifically on this point
althouth information found in the next section is also partly relevant.

Mitsubishi Rayon reported that they considered earnings and wages
in the light of the remuneration their competitors paid.

RPT reported that up to 1974 the main factor determining their
wages in France was the cost of living in accordance with an agreement
reached earlier between the social partners.   However, due to serious
drawbacks, they had to discontinue the agreement.   In 1980 RPT was
able, though, to accept a contract guaranteeing minimum wages for their
French subsidiaries and to increase the lowest wages in accordance with
varying criteria at the different plant levels.   Furthermore, RPT
introduced capital participation for employees and incentive pay
(plans d'intéressement and primes d'objectifs).

In the same sense, DMC reported that at the personal initiative of
the group's president they have implemented, in their thread-making
branch a system of employee participation in their capital stock
(système d'intéressement) for the management staff of their French
plants and the directors of their subsidiaries abroad.   This takes
the form of free distribution of negotiable shares within the limits

of 1 per cent of the group's capital.   The enterprise indicated that
this particular type of capital participation seemed to be unique in
the entire textile sector, both at home and abroad.

Wages, benefits and conditions of work in multinationals as compared to those offered by similar enter- prises or in the sector as a whole[2]

Situation in MNE host countries

Kanebo's subsidiary in Indonesia (KTSM) reported that official
statistics for a comparison with similar enterprises are not available
in Indonesia.   However, the textile companies with Japanese capital had
recently started talking about a unified method for determining these
conditions for their operations in the country.   Similarly, Kanebo do
Brasil was unable to make comparisons with other enterprises of similar
characteristics for lack of data.   Kanebo's subsidiary in Australia
(Lachlan) noted, however, there was no great difference in the wages
and working conditions among similar companies, whether national or
multinational, since they had to abide by the same award determined by
an agreement between management and trade unions of the relevant
industry and district.   Lotus, the subsidiary of Sam Hwa, reported
that its wages and other conditions of work are usually the same as
those of similar enterprises in the Philippines whether national or
multinational.   The Government of the Philippines held that some multinational enterprises in the clothing and footwear industry offer
incentive bonuses usually geared to production and wages that are
slightly higher than those required by law.   Generally, wages and
benefits offered by multinational enterprises are rather similar to
those in local enterprises in the same sector of business.

Some of the participating multinationals reported that their levels
of wages, benefits and conditions of work in host countries were above
legal requirements as well as the provisions contained in the collectively agreed contracts for the industry.   Thus, FISIPE, Mitsubishi
Rayon's subsidiary in Portugal, stated that its wage level was 13 per
cent higher than foreseen in the collective agreement for the industry,
but slightly inferior when compared with some other similar companies
of the same sector.   As concerns FISIPE's conditions of work and
benefits, they were better than those fixed by the contract and the
law and were quite affected by the policy followed in this field by the
major Portuguese shareholders in the enterprise (QUIMIGAL).   Enka
pointed out that its benefits were higher and more numerous than the
national standards foreseen in the relevant collective agreement.
However, additional benefits were fewer nowadays as they tended to
become more and more an integral part of collective agreements.

LSB, Enka's subsidiary in Spain, noted that its wage level was
considerably higher than that of its competitors.   Thus, the wages

for skilled workers in their fibre-producing units were about 20 per cent above the wages paid in other similar enterprises. While it could be said that conditions of work were, in general, comparable to those which existed in other enterprises of the same size and characteristics, the level of paid social benefits granted by LSB, such as the length of vacations and work hours occupied only a middle position when compared with other similar enterprises.

According to Viscosuisse (Rhône-Poulenc's subsidiary in Switzerland) regional differences in emoluments, a characteristic feature of the Swiss wage scene, did not exist in its case or for MNEs having sub-sidiaries in different parts of Switzerland. As social benefits and conditions of work were determined to a large extent by collective agreements, they too seemed to be rather homogeneous for the entire Swiss textile sector whatever the enterprises involved.

Only a few MNEs report of "special paid leave" as, for example, Kanebo do Brasil granting marriage leave, maternity leave, compassionate leave, while the Kanebo subsidiary in Australia (Lachlan), mentions, in addition to compassionate leave, long service leave and sick leave.

The Confederation of Australian Industry stated that fringe bene-fits above minimum award standards were in many cases negotiated at the individual enterprise level, and these may vary from enterprise to enterprise. However, the variations between the fringe benefits provided by multinational and national enterprises were not significant.

The Clothing and Allied Trades Union of Australia noted that it was not aware of differences in wages and conditions of work of MNEs with respect to comparable domestic enterprises.

The National Association of Industrialists, Colombia, was of the opinion that differences in labour conditions derive mostly from the size of the enterprise, whether multinational or not, within the sector under study.

The Federated Union of Employers, Ireland, indicated that wages, fringe benefits and conditions of work, including safety and health in multinationals operating in the textile sector compared very favourably with those in nationally operating enterprises.

The Irish Transport and General Workers' Union pointed out that the wages in Asahi, one of the sample enterprises, are somewhat better than those in other comparable multinational enterprises in the country. Comparable domestic enterprises did not exist.

According to the Korea Employers' Federation, in general, prevail-ing labour standards in MNEs are not different from those in local enterprises, since local labour laws are equally applied to both categories. However, some MNEs subsidiaries in the Republic of Korea

have established advanced practices which are not found in local enterprises.

In the view of the Malaysian Employers' Federation, as a general
rule, the terms and conditions of employment for workers of multinational enterprises are better than those of local companies in the
same industry. The minimum labour standards set by the Employment
Ordinance are, in a number of instances, improved upon through collective bargaining. For example, the average working hours per week in
the industry is 45.2 hours as compared with the statutory maximum of
48 hours; the average number of public holidays per year is 13.5 days
compared with the statutory minimum of 10, and the average duration of
paid annual leave (after service of 12 continuous months) is nine days
as compared with the statutory figure of eight days.

The Mauritius Employers' Federation said that the labour standard
of the workers has improved. Wages are higher than the rates fixed by
the Government or than those practised in comparable enterprises and
fringe benefits represented 40 per cent of wages.

The Trades Union Congress was unable to provide detailed comparison
on the wage conditions but revealed that wages, conditions of work as
well as non-wage benefits in the United Kingdom's textile, clothing and
footwear industries were much inferior to other sectors of the British
economy.

A differentiated view was presented by the ITGLWF in Brussels. It
was of the opinion that, although a lack of comparable data existed, the
general tendency seemed to indicate that not only wages were lower but
also conditions of work less good in the subsidiaries of MNEs in the
developing host countries as compared to those in their home countries'
activities. Nevertheless, compared with the situation prevailing in
the developing host countries, generally, conditions of work seem to be
better in MNEs while the wage rates were much on the same level as in
the comparable local enterprises. This was also confirmed, the ITGLWF
noted, by an ILO study on Kenya where it was found that in footwear,
clothing and make-up textiles, the labour costs per worker were much
the same in local and foreign firms.[3]

Multinationals provided also better labour conditions in some areas
when attracting persons formerly employed in the local small-scale
industry. It was found, for instance, for Tunisia that multinational
factories provided better employment conditions than previously available in the artisan sector.[4] On the other hand, while information for
all countries which textile, clothing and footwear multinationals are
operating was not available, ITGLWF could not confirm, from its
experience, claims that MNEs paid generally higher wages than other
enterprises.

Situation in MNE home countries

Mitsubishi Rayon held that their wage and benefits are similar to
those of competitors' enterprises in Japan.   DMC indicated that earnings
of their management staff are more or less equal to the average earnings
paid by similar enterprises in the same sector.   DMC's salaries for the
upper management staff in the company's spinning subsidiary are slightly
lower than the general average paid in the sector, while the contrary
applied to the weaving branch, TEXUNION.

The Confederation of German Employers' Associations (BDA) reported
that there was no difference in wages, fringe benefits and conditions
of work between MNEs and national enterprises as concerns the clothing
industry.   The same was true for the synthetic fibre sector which
compared favourably with the other sectors of the chemical industry.
Wages and condition of work in synthetic fibre enterprises were clearly
above average when compared to the textile industry.   The Organisation
noted that within all sectors of industry in the Federal Republic of
Germany, the shoe sector was at the lowest end of the wage scale.

The Textile Employers' Association felt that in France the wages
in MNEs are in line with those offered by other enterprises.   It seems
that in the MNEs the social benefits are higher than in other enterprises.

In the same sense, the Japanese Federation of Textile, Garment,
Chemical, Distribution and Allied Industry Workers' Unions (ZENSEN)
stated that there was absolutely no difference in wages or working
conditions between national and multinational enterprises in its sector.
Wages of large enterprises in the manufacturing industry in Japan were
about 10 per cent higher than those of the smaller enterprises, which
was also true for most of the multinationals as many of them were of a
larger scale.

The Swedish Trade Union Confederation said that the trade union
movement pursues the so-called wage solidarity policy.   This means
that wages and wage differentials should not be based on differences in
companies' profitability, or on the branch of the public service they
work in.   So far, the wage solidarity policy has been used primarily
to narrow the wage gaps within the ranks of the workers.   During the
1960s and 1970s this policy has benefited the members of the Swedish
Textile, Garment and Leather Trades Union.   This is reflected in the
following table:

Table IV-1: Monthly wages in Sweden

	1960	1965	1970	1976	1978	1979
Average for industry (men and women)	100	100	100	100	100	100
Textile, garment and leather industries (men and women)	79	82	85	89	90	91
Female workers' wages as percentage of men's wages in textile, garment and leather industries	70.2	77	82.9	88.8	90.6	91.5

Differentials in wages and conditions
of work by category or sex of workers[5]

Various participating enterprises, such as Mölnlycke, KTSM, Kanebo
do Brasil, FISIPE, LSB and all Asahi subsidiaries, stress that they do
not practice any discrimination by sex and that their wages are set
according to the job position and performance of workers. Kanebo do
Brasil notes further that its wages and salaries are specified according
to job grades as well as job categories: managers, maintenance workers,
operators, electricians and clerical workers. Mitsubishi Rayon reports
that their wage level is different by rank and position of workers as
well as years of service. Lotus in the Philippines notes that
differentials in wages, benefits and other working conditions for the
various job categories and for men and women are set in accordance with
the local labour law. Enka's subsidiary in Spain (LSB) states that
most of the company's wages, benefits and working conditions are
regulated by collective agreement. Benefits are unrelated to job
categories. The only exception is the old-age pension which is
calculated on the basis of the different wage levels.

The Clothing and Allied Trades Union of Australia reports that
working hours are different according to sex: while the average weekly
hours paid for males in the industry are 41.7 per week, working hours
for women are 38.8. Award hours are 40 per week. As the industry is
90 per cent female, the conditions of the industry are identical with
those of women workers, and it is particularly important to protect this
category of workers. The second important category equally linked with
the sex of the workers is the unskilled workers. Although workers in
the clothing industry generally experience similar conditions, in
general, unskilled workers tend to work in industries with poor conditions. The third important category is migrants. As in other
countries, migrants in Australia tend to be found in industries with

poor wages and labour conditions.   The fourth category of particular
relevance for the clothing industry is homeworkers who experience very
poor conditions.   The Union said that it was currently involved in a
campaign to assist homeworkers gain improved wages and conditions
through the use of state legislation since they were not covered by
collective bargaining.

The Irish Transport and General Workers' Union noted that there
were no special problems attached to the working conditions of any
particular group in the sector under consideration.

For the Republic of Korea it was noted by the Federation of Korean
Trade Unions that wages for men are more than 50 per cent higher than
those of women.   A number of protective employment restrictions also
exist for certain categories of workers.   Thus, a minor under 13 years
of age cannot be employed and night work is prohibited for those under
18 years of age according to the law.   The workers held further that
night work of women ought to be avoided.

The Japanese Federation of Textile, Garment, Chemical, Distribution
and Allied Industry Workers' Unions (ZENSEN) reported that institutional
struggles still have to be fought in order to win favourable legislation
for women workers to raise their status and protect motherhood which was
particularly important in this women-dominated sector.   The Union
participated actively in the application of the Minimum Wage Law and
Industrial Home Work Law in order to protect the unorganised workers
and to try to improve their wages and working conditions.   ZENSEN
mentioned that its next move would consist of the following: the
problems of temporary workers and part-timers in the sector.   Particular efforts would be made for a better degree of union organisation of
these categories.

The Government of the Philippines stated that the Labour Code and
Presidential Decrees on wages and allowances provide benefits and
conditions of work and minimum wages which are applicable to all workers
and/or employees in the private sectors: no distinctions are made
according to job categories and sex.   Wage levels for skilled, semi
and unskilled workers are determined in collective agreements.

Types of wage systems and benefits

Asahi's subsidiaries, INDACI, ASP, TPC, and ASF, pay their workers
on a monthly basis.   Kanebo's subsidiary in Indonesia (KTSM) applies,
in addition to the all-month rate, a day rate.   Kanebo's subsidiary in
Australia, Lachlan, pays the general workers by the week while managers'
salaries are calculated on an annual basis.   The clerical workers at
Lotus in the Philippines get their salaries monthly while manual workers
are paid on a daily piece-rate basis.[6]

As the majority of the MNEs explain, emoluments consist of a basic wage plus benefits. These are usually beyond the legal requirements and vary a great deal from company to company. Thus, the wage system of Mitsubishi Rayon in its Japanese plants consists of: (1) the basic wage, which is composed of a fixed minimum and an amount varying with the function performed; (2) allowances, ranging from residence, family, vacation, night shift, etc., allowances to post, commuting, shift, year-end and year-beginning allowances, an allowance for being on call, and one for working at the head office; and (3) additional wage payments.

As a complement to basic wages/salaries, Enka in Spain (LSB) pays the following allowances: a seniority allowance of 3 per cent of the last five years' earnings; an attendance grant amounting to 10 per cent of the basic salary; two additional monthly basic salaries (plus a seniority allowance), one in July, one at Christmas; a special grant payable in January (of 6 or 8 per cent of the basic salary) considered to be profit-sharing; and another special gratification in September, the amount of which is fixed through collective agreement. Shift-workers working in three shifts - and this includes practically all employees - receive a night shift allowance and, when working on Sunday, a Sunday allowance of 800 pesetas. Some of the LSB workers receive a special grant (the so-called "Bédeaux" grant), raising their wages by 13 per cent.

The Asahi subsidiaries in Ireland and the Republic of Korea grant supplementary food allowances and allowances for seniority and position. Additionally, a housing allowance is paid in the case of Asahi's subsidiary in Indonesia. All the Asahi subsidiaries distribute to their employees, in addition to regular wages, annual bonuses equivalent to approximately one month's wage, if financial circumstances permit. KTSM, Kanebo's subsidiary in Indonesia, grants the following benefits: long service allowance, allowance attached to a post, housing, overtime and family allowances, as well as an allowance for expatriates. In addition, bonuses to workers are distributed according to the business results of each fiscal period.

The Clothing and Allied Trades Union of Australia indicated that earnings, in addition to the basic salary, consist of payments by results and payments above the basic award. The Irish Transport and General Workers' Union reports on seniority-related payments as an important additional wage element. Thus, £1.20 is paid per week for each year of service subject to a maximum of five years which yields sizeable amounts after a number of years.

Aside from additions to basic salaries, there exists another category of benefits having no direct bearing on the wage level, but which determines to a large extent the quality of work and the living conditions of employees in the sector multinationals, i.e. the welfare and recreation facilities.[7] These social services were found to be important elements of working conditions both in the parent companies and in the subsidiaries of the participating multinationals. The facilities provided by the subsidiaries in developing countries may not always come up to the standards of the parent companies in the industrialised countries. It appears, however, to be fairly certain that they are on the whole better developed than those provided by local firms.

As the MNEs report, welfare and recreation facilities ranging from canteens (all Asahi and Kanebo subsidiaries and Lotus in the Philippines) and sports facilities (all Asahi subsidiaries as well as Kanebo's subsidiaries in Indonesia and in Brazil, Enka in Spain (LSB) and Lotus in the Philippines), to clubhouses (Kanebo's subsidiaries in Indonesia and Brazil) and summer camps/vacation houses (Kanebo do Brasil, Mitsubishi Rayon and FISIPE in Portugal, Mölnlycke, Enka in Spain (LSB)) and even to a company-owned hospital (Kanebo's subsidiary in Indonesia).

The importance of welfare and recreational benefits is confirmed by several union sources, which note at the same time the absence of certain facilities or social services. Thus, the Irish Transport and General Workers' Union indicated that, with respect to Asahi, recreation facilities are organised through the company's sports and social club. Transportation is arranged, however, only for female workers in the spinning plant. Likewise, no nurseries exist. The Clothing and Allied Trades Union of Australia mentions similarly that recreational facilities are provided in only a few firms, whether multinational or not, and that nurseries are not provided by any of the major firms. The Federation of Korean Trade Unions reported that almost all of the larger enterprises in the sector have dormitories, furnish one meal a day free of charge, and run schools and special industrial classes. In addition to commuters' buses, which large enterprises possess, it says that almost all enterprises have various recreational facilities such as a volley-ball court and table tennis facilities. All enterprises have their own arrangements for child and health care, such as nurseries and designated hospitals. Also, all enterprises have canteens. ZENSEN, Japan, indicated that vacation houses are generally available for the personnel and that a canteen exists at each plant. With regard to the latter point, it is confirmed by the ITGLWF that canteens are a common feature of textile MNEs in the Third World. Japanese MNEs in Asia, in particular, often provided schools and medical services in addition. On the other hand, it was ITGLWF's experience that there were very few nurseries or recreational facilities in MNEs in the Third World operating in the sector under study.

Social security practices of MNEs

The efforts made by MNEs in this field are normally determined by the following factors listed by order of importance: (1) national legislation, varying a good deal from country to country and especially between industrialised home and developing host countries; (2) collective agreements at the industrial, regional, national, or possibly, company level; and (3) MNE-specific welfare plans not covered by these.

As a rule, the standards set by law and agreements seem to account for the bulk of social security measures undertaken by MNEs in the textile, clothing and footwear sector.

In most industrialised countries and particularly in the home countries of the multinationals participating in the study, the social security benefits set up by law and/or collective agreements, such as pension schemes, sickness, disability and life insurance, income maintenance in the event of sickness and medical care, are well developed and afford workers a comparatively high standard of protection. In most of the developing countries this does not, however, appear to be the case, generally speaking, although some multinationals seem to offer various types of benefits.[8]

In this connection, Kanebo do Brasil mentions that it provides for free dental treatment of their personnel, and Mitsubishi Rayon's subsidiary in Portugal (FISIPE) provides complementary allowances in case of illness, hospitalisation, retirement and survival. Enka's subsidiary in Spain (LSB) grants in special cases (e.g. chronic diseases and/or mental trouble) extra allowances, the amount of which is fixed by a committee, composed of employer and worker representatives. LSB has, moreover, a special accident insurance for their employees when they are not totally covered by the public security scheme (in case of missions, for example). In addition, they grant a children's allowance for dependents under 18 years. LSB has also a supplementary retirement scheme for some of its managerial staff, and Viscosuisse, Rhône-Poulenc's subsidiary in Switzerland, provides retirement benefits to its employees in the form of a lump-sum payment.

The Clothing and Allied Trades Union of Australia reported that company pension schemes are provided by a few firms only and that the conditions of such schemes differ widely. The Irish Transport and General Workers' Union said that, in Asahi, no pension scheme exists as yet, though the company is committed, in principle, to the introduction of one. ZENSEN, Japan, indicated that a pension scheme, financed by regular contributions from both workers and management, has been in operation since 1966. According to the Government of the Philippines workers, upon their retirement, are entitled to pension benefits from the Social Security System, pursuant to the Social Security Act. In addition to this, they are entitled to retirement benefits from company-established retirement plans. The company retirement plan is established either through collective bargaining or other employment contracts, or in the absence of such collective bargaining agreements or contracts, it is voluntarily set up by the employer as a matter of policy or practice. Usually, company retirement plans are locally administered.

Redundancy measures

In view of the fact that in many countries employment in the sector has dramatically decreased over the past decade, it is surprising to

note that this question has received little attention in the replies
received from the enterprises.   It would appear, however, that
redundancy measures are mainly regulated at the level of national
labour legislation and in sector or industry-wide bargaining rather than
specifically at that of the enterprise.   Legal arrangements for
redundant workers appear to be rather widespread in industrialised
countries and not uncommon in a good number of developing countries.[9]

According to the Irish Transport and General Workers' Union, no
specific enterprise-level arrangements exist for redundancy and would
obviously have to be the subject of negotiation if this were to arise,
having regard to the negotiated settlements for the sector and the
country at large.

The French Federation of Textile and Allied Workers reported for
the participating French enterprises that no social security provision
existed in the event of redundancy other than what was contained in the
national collective agreement for the sector.

The Government of the Philippines reports that where employees are
separated by reason of redundancy, the employers are required by law
to pay separation pay to the employees concerned equivalent to one
month's salary for every year of service, a fraction of six months is
considered one whole year.

Mitsubishi Rayon said that they had no specific provisions for
redundancy benefits, nor did FISIPE, its subsidiary in Portugal, while
Viscosuisse, Rhône Poulenc's subsidiary in Switzerland, pointed out
that unemployment insurance was obligatory and thus covered the problem
of income maintenance in case of redundancies.

DMC noted that it was the policy of the whole group to favour, in
crisis periods, the transfer of workers to other jobs, re-employment
of redundant workers in other enterprises and early retirement.

In cases of plant closures, DMC would search for a buyer likely to
take over a maximum of employees.   In this connection, subsidiaries of
TEXUNION collaborated in the absorption of workers by subsidiaries in
the Federal Republic of Germany who had been made redundant in the
French subsidiary of the company.

The ITGLWF noted in this connection that in its international
experience there exists fear redundancy arrangements at the enterprise
level in respect to the sector.

Work organisation and hours of work

Owing to data limitation, comparison of working hours in MNEs with
the average hours worked in the entire sector[10] (textiles, clothing and
footwear, respectively) can only be made for some industrialised

countries.   For the developing countries where participating MNEs'
subsidiaries are located, industry-specific data are usually missing.
Information on other aspects of work organisation is rarely contained
in the replies.

It appears that, with the exception of Viscosuisse (Rhône Poulenc's
subsidiary in Switzerland) and Mitsubishi Rayon, the number of working
hours per week in textile and clothing is higher in the participating
MNEs than the average number of working hours for the respective
industry or sector as a whole.   In the synthetic fibre production,
which in most available statistics of hours of work is grouped with
the chemical industry, the average work-week tends to be shorter than
in the textile and footwear industries.

The Irish Transport and General Workers' Union reported that in
the sector being studied the work-week in MNEs in Ireland is generally
40 hours.   Shift operators are an exception to this who, because of
the nature of their work, have an average of 42 hours a week with the
extra two hours being paid at overtime rate.   The average working
hours actually worked for the whole of the Irish textile industry was
41.7 in 1982.[11]

The number of working hours in MNEs in developing countries seemed
to be much higher than in industrialised countries.   Thus, Kanebo do
Brasil reports of a 48-hour week while, in comparison, another
subsidiary in Australia, Lachlan, has a 43-hour work-week and the
average hours worked in the same lines of production in the home
country, Japan, amount to 41.3.   Lotus in the Philippines also reports
a 48-hour week while the average for the whole of the sector in the
developing home country (Republic of Korea) is 53 working hours[12]
(all data for about 1980).   In the Republic of Korea, excessive hours
were worked in MNEs, i.e. often 55-60 a week.   This seemed to correspond to the general practice in the country.[13]   In connection with
working time, the ITGLWF observed that in some countries, such as
Sri Lanka, high production quotas were set by enterprises requiring
workers to produce a certain number of clothing items a day.   This
amounted, in practice, to imposing compulsory overtime as the workers
were often kept in the factory until the required goals were met.[14]
Excessive hours were also found in some Asian export processing zones
and in Sri Lanka the ILO's Convention on Night Work by Women (Nos. 4
and 89 (Revised)), prohibiting women from being used on night shifts
had recently been repealed[15] (see also the next section in this chapter
on these zones).

Generally speaking, the hours of work and the work organisation
situation in the clothing industry in developing countries was much
worse than in the textiles.   The clothing industry was more labour
intensive and the companies had tight delivery dates in response to
market and fashion changes.   Also, the companies tended to be smaller
than the textile companies.   This resulted in longer hours of work and
in the danger of a greater degree of exploitation of workers.   It was

reported for one MNE in India (not participating in the study) that its basic working week consists of six working days of eight hours each, on a revolving shift basis, and that no extra pay was given for shift work.[16]

With a view to other aspects of work organisation, such as piece work, shift work[17] and initiatives taken towards new forms[18] of work organisation - for example, the introduction of flexible working hours - the following picture emerges:

The five Asahi subsidiaries and Kanebo's subsidiary in Indonesia (KTSM) note that no piece-work system is used. Most of the MNEs reported of a three or four group shift-work system (all the Asahi subsidiaries, KTSM and Kanebo's subsidiary in Australia (Lachlan)). The Irish Transport and General Workers' Union noted that in the fibre plant of Asahi the vast majority of operators work the four-shift continuous cycle throughout the year with no close down of the plant. The Sam Hwa's subsidiary in the Philippines, Lotus, reports to the contrary that they were unable to introduce a shift or overtime work system due to the refusal by local employees. Generally, in highly automated factories in the sector (textiles, fibre products), capital-intensive equipment seems to be utilised often, 24 hours a day, and in one RPT factory which used to employ 200 workers, seven are now sufficient.

Only one participating MNE reported that it used flexible working hours, i.e. Enka's subsidiary in Spain (LSB) who introduced them for their administrative and technical personnel. Viscosuisse created recently autonomous work groups in some of their workshops. The management points out that further trials of this kind are under way. Mölnlycke noted that part-time work arrangements were increasing. The enterprise has also set up special production groups, often upon the initiatives of the workers themselves.[19]

Occupational safety and health

The replies received indicate that safety and health measures are a priority concern of multinationals in the sector. Their records are similar or compare favourably with other enterprises in the industry.[20] However, a number of unresolved problems are referred to in the trade union replies.

The Confederation of Australian Industry reported that safety and health standards are prescribed by national awards and/or by the relevant legislation applicable in the state in which the enterprise operates. These standards have equal application to multinationals and national enterprises. There is no difference in the manner in which the standards are applied or in the procedures followed for the maintenance of safety and health standards for employees of multi-nationals as compared with national enterprises.

The Clothing and Allied Trades Union of Australia noted that there were many problems which are not sufficiently addressed by the existing safety and health standards, such as muscular over-use, excessive noise, back and leg strain, eye strain, chemical exposure, dust, mental stress, use of analgesics, urinary tract infection. Deviations from normal practices by multinationals are not known to the union. The National Confederation of Industrial Workers, Brazil, noted with a view to Kanebo's subsidiary that optimal conditions existed in the enterprise as regards hygiene and comfort. The number of occupational accidents is almost zero. The Amalgamated Clothing and Textile Workers' Union (ACTWU), Canada, reported on its part that while the Canadian clothing and textile industries are modern and efficient compared with production facilities in the Third World, health problems associated with the materials used in production are still very much present. The Irish Transport and General Workers' Union observed that because of the sensitive nature of the industry and the chemicals and acids used, the Asahi's subsidiary operating in the country puts emphasis on safety measures. An active safety committee, with a heavy worker involvement, is in operation and a safety officer is employed. The factory is also inspected regularly by the industrial inspectorate.

Lotus in the Philippines reported that its safety and health provisions are in accordance with the relevant local laws; the Asahi subsidiaries, INDACI, ASP, TPC and ASF, noted that they respected and followed the relevant ILO safety and sanitation standards and codes of practice; Kanebo's subsidiary in Indonesia (KTSM) likewise noted that the company abides by the ILO standards for safety and sanitation in respect to noise, dust, etc.21 In the case of Kanebo's subsidiary in Australia (Lachlan), safety and health standards authorities with jurisdiction are the Department of Labour and Industry (State) and the local council (town). The Factories, Shops and Industries Act, 1982, and the Noxious Act are mentioned as jurisdictional Acts.

Collectively agreed safety and health standards seem rarely to exist for the enterprises participating in the study. The most important norms in the safety and health field are those found in the legislation of the host country. In this connection, Kanebo do Brasil observed that safety and health provisions are enacted by the governmental enterprise law and that they are not part of the collective bargaining agreement with labour unions, while Lachlan pointed out that the award for individual unions sometimes sets forth the minimum standards of working environment and owrking conditions.

A common feature in the majority of the participating MNEs is the existence in their plants of joint safety and health committees, whether these are prescribed by national law or collective agreement or not. Their main principle is the inclusion of workers' representatives in the control of the application of relevant protective standards.

Kanebo's subsidiary in Australia (Lachlan) stated that discussion about occupational safety and health issues take place at the company's safety council, consisting of the plant manager, workshop supervisors and worker representatives, while Kanebo do Brasil indicated that the establishment of an enterprise safety committee is compulsory under the enterprise law. This committee is responsible for the adoption of practical solutions to safety and sanitation problems. The members of the committee are employers, workers and medical doctors in the event of workers' accidents. Mitsubishi's subsidiary in Portugal (FISIPE) also has a safety committee at the company level which includes workers' representatives. At the national level, the enterprise also has to report to the Public Health Service. Mölnlycke reported that in all its workplaces there is a labour safety organisation. Enka's subsidiary in Spain (LSB) noted that all enterprises employing more than 100 wage earners had to set up, by law, a safety committee composed of management and workers' representatives. The functions of the safety committee consist of implementing the legally-defined safety and health protection measures; supervising/controlling their correct application; actively participating in fire and accident prevention; informing management of potential dangers due to defective machinery or bad state of working instruments; promoting vaccination campaigns, etc.

The exact functions of the safety committees vary a great deal from country to country, depending on the different legal or other require-ments. Where safety committees are not compulsory by law or collective agreement, their scope is determined by MNE-specific practices in this field. DMC reported that the rates of risk as published by the various subsidiaries of the group were comparable to the national average rates of the sectors in question. It further noted that each of their French subsidiaries had a safety committee which met regularly to exchange experience on occupational safety and health matters. This sort of formal consultation does not exist at the level of DMC's foreign-based subsidiaries. DMC affirms, however, that an informal transfer of safety techniques takes place at the management level. This applies especially for information transferred from headquarters to the subsidiaries in developing countries. The "Safety Delegation" of RPT participates in the choice, recruitment and training of the company's safety personnel, sets up security objectives and supervises their implementation.

The Malaysian Employers' Federation reports on three unidentified multinational enterprises in the sector. As regards the first enter-prise, a textile company, great emphasis is laid on both safety and health matters. All employees are provided with suitable work clothes, i.e. caps, shirts, trousers/skirts, shoes, including safety shoes where necessary. Regular checks are carried out to ensure that employees wear these uniforms. A full-time safety supervisor is employed to ensure that fire-fighting equipment is in working order. Additionally, a safety committee exists to see to it that safety is maintained at all times. Signboards are displayed all over the factory reminding employees not to smoke or litter and to ensure that they follow the existing safety rules when operating machinery. Any accidents that may occur are investigated by the safety committee and, where necessary, immediate remedial action is taken.   A 24-hour clinic, with a full-time nurse in attendance, is provided at the factory. There are company-appointed doctors in the city where employees are sent for medical check-ups and treatment.   All employees are entitled to free second-class hospitalisation at government hospitals to the maximum of $900 per year per person.

As regards the second multinational, likewise a textile company, the safety and health measures include the provision of caps to female employees, and safety shoes to employees handling heavy items.   Ear plugs are put at the disposal of workers in areas with a high noise level, and face masks exist for dust protection.   Fire drill is given once in every two to three months and regular training to the company fire brigade.   The works safety committee meets regularly, chaired by the mill engineer.

In the third multinational, a footwear company, safety measures include instructions to employees how to perform their respective operations and precautions to be taken during working hours.   The department supervisor and the department heads regularly follow up these to ensure that the employees follow the safety procedures.   Periodic maintenance and safety checks are conducted by a maintenance team on a regular basis.   As regards health protection, all employees are sent for medical check-up prior to confirmation of their contracts, followed by regular check-ups whenever necessary.

In its reply, the ITGLWF provides some further information on the particular safety and health issues in the industries covered and the problems found with MNE subsidiaries in developing countries.   According to them the main problems are connected with noise, dust, fumes, toxic chemicals and unguarded machinery.[22]   For example, with regard to dust extraction, there was still much to be desired in many plants. Industrial unrest had occurred in connection with insufficient safety and health protection in MNE subsidiaries.[23]

Additionally, according to the Federation, a common form of physical stress for workers in the textile and clothing industries was over-exertion in highly repetitive tasks.   Workers were often required to do the same type of twisting, pulling and pushing movements of tools and materials hundreds - and sometimes thousands - of times per day.[24] On the whole, textiles would appear to be the industry with higher risk in the sector, with the situation being much the same throughout the world.   There was much less risk in the clothing industry and in the shoe industry, where a special risk was associated with glue.   But unguarded machinery was a risk in the textile and footwear industries and in the clothing industries - fingers punctured by sewing-machine needles were common.   A particular problem in many of the Third World countries was that the labour inspectorates were not sufficiently well staffed.   According to the ITGLWF in Niger, for example, there was only one factory inspector for the entire country.   In some cases there were also problems connected with competence and integrity of inspectors and

the Government's determination to have safety and health standards
applied.

The ITGLWF felt that, in general, the larger enterprises - multinationals or not - had a more rational layout of their plants; they
were usually cleaner and better managed.   All this reflected better
standards of safety in the enterprise.   The larger MNEs sometimes had
standard equipment which they would use throughout the world, including
satisfactory protective devices.   Also, the more recent MNE implantation
in the developing countries tended to have more modern and safer equipment.   Man-made fibre producers, in general, fell in this category.
This was in contrast to the older companies that tended to use outdated
machines in the textile industry, which were often less safe.[25]

Wages and labour conditions in export
processing zones in the field of
textiles, clothing and footwear

An increasing amount of production in many developing host
countries is carried out in export processing zones (EPZs).   These
zones, in which multinational enterprises dominate in the form of
subsidiaries or joint ventures, have proliferated in the developing
regions of Asia and Latin America and to a smaller extent in Africa.
In the Asian region, the number of EPZs has risen from only a few in
the 1960s to 26 in 1981, and about ten more were scheduled to start
operations in 1982/83 with some 30 more in various stages of planning
and implementation.   In Asia, at least, EPZ-based electronics and
garment/textile enterprises together accounted for more than two-thirds
of total zone employment in Malaysia, the Philippines and Sri Lanka,
and a similar pattern can be assumed for other Asian countries.   Total
EPZ employment in Asia can be estimated at over 500,000 workers and at
1 million world-wide at present.   The bulk of workers in the zone
consist of low-skilled young females, a labour market group considered
particularly vulnerable in many countries.   Considerable interest
attaches therefore to their wages and working conditions.[26]

Working conditions in EPZs can be explained largely by the
occupational structure and the characteristics of the majority of
workers in these zones.   As a result of the nature of the zone
production, most of the jobs are restricted to simple operative tasks.
In Masan (Republic of Korea), for instance, operative workers accounted
for 89 per cent of total zone employment, in Katunayake (Sri Lanka) for
88 per cent, and in Penang (Malaysia) for about 84 per cent.   Most of
these operative jobs were performed by female workers whereas men pre-
dominated in the higher echelons.   In Malaysia, for example, in 1979
over 75 per cent of the administrative and technical jobs were performed
by male workers.   Among the unskilled and skilled workers only 15.5
and 6.3 per cent respectively were male.   Similarly, in the Republic
of Korea, all the engineers and technicians were male, as compared to
only 13.6 per cent of the unskilled labourers.

The promotion prospects for unskilled female workers in the EPZs are usually restricted. Almost all of them start working as factory floor operators and because of the virtual absence of an internal job ladder they remain in this position until they stop working in the EPZs. The skills which they learn from their jobs are acquired in a matter of weeks and peak productivity is generally reached after only a couple of months. In view of the low skill contents of the jobs, there are also very few transferable skills which might give the outgoing female workers a competitive advantage in the search for alternative employment.

With regard to the wages of the zone workers, it has often been claimed that they tend to be very low. This is certainly correct if one compares them with the wages paid in similar sectors in the industrialised countries. Naturally, this type of comparison is debatable because of the different general economic context in the countries concerned. Nevertheless, in comparison to the wage level in other formal sector employment in the Asian developing countries, wages paid by EPZ firms tend also to remain on the low side. However, this is not because EPZ firms were paying below prevailing national wage rates. It reflects rather the composition of the workforce: the category of workers predominantly employed in the zones (young, female and unmarried workers) is among the lowest paid in the local labour market. Female wages are usually less than half of the male wages; in some countries this amounts to about a quarter or a third. Young workers also receive lower wages than workers with longer professional experience. As a result of the high concentration of workers which combine these two characteristics, wages in EPZs tend to be below the national average. For workers of the same age, sex and sector, however, hardly any significant differences could be discerned between the wages inside and outside of the export processing zones. In the electronics sector in Malaysia, and in the garments sector in Sri Lanka, earnings seemed to be even slightly higher inside the EPZs for the same category of workers. In Bataan (Philippines), on the other hand, zone wages were slightly lower than the wages paid nation-wide for the same category of workers. This might have been due to the fact that the region around the Bataan EPZ was a typical labour-surplus area. See in this connection table IV-2 below.

In spite of their low position in the national wage structure, most of the female workers interviewed for a survey carried out by the ILO's Asian Regional Team for Employment Promotion (ARTEP) in 1979-81, who had previously held employment, still reported significant income gains resulting from their recruitment by zone enterprises. In Malaysia, for example, the average monthly wage rates for female workers thus increased from M$154 to M$201. In Sri Lanka also, reported income gains due to employment in the zones were considerable. In the Philippines, average daily earnings increased upon recruitment in the zones from 22.6 pesos per day to 30.5 pesos per day. As a matter of fact, wages obtained in the zones were generally considerably higher than what could be earned by similar workers in the rural areas or in the informal urban sector. In Malaysia, the average income derived

Table IV-2: Daily wages of women workers in the Bataan EPZ (Philippines)
(textile and clothing operations, 1980)

	US$ (converted from local currency)		
	Basic wage	Allowance	Total
Regular workers:			
- lowest	1.95	1.03	2.98
- average	2.03	1.60	3.63
- highest	2.18	1.60	3.78
Casuals (1-6 months)	1.60	-	1.60
Trainees (1-3 months)	1.37	-	1.37

Source: Data received from ITGLWF.

for females working in the zones was M$201 per month while the poverty line income for urban households can be estimated at M$316 per month (US$137).   However, wages below the poverty line were none the less acceptable to secondary workers, i.e. workers complementing the earnings of the primary breadwinner of the family.

Another characteristic of the zone workers is that their average length of employment in the zones rarely exceeds a few years which results in a high labour turnover.   It must be mentioned, however, that the age at which female zone workers give up their jobs coincides very much with the mean age of marriage.   Also, long average working hours can often be observed and a high proportion of earnings is accounted for by overtime and incentive payments.

Hours of work are an element of working conditions which is relatively easy to measure in EPZs.   ARTEP data on the distribution of hours worked per week in the EPZs of Sri Lanka, Malaysia and the Philippines are summarised in table IV-3 below.

It can be inferred from the table that in Malaysia and Sri Lanka the work burden measured by the length of the working week does not deviate significantly from the national average for the manufacturing industry (Malaysia: standard working week - without overtime - 45 hours in 1980; Sri Lanka: standard working week - 45 hours in 1980, hours paid for 52.6 in 1979 and 45.3 in 1980).   In the Philippines, on the other hand, in comparison with the national average in the Bataan EPZ

Table IV-3: Distribution of hours worked per week in the EPZs in
Sri Lanka, Malaysia and the Philippines (1980)

	Sri Lanka	Malaysia	Philippines
Below 40	0.1	1.0	-
40-44	10.4	31.8	-
45-48	43.5	43.3	54.4
49-54	29.1	17.9	12.2
Over 55	16.9	6.0	33.3
Total	100.0	100.0	99.9

Source: ARTEP documentation; reproduced in Maex, op. cit., p. 56.

was much higher with about 53.9 hours. Almost one-quarter of the
workers in the Bataan Zone actually worked more than 60 hours per week
and 5 per cent even more than 70 hours per week. Very long hours of
work also seemed common practice in the EPZ of Masan (Republic of Korea).
According to a survey undertaken in 1977, 50 per cent of the workers
there worked more than eight hours per day and 30.1 per cent even more
than 15 hours per day.[27] Still longer hours of work, often as the
result of overtime, would seem to be a widespread general phenomenon
in developing countries.[28]

Surveys also show that shift work is proportionally much more
common in the EPZs than in the rest of the economies of Asian developing countries. Some countries, including Malaysia and Singapore, have
waived existing legislation against night work for women in order to
enable zone enterprises to operate three shifts of women workers per
day. A certain leniency at times by the authorities regarding the
respect of labour regulations in the zones is also an impression gained
from the available studies.

In Malaysia, night shift work has now become a common feature.
According to the above-mentioned ARTEP surveys, almost half of the EPZ
firms were operating three eight-hour shifts daily. Another 25 per
cent worked on a two-shift basis. The incidence of shift work was
equally high in the Bataan EPZ in the Philippines, and in the electronics
firms in Singapore. As elsewhere, social problems of shift work also
exist in the EPZs, related to insufficient rotation of shifts.

The before-mentioned surveys have clarified for some of the export processing zones in Asia the characteristics of th workforce, wages, hours of work and related aspects. Still, the field of labour conditions and labour relations in the zones needs further research in particular as regards other developing regions.[29]

Notes

[1] For procedures for the establishment of minimum standards in the clothing industry, see ILO: General report, Report I, Second Tripartite Technical Meeting for the Clothing Industry, Geneva, 1980, Ch. I, pp. 15-19; in the leather and footwear industry: idem: General report, Report I, Second Tripartite Technical Meeting for the Leather and Footwear Industry, Geneva, 1979, Ch. II, pp. 40-45.

[2] General information on wages in the industries under study can be found in idem: General report, Report I, Textiles Committee, Tenth Session, Geneva, 1978, Ch. XIII, pp. 97-98; idem: Report III, Ch. II, pp. 40-57; idem: General report, Report I, Second Tripartite Technical Meeting for the Clothing Industry, op. cit., Ch. XI, p. 127; idem: General report, Report I, Second Tripartite Technical Meeting for the Leather and Footwear Industry, op. cit., Ch. XIII, pp. 155-156; and idem: Report III, Chemical Industries Committee, Ninth Session, Geneva, 1982, Ch. II, pp. 22-44 (as regards synthetic fibres).

[3] idem: Employment, incomes and equality: A strategy for increasing productive employment in Kenya (Geneva, 1972), table 7, p. 448.

[4] ITGLWF: The international division of labour and international trade in textiles, clothing, shoe and leather products (including outward processing); Discussion document, Part One: Outward processing in the textiles, clothing and shoe and leather industries (Third World Congress, Vienna, 6-10 October 1980; mimeographed), p. 15.

[5] In this connection, it might be recalled that Resolution No. 63, adopted by the Textiles Committee, concerns the wages of women employed in the textile industry, which referred specifically to the elimination of unjustifiable differences between men's and women's wages, Official Bulletin (Geneva, ILO), Vol. LII, 1969, No. 1, p. 116; and ILO: General report, Report I, Textiles Committee, Tenth Session, op. cit., Ch. III, pp. 21-27.

[6] For systems of remuneration in the textile sector, see idem: Report III, a general review of the Textiles Committee, Tenth Session, Geneva, 1978, Ch. II, pp. 43-50.

[7] For general information on such social services in the leather and footwear industry, for example, see idem: Report III, Second Tripartite Technical Meeting of the Leather and Footwear Industry, Geneva, 1979, Ch. IV, pp. 27-31.

[8] Summary of second government reports on the effect given to the Tripartite Declaration of Principles concerning Multinational Enterprises and Social Policy submitted to the Committee on Multinational Enterprises (Geneva, ILO; doc. GB.224/MNE/1/1/D.1).

[9] For a general discussion of this aspect, see also ILO: General report, Report I, Textiles Committee, Tenth Session, op. cit., pp. 101-103.

[10] As regards hours of work in the industries of the sector, see idem: General report, Report I, Textiles Committee, Tenth Session, op. cit., Ch. XIII, pp. 98-100, Ch. XI, p. 149; idem: General report, Report I, Second Tripartite Technical Meeting for the Leather and Foot-wear Industry, op. cit., Ch. II, pp. 45-48; idem: Report III, Ch. III, pp. 19-21; and idem: General report, Report I, Second Triparte Technical Meeting for the Clothing Industry, op. cit., Ch. XI, p. 127.

[11] idem: Year Book of Labour Statistics, 1981 (Geneva, 1981).

[12] ibid.

[13] In 1976, a trade union paper in the Republic of Korea stated:

Under the provisions of article 57 of the Labour Standard Law, women workers should not work more than ten hours a day, more than 54 hours a week, nor more than 200 hours a month, but they work 350 hours a month in some establishments surveyed. This is believed to result from employers' schemes to conceal low wages, and from the ignorance of women workers themselves about their health control rights. There must be measures to protect women workers as mothers of the rising generation.

ITGLWF: Employment of women, Third World Congress, Vienna, 6-10 October 1980, p. 23.

[14] See also G. McCredie: "Body space only", in Guardian Third World Review, 19 Mar. 1982, p. 9.

[15] C. Ford: "Value added: Free trade zones in Sri Lanka", in Free Labour World (ICFTU), 1981, No. 4.

[16] The ITGLWF refers, in this connection, to a publication of A. Sinclair: Sewing it up: Coats Patons' multinational practices (Edinburgh, Scottish Education and Action for Development, 1982), p. 15.

[17] See also for general aspects in the industry, ILO: Report III, Textiles Committee, op. cit., Ch. I, pp. 3-39.

[18] ibid., Ch. III, pp. 60-78.

[19] For trends in new systems of work organisation in the chemical industries, see idem: Report III, Chemical Industries Committee, op. cit., Ch. III, pp. 59-62.

[20] For safety and health aspects in the leather and footwear industry in general, see idem: Report III, Second Tripartite Technical Meeting, Geneva, 1979, Part II, pp. 35-60.

[21] In this context, reference should be made to ILO Resolution No. 69 concerning the obtaining, by the ILO, of information on the conditions of life and work of textile workers, Conclusion No. 66 concerning safety and health in the textile industry, and the informa- tion furnished by governments concerning the action taken, Official Bulletin, Vol. LVII, 1974, Nos. 2, 3 and 4, pp. 189-190 and p. 184; ILO: Report I, Textiles Committee, op. cit., Ch. V, pp. 33-38 (see also pp. 59 and 60 of the same report).

[22] The ITGLWF refers, in this connection, to the study by Sinclair, op. cit., p. 16.

[23] On the other hand, according to ITGLWF, workers often feared reprisals if they complained about safety measures. (Information provided by the ITGLWF for the Philippines.)

[24] For garment workers, the ITGLWF went on to point out that the strain on their hands, wrists and arms from highly repetitive needle- work had been linked by scientists to the development of various types of serious disorders: (i) tendonitis (or "tenosynovitis"), a painful swelling of the tendons due to repeated use of the tendons in certain stressful movements, such as twisting, bending or jerking of the arm or hands; (ii) carpel tunnel syndrome, a deterioration of the nerve leading to the thumb, pointer and middle finger, due to repeated strenuous bending of the wrist, especially when done in conjunction with pinching/grasping motions of the fingers; and (iii) bursitis and "tennis elbow" (or "epicondylitis"), a painful swelling of the membranes around the bones in joints, such as the elbow or shoulder, again due to repeated, prolonged pressure on the joint. For sewing-machine operators, inspectors, folders, packagers and others who handle literally thousands of garments per day, these symptoms could become so intolerable as to cause temporary or total disability.

[25] The subject of safety and health standards of MNEs in their various places of location, especially developing countries, of exchange of information between headquarters and subsidiaries, management and workers, and of co-operation with national authorities has received an in-depth treatment in ILO: Safety and health practices of multinational enterprises (Geneva, ILO, 1984).

[26] See, in this connection, R. Maex: Employment and multinationals in Asian export processing zones, Multinational Enterprises Programme working paper no. 26 (Geneva, ILO, 1983). This section draws mainly on this study, which incorporates findings of surveys undertaken by the ILO Asian Regional Team for Employment Promotion (ARTEP).

[27] P. Tisser: "Conditions de travail et zones franches d'exportations dans quelques pays d'Asie", in Critiques de l'Economie, No. 14, Jan.-Mar. 1981, p. 129.

[28] "Where overtime is a veritable institution", in ILO Information, Feb. 1983, p. 6.

[29] Similar studies for countries in Latin America and Africa are to be carried out in 1984/85 under the ILO's Multinational Enterprises Programme.

CHAPTER V

LABOUR RELATIONS

Membership in national employers' organisations and involvement in their activities

The majority of MNE subsidiaries covered by this study reported that they were affiliated to one or several employers' organisations in the respective host country.   INDACI, Asahi's subsidiary in Indonesia, stated in this respect that it was an active member of the Indonesian Textile Association as well as of the Japan-Indonesia Joint Venture Enterprisers' Association.   KTSM (Kanebo's subsidiary in Indonesia) mentioned that, in addition to these organisations, it was also affiliated to the Japanese Textile Joint Venture Association (Ahiru-kai).

Lotus in the Philippines, a subsidiary of Sam Hwa, reported that in the home country, Sam Hwa is affiliated to the Korean Employers' Federation; Lotus itself is not affiliated to any national employers' organisation.   Kanebo do Brasil indicated that there was no employers' association to which it could be affiliated.

Enka pointed out that their subsidiaries - in accordance with the basic policy principles of the enterprise - conformed in labour relations matters with the practices of other local enterprises.   Mitsubishi Rayon indicated that subsidiaries were members of the various national employers' organisations where they operated.   Its subsidiary in Portugal (FISIPE), covered by the present study, is thus affiliated to the Portuguese Association of Industrial Companies of Chemical Products.

Viscosuisse, a Swiss-based subsidiary of Rhône-Poulenc reported that the enterprise was a member of the relevant employers' organisations both at the national and at the regional levels.   At the national level, these were the employers' association of the textile industry and the association of the Swiss synthetic fibre industry as well as the Central Chamber of Commerce of Switzerland.   At the regional level, the company is, inter alia, a member of the Industrial Association, Lucerne, the Commercial Board of Directors, St. Gallen, the Employer's Association of the Rhine Valley and the Chamber of Commerce and Industry, Aargau.

Several enterprises commented on their ways of participating in the local employers' organisations.   Enka's subsidiary in Spain, LSB, for example, which is a member of the regional Catalonian employers' organisation "Fomento del Trabajo Nacional" - one of the founders of the biggest Spanish employers' organisations, Confederación Española de Organizaciones Empresariales (CEOE) - noted that it entertained with both associations exchanges of information and advisory services in all labour/management relations matters.

Lachlan, Kanebo's subsidiary in Australia, indicated that the
enterprise takes a particular interest in the following activities of
the Chamber of Manufacturers of New South Wales (of which Lachlan is
a member): (i) negotiation of revision of the award with trade unions;
(ii) notification of the decisions concerning the award to each
enterprise; (iii) answering questions concerning labour relations.

The Textile Employers' Association of France confirmed that the
five largest textile MNEs were members, although their level of
participation was low.

Policies and decision-making levels
in labour relations matters

The majority of parent companies and subsidiaries explicitly
emphasised that, in general, policy-making in labour relations matters
is decentralised, i.e. is the competence of their subsidiaries or
affiliates in the various countries. However, involvement in one way
or other by the parent company is found exceptionally in problem cases
and at times final approval is given by it. Normally, however,
headquarters seem to have in this connection an advisory or co-
ordinatory role.

The subsidiaries of Asahi (INDACI in Indonesia, ASF and ASP, both
in Ireland, and TPC in the Republic of Korea) indicated that in general
they are themselves fully responsible in labour relations matters. The
parent company in Japan added that while this autonomy was respected,
Asahi may take appropriate measures in close co-operation with its
affiliates (joint ventures) concerned where solutions were not obtained
by the latter. KTSM, Kanebo's subsidiary in Indonesia, stated that not
only the Indonesian laws were taken into account but also the policy of
the parent company kept in mind when dealing with problems in labour
relations. Important industrial relations matters were reported to the
parent company for its views prior to final measures being taken by the
subsidiary. The parent company, Kanebo, indicated in the same context
that local subsidiaries and joint ventures abroad were fully responsible
for the handling of local labour relations. The parent company received
only reports on these matters. Mitsubishi Rayon stated that in the case
of FISIPE (its subsidiary in Portugal) the responsibility in labour
relations matters remained fully with the president of FISIPE.

In the case of Rhône-Poulenc Textile (RPT), the central management
of the group noted that it had a certain advisory and co-ordinating
function with a view to the labour relations of their subsidiaries which
otherwise were autonomous; likewise each division retained autonomy in
this field. For instance, RPT had developed its own, very particular
labour/management consultation and negotiation mechanisms.

According to Dollfus-Mieg & Cie. (DMC) no general policy in labour
relations has been defined at the central level of the group. As a
consequence, labour relations practices differ to a certain degree from

branch to branch.   A strong general tendency towards decentralisation
of responsibilities in labour relations can be observed throughout the
group.   As regards the Texunion Branch and the thread-making branch
there is complete decentralisation of labour relations responsibilities
in their foreign subsidiaries.

Concerning the French plants of the thread-making branch, which
consists of the oldest subsidiaries of the DMC group, there had been a
long-standing tendency to centralise the decision-making process in all
matters.   Over time subsidiary management has been delegated more and
more decision-making power in the social field.   However, subsidiary
managers still had the obligation to report to headquarters, particularly
when their decisions might also have labour relations implications for
other subsidiaries of the group.   In extreme cases, central management
may modify a specific decision or advise the subsidiary management not
to take a similar decision again if it was felt that the consequences
of the decision taken by the subsidiary would create unacceptable
precedents for labour relations matters in the entire group.

Concerning the French plants of the Texunion Branch, although
decision-making is formally delegated to subsidiary managers, they
nevertheless have an obligation to inform the central social relations
management of Texunion about any decisions taken.   After this information has been given, consultations may follow and guidance be offered.
It was noted in this connection that in the French Texunion subsidiaries
there are no special personnel and labour relations managers.   These
functions are fulfilled by the technical manager in charge of production.
This situation can lead to a closer contact with the specialised central
management of the branch.   Thus the Texunion Branch has set up a social
studies committee with the participation of the technical managers of
the subsidiaries, which is an instrument for co-ordination, exchange of
experience and guidance by central management.

DMC stressed at the same time that at the central level of the
group, there is no separate department for the management of labour
relations which would formally control the different branches of the
group.   None the less, informal contacts between labour relations
managers of the branches and the president of the group exist in all
matters.   They have led to the definition of general principles
according to which decentralised decision-making should be carried out
in the subsidiaries.

The Japan Federation of Employers' Associations noted that most
of the multinationals have adopted the policy that local management be
delegated substantial authority regarding labour relations matters.
Such a policy was essential for the achievement of solutions or settlements through negotiations or collective bargaining which were carried
out locally.

Another question of interest is whether and to what extent foreign
subsidiaries may adopt certain labour relations practices and methods of
the parent company.

In this connection, KTSM, Kanebo's subsidiary in Indonesia, notes that personnel and labour relations practices of the parent company were followed as far as general principles were concerned while naturally abiding by local laws and rules. These having become more developed over the years there was now a strong tendency by subsidiary management as well as labour to establish their own policy and practices as much as possible, independent from those prevailing at the Japanese parent companies. Kanebo do Brasil reported, too, that they adopted the labour relations and personnel management practices of the parent company as much as possible within the framework of the legal requirements of the host country. As a result the company feels that its labour relations are superior to those of many other companies in Brazil.

The Korean Employers' Federation pointed out that some subsidiaries of MNEs in the Republic of Korea had introduced, for example, certain advanced practices in operating joint labour/management methods which were not found in local enterprises.[1] These were expected to contribute to the improvement of prevailing local labour practices.

On the contrary, Mitsubishi Rayon indicated, as FISIPE itself, that for this subsidiary in Portugal there was no transfer of labour relations and personnel practices from the home to the host country.

No such transfer was also noted in the case of LSB, Enka's subsidiary in Spain. LSB's labour relations policies were fully independent from those of headquarters, a consequence of the subsidiaries' adherence in labour relations matters to existing practices and regulations prevailing in the host country. In particular the regulations of the "Estatuto de los Trabajadores" of 10 March 1980 constituted a major framework for labour relations in Spain. Lachlan (Kanebo's subsidiary in Australia) also reported that except for senior expatriate personnel, they abide fully to labour/management relations and customary practices in the host country.

The Confederation of Australian Industry was of the opinion that where awards or legislative requirements existed, MNEs observed them to the same extent as national enterprises as governments made no distinction in their application. Furthermore, as regards matters not settled by legislation, most MNEs adjusted to the local circumstances so that their practices were identical to those prevailing in the host country. The effect of this attitude was stable industrial relations which had prevailed in the industries concerned and reflected the expressed policy of equal treatment pursued by the employers' organisations on this issue.

The Government of Ireland indicated that it did not differentiate between multinationals and other companies in labour relations legislation. To its knowledge no particular provisions or procedures transferred from the home country seemed to govern labour relations in Asahi's subsidiaries (ASP and ASF) in Ireland.

Referring particularly to the latter subsidiary, ASF, the Irish Transport and General Workers' Union considers that its standards of industrial relations are positive, and are clearly influenced by the parent company's thinking: an indication is that since 1977 when the Asahi plant opened, it has had a strike-free record. Despite the recession in the textile industry, the union has been able to secure pay increases in the last few years; and the Asahi wages are above those of the other synthetic fibre plants in the country. The company seems fully aware of its social responsibility and the social devastation which would result from a close down of its operations, says the Union.

The Clothing and Allied Trades Union of Australia notes that while MNEs are normally larger and better organised and, on the whole, more capital intensive, they are very similar to the local firms in the sector with respect to their labour and social practices. MNEs tend to comply with law, custom and practice of the Australian industrial relations in the sector; no more, no less.

The French Confederation of Christian Workers notes that in its experience local labour legislation and practices as well as collective agreements are respected by the multinationals operating in the sector, which is seen in part as the result of the vigilance of the trade unions concerned.

The Spanish State Federation of Textiles and Furs notes that headquarters do not intervene in the daily management of labour relations in the subsidiaries. In this area, the foreign subsidiaries strictly abide by the Spanish labour legislation without trying to bring any improvement to the legal requirements. Also, while long-established multinationals which had operated in the earlier Spanish industrial relations setting tended to be more paternalistic, more recently-established enterprises accepted negotiations with the unions more readily.

The International Textile, Garment and Leather Workers Federation (ITGLWF) noted that the general claim of multinationals in the sector that their foreign subsidiaries were autonomous in industrial relations matters was not correct in all respects. In particular, as regards the question of trade union recognition, some company-wide tendencies can be observed for a number of enterprises. Where these are negative they have often given rise to international trade union action.

While practically all answers stress the dominance of local factors for the management of labour relations in the multinational enterprises, which explains the broad autonomy of subsidiary management from the parent company, this does not seem to contradict other evidence regarding particular management styles of companies which prevail throughout the various entities. Factors related to such enterprise-wide approaches concern, for instance, pay systems, career development, attitudes towards unions or employers' organisations, etc. which in certain cases can be traced to practices first developed at the parent company.[2]

Modern communication possibilities have also been noted as making it important for multinational enterprises to take on some matters of principle a common position wherever they operate, sometimes in order to avoid prejudicial repercussions in other parts of the enterprise.[3]

Unionisation and trade union recognition

According to the reply received by the Malaysian Employers' Federation, the majority of the multinational enterprises in the sector are unionised, i.e. have accorded recognition to the appropriate trade union. In their dealings with trade unions, these companies were fully integrated with the custom and practice for collective bargaining and observed the existing labour legislation and practices.

On the other hand, the Mauritius Employers' Federation noted that workers in the establishments of one footwear MNE are not unionised. However, the company had a Joint Industrial Committee which consists of six representatives of the workers and two representatives of the employer. This means of communication with the personnel, according to the Federation, has proved to be effective.

According to the Clothing and Allied Trades Union of Australia, MNEs in the clothing industry in Australia are required by law to recognise trade unions and actually do so. Some of the trade union rights are governed by both legislation and awards of the Arbitration Commission, others are a matter of custom and practice. MNEs in the clothing industry behaved similarly to domestic firms, but unless pressured, abided only by the letter of the law. The Union adds that approximately 80 per cent of employees in the industry are its members; this is fairly uniform across most plants with very small plants experiencing lower levels of unionisation and some large plants 100 per cent.

Workers are represented at a plant, enterprise, regional and national level by the union and at an international level by the union's affiliation to the International Textile, Garment and Leather Workers' Federation. In addition, the union is affiliated to the Australian Council of Trades Unions, which is in turn affiliated to the International Confederation of Free Trade Unions.

The activities of employees in MNEs who are members of the union are co-ordinated by the union. The aim of the union is similar for employees of MNEs and of domestic firms and is, generally speaking, to protect and advance the industrial interests of the members.

The French Confederation of Christian Workers noted that the question of union recognition as other industrial relations matters were determined by the country's labour legislation. The French Federation of Textile and Allied Workers, referring to the Texunion branch of DMC, mentioned that personnel delegates and works' committees were the official bodies of workers' representation in the enterprise. However, the latter was favoured by management as it tended to be less militant. Union members are elected to both functions but the trade union as such is not represented. In the case of Dollfuss Mieg & Cie. central enterprise committees exist at the level of each major enterprise of the group in France. This organisation, founded in French law, does not permit the union organisations concerned complete information or representation for the group as a whole whether at the local or at the national level. (In this connection, the trade union makes reference to four DMC enterprises in various lines of production in the Mulhouse region employing a total of 4,000 workers for which no common workers' representation exists.) The DMC group applies labour legislation in force in each country of implantation. This implies a considerable diversity in information provisions and workers' representation throughout the company which negatively affects action possibilities for the workers.

Membership in trade unions in the textile, clothing and footwear sector is reported to be variable from one enterprise to another but is generally low as compared to the total industry average. According to the French Federation of Textile and Allied Workers some 30 per cent of the textile and clothing workers are unionised, most of them by the General Confederation of Labour (CGT).

The Irish Transport and General Workers' Union indicated that approximately 90 per cent of the workforce in the sector is organised, the exception being managerial, supervisory and clerical staff. As regards the Asahi subsidiary, the union mentions that workers in each section/shift are represented by elected shop stewards. This group of shop stewards (from the Fibre and Spinning Plants) comprise the Section Committee of the union who attend major plant negotiations with the union official. All of the workers' representation, therefore, is at plant level. However, there are times when only the Fibre Plant or the Spinning Plant is affected and so only the shop stewards from each of these plants attend. All of the shop stewards are kept informed of the overall situation at the Section Committee meetings. A major concern of the shop stewards is the improvement of wages and working conditions and the representation of members who find themselves in difficulty with the company for one reason or another.

The Japanese Federation of Textile, Garment, Chemical, Distribution and Allied Industry Workers Unions (ZENSEN) noted that workers in major and medium-sized enterprises (especially in chemical and synthetic fibres, and in the spinning industry) have high organisation levels which at times include the total workforce. However, the rate of organisation is low in smaller enterprises. In general, a little over 20 per cent of the workers in the whole textile industry are organised.

At the enterprise level, including multinationals, joint consultation systems have been established. At the local level, joint and sometimes tripartite meetings are held to discuss questions of common

interest.   At the sectoral level, i.e. for the whole textile industry,
joint meetings or conferences are held for the same purpose.   At the
national level, union representatives are dispatched to the Textile
Industry Council, which is the advisory organ to the Ministry of
International Trade and Industry.   ZENSEN has set up a joint Japan
Textile Industry Conference including the 14 trades organisations of the
textile industry.   It also mentions expressly that it sends representatives to attend the ILO's tripartite technical meetings for both the
textile and the clothing industries.

The union knows of no example of a formal union organisation
council set up for a multinational enterprise as a whole in the sector.
However, very often the representatives of Japanese trade unions in the
home country visit the overseas subsidiaries of individual enterprises
and have meetings with the local trade union or other representatives
of local workers, aiming at promoting friendly relations and solutions
to labour problems.   At the international level, information is
exchanged with the International Textile, Garment and Leather Workers'
Federation (ITGLWF) and its Asian Regional Organisation (TWARO), and
policies are jointly co-ordinated.

ZENSEN is active in assisting its counterpart unions at Japanese
subsidiaries overseas to organise workers.   A tripartite council on
MNEs in Japan agreed in May 1975 that each party should not hinder
workers at Japanese subsidiaries overseas in their effort to organise
themselves in the union.   Japanese trade unions formed a trade union
council for multinational companies in April 1974 to strengthen their
activities on MNEs.

The Federation of Korean Trade Unions noted that 82 per cent of the
workers of Sam Hwa, i.e. more than 8,000 out of 10,000, are affiliated
to the trade union in this enterprise.   In general terms, however, only
25 per cent of the workers in the textile industry are unionised.   It
is the local practice that unions are organised at the plant and the
enterprise levels.

The Textile Trade Union in Portugal, SINDETEX (UGT), holds that
multinationals, in view of the economic resources, compare well with
other enterprises in the sector in the social and industrial relations
field.   However, there are general problems for the expression of
interest and participation of workers in the country which are obviously
reflected, says the union, in the relations with enterprises.

The Spanish State Federation of Textiles and Furs observed that the
labour unions in Spain are fully integrated in the political system.
The behaviour of MNEs relating to trade union recognition was dependent
on the ability of the unions to make their claims prevail not only with
the personnel manager but also with management as a whole.

In Sweden, according to the Swedish Trade Union Confederation, some
95 per cent of the workforce is organised by the Textile, Garment and
Leather Trades Union.   The Swedish law on co-determination is a centre

piece for labour-management relations. This law also provides for the right to information for the unions on all questions, the right to joint decisions and a right of veto in certain cases. The law on the status of shop stewards is likewise important.

Generally speaking, as regards trade union recognition, the ITGLWF did not see any particular problems as far as the situation in home countries is concerned. In the United States trade union rights and influence varied, however, from state to state. Unionisation problems may occur, for instance, when a European-based MNE with a good labour relations policy at home opened up in the little-unionised South.

As regards trade union recognition and respect of trade union rights in the developing host countries, it was the experience of the ITGLWF that problems decrease with the size of the company, whether multinational or not. Larger companies were normally found to be better equipped for the industrial relations function. There were more transgressions in the clothing sector with its relatively small size and, sometimes, family-owned nature than in the textile or footwear industries. Occasionally problems had been found with enterprises which, although they accepted unionisation at home, tried to avoid it in developing countries for cost reasons. The ITGLWF had found proportionately more problems with multinationals from the developing world, probably because they were smaller.

Trade unionisation in the textiles, clothing and footwear sector varied very much from country to country. However, it was high for the textile industry in practically all African countries. In Asia, the situation varied in line with the level of union organisation. Thus the unionisation rate in India was high, while in Indonesia, the Philippines and Thailand the opposite was true as unions only started developing. Especially in the textile industry, the unions in all parts of the world tended to affiliate to a high degree with the inter-national sectoral unions. Via this affiliation, the ITGLWF, for instance, had a base of over 600,000 workers in Africa and of more than 2 million in Asia.

International information and co-ordination of activities with respect to individual multinational enterprises were among the most important activities of the sectoral international union organisations. The ITGLWF had launched campaigns regarding individual enterprises.[4] In contrast to international trade secretariats in other sectors it had not been found possible to organise permanent World Councils regarding individual multinations in the sector being studied, since they would be too expensive. However, ad hoc meetings were organised for this purpose.

Likewise, the Trade Unions International of Textile, Clothing, Leather and Fur Workers (TUI) notes that it has created co-ordination committees for individual multinational enterprises, such as Dollfus-Mieg, Agache-Willot and Bata to achieve the co-ordination of trade union action which was for the moment limited to each continent. One of the main functions of this committee is information provision but also the expression of concrete solidarity.

Systematic information by company was thus provided regarding practices in the field of employment, wages, vocational training and attitudes towards unionisation. This would give a basis for the elaboration of a programme of common union claims in all the subsidiaries of a company. It was felt in particular that the co-ordinating role of the Committees should be recognised by the multinationals within the framework of collective bargaining.[5]

Collective bargaining

Mitsubishi Rayon negotiates at an industry-wide level with the Mitsubishi Rayon's labour union, which is a member of the Japan Textile Companies' Labour Union to which all unions of the Major Japanese synthetic fibre manufacturers are affiliated. According to the Japanese Federation of Textile, Garment, Chemical, Distribution and Allied Industry Workers' Unions (ZENSEN), this is the general pattern in the sector. The collective agreement determining the working conditions of the Mitsubishi Rayon's subsidiary in Portugal, FISIPE, was negotiated and signed between the employers' associations and the sectoral chemical unions' organisation. No negotiations take place at the company level, although there are sometimes revindications for such bargaining.

In the case of LSB, Enka's subsidiary in Spain, bargaining is done at the company level. Negotiations resulting in a collective agreement take place annually between the management of the subsidiary and a committee consisting of works' council representatives of the different plants of the subsidiary. In the case of Viscosuisse, Rhône-Poulenc's subsidiary, collective agreements are also binding at the company level. They are concluded between the enterprise and the six unions to which their individual workers are affiliated. In these negotiations, the participating union representatives are at the same time members of the works' committee. The collective agreement covers wage earners while salaried employees hold only individual work contracts.[6]

The Clothing and Allied Trades Union of Australia indicates that industrial relations proceed on a two-tier level with the arbitration system forming the basis and collective bargaining supplementing the arbitration system. Such bargaining is conducted between the union and the employer organisation at the level of the whole industry. Changes in the field of labour relations are dealt with through arbitration systems and through bargaining with employers' organisations.

The Amalgamated Clothing and Textile Workers' Union (ACTWU) Canada, reported that collective bargaining occurs, as prescribed by provincial legislation. About one-third of the clothing and textile industry is organised and the bargaining units tend to be at the plant level. Union shops are usual.

According to the <u>French Confederation of Christian Workers</u> (CFTC)
collective agreements are concluded at the industry level. Little
improvement has been achieved, however, in recent years owing to a
refusal to modify agreements from the employers' side.   The French
<u>Federation of Textile and Allied Workers</u> confirms this general bargain-
ing pattern, which is also valid for Texunion Branch of DMC, and notes
that region, plant, enterprise or group level collective bargaining has
never happened despite reiterated requests from the General Confederation
of Labour (CGT).   Occasionally, negotiations have been held at the
level of the enterprise in connection with particular employment problems
especially after labour disputes.   These usually involve plant level
management and personnel delegates.   It was found by the union that in
such cases the local management only transmits the position of the
higher level management.

According to the <u>Irish Transport and General Workers' Union</u>,
collective bargaining in the sector continues at local (plant) level even
though national wage agreements and understandings set the main wage-
level increase.   The union has been able to secure wage increases at
plant level through collective bargaining.[7]   The union also conducted
a joint job evaluation exercise with the assistance of the Irish
Productivity Centre which provided a further opportunity for collective
bargaining on wages to secure further increases.

The <u>Federation of Korean Trade Unions</u> notes that workers' representatives of the rubber workers union in the Pusan region of the Republic of
Korea, where Sam Hwa is located, negotiate the collective agreement with
the plant-level management.   Collective agreements on job security,
productivity bargaining, etc. are concluded according to the Labour-
Management Council Law.   There also exist collective agreements
stipulating the necessity of consultation with the trade unions when
workers are to be dismissed in enterprises in the sector.

In Nigeria it was indicated that collective bargaining was done
through the trade unions on behalf of the plant workers.[8]

The <u>Trades Union Congress</u>, United Kingdom, indicated that the
bargaining structure within multinationals in the sector is mostly plant-
based within a framework of sector-level agreements as regards the
textiles, clothing and footwear industries.   Few enterprise-level
negotiations (i.e. for all British plants of an enterprise) take place.
Where such arrangments has existed in some companies, e.g. Courtaulds,
they have now been dissolved.   At an international level, there are no
trade union bodies negotiating company-wide with any of the multinationals concerned.   (This is true, however, for all multinationals
in the sector, wherever they operate.)[9]

The <u>ITGLWF</u> noted in this connection that although fully fledged
international collective bargaining did not exist in the sector, the
role of international trade secretariats was important for local
bargaining.   The ITGLWF was often able to inform local unions of
fringe benefits which particular multinationals provided in other

locations or what elements were negotiable.   Similarly, the provision
of company profiles to members in the various countries could help in
bargaining efforts.   Of considerable use for the harmonisation of
union claims were international seminars.   A seminar for Asian members
had adopted at 34-point common African collective bargaining platform
regarding such matters as trade union representation, equal pay for men
and women, working hours, bonuses and safety and health conditions.
A bargaining problem in many developing countries was that enterprises,
including multinationals, tended to adhere to the rates set by the
minimum wage legislation where this was strictly applied by the local
government.   Some larger enterprises were, however, more amenable to
accept a slightly higher wage level.

Information and consultation practices [10]

Between enterprises and workers

While collective bargaining provides an essential occasion for
institutionalised labour/management relations in multinational and
other enterprises, information and consultation practices also play an
important part but seem to differ more widely in particular as far as
contacts with trade union organisations are concerned.   These variations reflect to a great extent differences in the general industrial
relations setting.

In the case of Rhône-Poulenc a central joint consultation panel at
the level of the group in France, has been set up (comité des sociétés
françaises du Groupe Rhône-Poulenc) consisting of central management
and workers' respresentatives, the latter being elected by the works'
committees of the MNE's French subsidiaries.   The panel has no
bargaining functions.   During its semi-annual meetings, views are
exchanged on the structural evolution of the group, its economic
activities, strategies and general tendencies, and on employment and
security matters.   Information is also disclosed on the development of
the foreign subsidiaries of the group.   The foreign subsidiaries of the
group are, themselves, not represented on this panel.

Rhône-Poulenc Textile reported that they had a unique consultation/
negotiation forum, the so-called "Collège des délégués syndicaux" (a
committee consisting of union delegates) which meets every four months.
Its workers' representatives are designated by the unions represented in
the enterprise.   The forum examines all RPT-specific problems relating
to employment, wages, working conditions, application of the collective
agreement, etc., i.e. problems which cannot be directly dealt with at
the different plant levels.   Due to this form of consultation/
negotiation, plant-specific problems can be examined at an intermediate
level without being submitted to the central management level of the
MNE via the above-mentioned central joint consultation panel for the
group.

In Rhône-Poulenc Textiles there exists, in addition, a quarterly consultation panel where management-related problems are discussed betweeen the central management of the group and the union representatives of the higher level staff (cadres).

Viscosuisse, Rhône-Poulenc's subsidiary in Switzerland, reported regular contacts with a view to renegotiating, adapting or modifying the current collective agreement. As regards the release of information, they mentioned that the unions were usually informed via the members of the works' committees, not directly by the company. However, information was provided directly to the unions on matters with particular importance.

The Government of Switzerland adds that agreements and procedures concerning consultation with workers and information disclosure are concluded directly between the employer and the trade unions in accordance with the Swiss collective bargaining legislation. The public authorities do not intervene in the collective bargaining process, and this rule also applied to MNEs.

In the case of LSB, Enka's subsidiary in Spain, contacts with the various unions to which their workers are affiliated are said to be of a more sporadic nature so far. The situation would change as the current collective agreement provided for the recognition of all legally admitted trade unions. In this connection the position of a union representative within the enterprise had been created who would represent the respective union vis-à-vis management. In the future, the representative would, in principle, also serve as the contact point in all discussions between management and the union.

Information disclosure to workers' representatives takes place at the level of the works' councils of each plant of the enterprise. Information is disclosed quarterly on: (i) the development of the market in the branch (at home and abroad); (ii) the economic situation of the enterprise with regard to production and sales; (iii) the future production programme; (iv) probable employment prospects; (v) the extent of absenteeism and its reasons. The balance sheet is disclosed once a year together with the annual report of the enterprise. Information on specific subjects is submitted monthly to various joint commissions such as the allocation of emergency credits; vocational training and training in the field of human relations; safety and health (studies, measures and prevention); new technologies and organisational aspects of the enterprise.

LSB added that general information on industrial relations was available through the Ministry of Labour and Social Security as well as from the employers' organisations and professional associations of managers of which the enterprise is a member. Conferences and seminars also played an important role in this respect to which the enterprise contributes.

Mitsubishi Rayon noted in the same context that its contacts with the labour union are frequent and the information disclosed for negotiation was a regular and very developed activity. FISIPE, their subsidiary in Portugal, indicated that they have contacts with the unions either directly or through the employers' association. Consultation and information practices in this connection existed essentially with QUIMIGAL, one of their main shareholders. The information provided to workers' representatives for collective bargaining negotiation purposes was very wide and its extent fixed by the Portuguese legislation.

KTSM, Kanebo's subsidiary in Indonesia, indicated that contacts with trade unions as such are very rare. At the company level, some subjects of common interest are discussed between workers and the employer in permanent or temporary subcommittees. Subjects discussed in this way were: improvement of working conditions; welfare of employees; management policy, business plans, etc. Employees having a personal problem or a complaint address themselves to the personnel manager or the department manager. As concerns general information on labour relations matters, KTSM mainly obtains its needs from the national organisation of labour unions or the industry unions' organisations, etc. Managing officials and economic papers and magazines also serve as sources of information.

Kanebo do Brasil stated, too, that there are no periodical or standing information or consultation practices with unions or other workers' representatives. Consultations and negotiations are held and information is provided when found necessary.

Asahi's subsidiaries in Indonesia (INDACI), Ireland (ASP and ASF) and the Republic of Korea (TPC) reported that institutionalised contacts with unions or workers are rarely found necessary. In case an employee has a problem the supervisor was normally asked for advice.

The Clothing and Allied Trades Union of Australia notes that the requirements of companies to inform and consult with employees are governed by the provisions of the Clothing Trades Award. Consultation is not required on every aspect of company policy, however, such matters as the setting of payment-by-results systems require consultation.

In cases of shut-downs consultation is not required by law. However, custom and practice require that the union is informed of impending shut-downs. As regards reduction of workforce which occurs as a result of shut-downs or retrenchments, again by custom and practice, the union is informed. A similar practice is followed in respect of transfers of production.

As regards the social consequences of these decisions, the union is informed but not necessarily invited to participate in the decision-making process of the above features. In the view of the union, firms

in the clothing industry, on the whole, take litte responsibility for
the social consequences of their actions: in general that is left to
the government.

The Amalgamated Clothing and Textile Workers Union (ACTWU) notes
for Canada that the union has the right under most agreements to demand
a review of the production quotas for piece workers. However, there is
no real worker participation in any aspect of plant management or
corporate decision making.

As regards the Texunion Branch of Dollfus Mieg, the French
Federation of Textile and Allied Workers notes that there exists no
provisions for informing trade unions although such information may be
requested on specific occasions such as the closure of a plant.
Efforts were made by the enterprise to inform especially higher staff
categories (cadres) and department chiefs of enterprise developments.
Such information and consultation was, however, mainly given with a
view to improve productivity and to reduce production cost.

The information given to plant-level representatives of the workers,
i.e. works' committees and personnel delegates were often connected with
the economic reasons advanced for the reduction of working hours, cuts
in the workforce or plant closures. These were normally initiated by
management and motivated by the economic conditions or competition
entailing the loss of markets while there was never a reference to the
transfer of production abroad which, as was found out afterwards,
occurred nevertheless.

The French Confederation of Christian Workers recalls in this
connection that economic information on the enterprise has to be given
to workers' committees four times a year under the provision of labour
law.   Consultations on questions of workforce reductions, transfers of
production, etc. were, however, only undertaken after headquarters had
made its decisions on these matters.

Consultations and negotiations on the social consequences of
plant closures were undertaken only after these had already been
decided by group management.   A further problem was that such decisions
were taken by group management while consultation on the social
consequences were held at the level of the local plant only.   This had
led to the fact that workers' representatives had never been able to
impede a plant closure but only to negotiate on financial compensation
or re-employment of the affected workers.   At the utmost a delay in
the execution of the decision to close might have been obtained.

In a similar vein, the Trade Unions International of Textile,
Clothing, Leather and Fur Workers was concerned about production
transfers even from modern plants to developing countries, including
Brazil and Thailand, which they had observed also for Rhône-Poulenc.

On the contrary, the Japanese Federation of Textile, Garment,
Chemical, Distribution and Allied Industry Workers' Unions (ZENSEN)

reported that in cases of workforce reduction, shut-downs, etc. prior
consultation normally took place between labour and management in the
enterprises and it was a premise that these matters should also be
approved by the trade union.   As regards general arrangements for
information and consultation with workers, it is difficult to generalise
for the Japanese enterprises in the sector.   However, joint consultation systems had made progress.   An extensive range of subject matters
are dealt with and the trade union is usually consulted on them.

With respect to one of the enterprises studied, the subsidiary of
Asahi (ASF), the Irish Transport and General Workers' Union indicates
that any problems which arise either on their part or the company's are
fully discussed.   Any changes proposed by the company are taken up with
the union and shop-floor representatives before they are made, where
such changes would affect the conditions of the workers.

As regards workforce reductions, shut-downs or short-time working,
consultation would certainly take place.   But workers representatives
would not be involved in the initial decision.   Lengthy consultation
and negotiation about the effects of such changes would have on the
workforce would take place.   As regards a recent period of short-time
work, which was introduced briefly, the union was able to negotiate
payments to workers to cushion them against the resulting initial
shortfall in social welfare payments.

Covering the questions more generally, the Government of Ireland
indicated that employees' rights to information and consultation from
their employers on decisions affecting them are primarily a matter for
free negotiation and collective bargaining.   However, there is provision in a number of statutes for mandatory consultation with employees,
e.g. (1) the Protection of Employment Act, 1977, which requires that
employees be informed and consulted regarding proposed redundancies;
and (2) the Safeguarding of Employees' Rights on Transfer of the Undertaking - European Communities Regulations, 1980, which requires that
workers be informed and consulted regarding transfer of ownership of
undertakings, businesses or parts of businesses, which entails a change
of employer.

As regards increasing employee involvement through access to information, suggestions for voluntary codes applicable to all enterprises
have been included in a discussion paper on worker participation,
published in 1980.   Under the 1980 National Understanding for Economic
and Social Development, the Irish Government has undertaken to initiate
discussions with the social partners on the content of a voluntary code
of information disclosure.   The principle of a voluntary codes of practice on information disclosure, consultation, etc., is favoured, bearing
in mind that the ILO's Tripartite Declaration of Principles concerning
Multinational Eneterpises and Social Policy was the result of thorough
research and extensive consultations with all interested parties.

The Federation of Korean Trade Unions notes that information
gathered at the Federation is given to the local trade unions, which
use it as the basis for policy suggestion at the company level.   As

regards management decisions on shut-downs, reduction of workforce and the like, the workers' representatives in the companies concerned are informed through the labour/management council.

The Spanish State Federation of Textiles and Furs (UGT) indicates that information and consultation requirements are set out in the Spanish labour legislation and the same applies for the specific questions of workforce reductions, closure of plants, etc. It regrets at the same time the absence of information on the activities of multi-nationals as a whole and on the strategies followed by them and by the governments in the various countries of operation.

The Swedish Trade Union Confederation informs that the law on co-determination came into force on 1 January 1977. It states that the employer no longer has the right to "direct and allot work". The employer's sole right to make decisions at workplaces has been curbed through negotiated agreements in line with this legislation. The co-determination law covers all aspects of employer/worker relations at work whether in multinational or other enterprises.

The co-determination law gives the workers the right to be represented in different levels of the management of a firm. The Confederation adds that the employer is obliged to call for negotiations with the union before making decisions on major issues including shut-downs, reduction of personnel, short-time work, etc. The employer is also required to keep the local union organisations informed about production progress, the company's finances and personnel policy.

The Trades Union Congress is of the view that in the United Kingdom no effective consultation or joint decision-making at national or inter-national levels within the multinational enterprises exists in the sector. During the last two years the textile, clothing and footwear industries have undergone a fundamental transformation and heavy job losses have occurred. Despite the serious implications of these developments to the workforce in the British textile, clothing and footwear industries, none of the multinational enterprises concerned has attempted to plan jointly adjustment policies with the trade unions concerned, says the union. Trade union participation in discussions on corporate restructuring has been minimal. Where such discussions have occurred, they have taken place after management had already reached their own decisions on the appropriate course to follow.

Moreover, consultation and joint decision-making at the inter-national level within the multinational group is non-existent. However, the multinational enterprises in this sector do not discourage trade union organisation in their operations any more than other companies.

In the experience of the ITGLWF, there is no doubt that information/consultation arrangements between multinational enterprises in the sector and workers' representatives/unions are much better in the enterprises' home countries than in their host countries - although

detailed information on actual MNE practices was often not available.
In the developing countries exceptions existed where unions are strong.
As a general rule it seems to be true - and this applies to home as well
as to host countries - that there is no workers' participation in
decision-making as regards shut-downs: they happen and the workers
can rarely prevent them. Workers are often only informed at the last
minute of such decisions. The ITGLWF observes that there had been no
recent closures in Africa, while many were taking place in Asia.

Between enterprises and governments

The answers received from the various respondents lead to the
conclusion that specific statutory provisions or other arrangements for
information/consultation between MNEs and governments are the exception.
In most cases, governments refer to the relevant provisions of national
labour law which applies to all enterprises.

The Government of Colombia notes that multinational enterprises are
held to inform and consult the Ministry of Labour and Social Security
as required regarding questions of employment, vocational training,
social and working conditions as well as industrial relations.

It is reported for Hong Kong that there are no statutory requirements, nor arrangements and agreements for information and consultation
with MNEs. The Labour Department offers advice on employment,
training, working conditions and labour relations questions to any
enterprise in need of such advice.

The Government of India notes that no agreements or arrangements
on information/consultation with multinationals exist. It may,
however, be mentioned that under the Apprentices Act, 1961, which is
equally applicable to MNEs and national enterprises, it is obligatory
for all employers in the specified industries to engage apprentices
as per the prescribed ratio in the designated trades. Certain textile
trades groups and the leather craft trades are among the designated
trades.

The Japanese Government indicated that no consultation machinery
is established for labour relations matters between the Government and
the Japanese undertakings in the textile industry having subsidiaries
abroad. Nevertheless, the representatives of the employers' organisation, which includes parent companies, were among the members of
tripartite meetings on labour problems in multinational enterprises,
and in this forum the Government, the employers and the workers exchange
their views.

On the other hand, the Government of Malaysia says that there are
arrangements in practice for information and consultation with such
enterprises in respect of labour relations questions.

The Government of Mexico reports that in conformity with article 153-V of the federal labour law, both national and multinational enterprises are under the obligation to submit, for approval by the Minister of Labour and Social Security, their training plans which are to be established by agreement with the workers. Article 153-Q of the law sets out conditions which have to be abided by in these plans.

The Government of the Netherlands notes that there are no other arrangements for information and consultation with multinational enterprises than those generally applied in tripartite contacts.

The Government of Nigeria states that the Federal Government, through the National Labour Advisory Council (NLAC) and other bodies, holds regular consultations with employers' and workers' representatives from all industries before laws or policies affecting employment, training, social and working conditions and labour relations are formulated. Following such consultations, some multinational enterprises in the textile, clothing and footwear industries are voluntarily embarking on housing schemes for their workers. The Federal Government has promised to provide free land and infra-structural facilities to make the housing scheme a success.

The Government of Spain notes that there are no special arrange-ments for information and consultation with multinational enterprises in the sector.

The United States Government notes that no special government agreements and arrangements on these matters exist for MNEs. The National Labor Relations Act and other laws concerning these matters apply to both national and multinational enterprises. Such matters may also be addressed in collective bargaining agreements on a case-by-case basis.

Grievances and labour disputes

The Asahi subsidiaries in Indonesia (INDACI), Ireland (ASP and ASF) and in the Republic of Korea (TPC) reported that, while formal dispute procedures existed, complaints and disputes are generally settled in the enterprises by way of discussion between: (i) the employee and his section manager; (ii) section managers and general managers; and (iii) general managers and personnel managers. The level at which these discussions take place depends on the nature of the complaints brought forward.

In the case of KTSM, Kanebo's subsidiary in Indonesia, complaints and disputes are resolved as follows: first, a solution is sought between the complaining worker and his direct supervisor; then, if no settlement can be reached at this level, the problem is discussed between the worker and managers at higher levels. If a settlement is not reached here either, the complaint is put forward to department managers in the case of non-staff workers and to the directorate in case of staff workers.   Management makes the utmost effort to find a solution.   However, if a solution can neither be found at this level, consultations take place between management and the union, or the solution is entrusted to a third party who acts as intermediary: the intermediary shall be the Indonesian Labour Ministry in accordance with Act No. 22 of 1957.

Kanebo do Brasil reported that with regard to complaints concerning safety and health matters the standing organisation in the company for this was the safety committee.   At the industry-wide level, the District Court for Labour Issues makes final decisions about grievances and disputes presented by the trade unions.

The National Confederation of Industrial Workers, Brazil, indicated with a view to Kanebo do Brasil that the number of labour complaints lodged each year is extremely low, almost non-existent.   The Ministry of Labour, the divisional trade union and other governmental bodies have found no irregularities in the activities of the undertaking, which strictly observes the provisions of the legislation governing industrial activities.

The Sam Hwa's subsidiary in the Philippines, Lotus, reported that there has been no labour dispute since Sam Hwa took over the company in 1977, as the company strictly conformed to the local labour laws and had made great efforts to improve working conditions.   However, the ITGLWF notes that certain labour disputes have arisen in this period.

Mitsubishi Rayon indicated that complaints from workers are submitted through Mitsubishi Rayon's Labour Union.   In the same sense, their subsidiary in Portugal (FISIPE) reported that complaints or grievances are made to the management of the company through the unions or the workers' representatives in the plan and usually settled at that level.

In the case of Viscosuisse (Rhône-Poulenc's subsidiary in Switzerland), complaints can be submitted to the enterprise works committee, the plant level works committee, the safety and a canteen committee, depending on the issue.   These committees, which exercise mainly an advisory function, put the complaints forward to the competent management level.   Complaints handled by the committees must be of a collective nature.   Individual complaints have to follow the established hierarchical channels.

While the replies received for the study do not permit a full picture to be gained of general procedures and labour disputes in multinational enterprises in the sector, it may be mentioned that it can be concluded from the follow-up survey to the Tripartite Declaration of Principles concerning Multinational Enterprises and Social Policy for 1980, 1981 and 1982 that in the vast majority of cases the procedures followed by MNEs are those provided for in national legislation and/or in collective agreements.[11]

Other issue areas and developments

The question regarding other factors, issues and developments connected with the social and labour practices of multinational enterprises in the textile, clothing and footwear industries has received only a few replies.   In a number of union replies, problems in export processing zones have been raised as a particular factor affecting industrial relations.   (The working conditions aspects of these zones have already been dealt with in Chapter IV above.) According to the ITGLWF, a major concern is the difficulty to organise the workforce in these zones.   In some countries of South-East Asia, textile workers in general are comparatively well organised, while in the zones union membership is at a very low level.[12]   Sometimes a practical ban on unions existed.[13]   Long working hours and an intense pace of work were other problems also referred to in the response of the Trade Unions International of Textile, Clothing, Leather and Fur Workers.[14]   The spread of export processing zones in such developing countries, in which textile, clothing and footwear manufacturing predominate, is a deeply worrying phenomenon to the Trades Union Congre in the United Kingdom.   It is considered that such EPZs are encouraging the neglect of fair labour standards by multinational enterprises.

The Clothing and Allied Trades Union of Australia and the Irish Transport and General Workers' Union are concerned about the effects which imports from EPZs may have on the employment in both countries and points to the existence of tariffs and quotas for imports from countries with low labour costs.

Likewise, the Japanese Federation of Textile, Garment, Chemical, Distribution and Allied Industry Workers' Unions (ZENSEN) notes that EPZs raise a number of special issues, in particular where unions are not recognised.   There is also a general suspicion that fair working conditions are often flouted.   The union felt that the ILO should see to it that these practices are abolished.

Another special problem area identified in some replies is labour relations in multinationals operating in South Africa, in particular in connection with recognition of Black trade unions.

It is stressed in various replies, i.e. in those of ZENSEN, Spanish and Australian unions, that the problems connected with homeworkers employed by multinational and other enterprises remain unresolved and that there seems increasing recourse to this cheap and widely un-protected labour force.

A number of replies such as those of ZENSEN, Clothing and Allied Trades Union of Australia and the ITGLWF refer to problems of job security and income maintenance for redundant workers in the textile, clothing and footwear industries as a problem affecting workers, and industrial relations, both in the developing and in the industrialised countries.   In the industrialised countries, a slight improvement as

regards at least income maintenances is noted in some of these replies
thanks to improved redundancy schemes and unemployment benefits partly
related with better legislation (including the EEC Directive on mass
dismissals) and partly to better provisions in collective agreements.
Such developments are not found in the Third World countries.

While concern for employment and the possibility to obtain
improvements in wages and labour conditions was expressed in various
replies as a result of continued imports from low-wage countries (Irish
Transport and General Workers' Union, French Federation of Textile and
Allied Workers, and ZENSEN) it is noted in other replies that such
problems exist also in many developing countries (such as the reply of
the Trade Unions International of Textile, Clothing, Leather and Fur
Workers).   It would, therefore, be justified to say that the sector as
a whole experiences continued restructuring and crises.

Experience with the principles established
in the Tripartite Declaration of Principles
concerning Multinational Enterprises and
Social Policy

Taking account of requests contained in resolutions adopted[15] by
various industrial committees or analagous bodies for the sector, a
question to this effect was introduced in the schedules sent to the
respondents of the present study.   In a good number of replies, the
value of these principles, which set out standards in the fields of
employment, training, conditions of work and life and industrial
relations, which governments, employers' and workers' organisations and
multinational enterprises themselves are recommended to observe on a
voluntary basis, was also confirmed for the industries in the sector.
However, it would appear from other replies that the Declaration is
still not sufficiently well known by various addressees, and in several
communications problems with its application have been referred to.

The Confederation of Australian Industry observes that experience
in the textile, clothing and footwear industries would indicate that
the multinationals operating in the country are cognisant of the
desirability of acting in accordance with the principles set out in the
Declaration.   It goes on to note that the structure of the industrial
relations system in Australia provides for the rights of workers to be
duly recognised.   Avenues exist, and are utilised, allowing for the
examination of industrial problems and for their ultimate resolution.
The industrial framework is such as to provide adequate opportunity
for the safeguarding of the rights of individuals as contemplated by
the principles embodied in the Declaration.   All the evidence supports
the fact that multinational enterprises conduct their affairs in
accordance with the accepted standards in their areas of operation,
being standards which apply equally to national enterprises in these
industries.

The Textiles Employers' Association in France felt that the Declaration was perhaps not so well known as it ought to be, due to the fact that there were few MNEs in the sector.

The Confederation of German Employers' Associations as well as its relevant affiliates in the industries concerned notes that the Declaration is fully recognised and respected by the enterprises in the textile and clothing, chemical fibre and shoe industries of the Federal Republic of Germany. In the same vein, the Japan Federation of Employers' Associations notes that Japan-based multinationals in the sectors covered and in other sectors have endeavoured to increase employment opportunities and standards, especially in the developing countries, taking account of local government policies and objectives. This is in keeping also with the Japanese-style employment philosophy which places priority in providing stable employment. Efforts were also made to extend equality of opportunity and treatment in employment.

The Malaysian Employers' Federation reports that the principles embodied in the Declaration are largely recognised and followed by virtue of the local labour legislation and the terms and conditions agreed upon during collective bargaining. There has been no instance so far where a trade union has complained that these principles have not been observed.

The Nigerian Employers' Association stresses the compatibility with the Declaration of the existing practices including the rules laid down in the procedural and collective agreement between the Nigerian Textile Employers' Association and the National Union of Textile, Garment and Tailoring Workers of Nigeria. The organisation also refers to the need for wider diffusion of the Declaration.

Finally, the Central Union of Swiss Employers' Associations indicates that no problems have been experienced with the application of the Declaration in the Swiss textile industry.

Among the multinationals participating in this study, Enka is of the opinion that the principles of the Declaration do not require changes in the policies and practices followed by the company. These and the OECD Guidelines for multinationals are regarded as elements of the policies established by the enterprise. The Guidelines have been expressly accepted also by Enka's major shareholder - Akzo, Netherlands.

Viscosuisse (Rhône-Poulenc's subsidiary in Switzerland) indicates that industrial relations in all of its plants are, of course, in line with international norms and refers in this context to the collective agreement for the sector which it has concluded with six union organisations in Switzerland.

A number of other enterprises, in particular the subsidiaries of Asahi in Indonesia (INDACI), in Ireland (ASP and ASF), in the Republic of Korea (TPC) and of Kanebo in Indonesia (KTSM) and in Australia

(Lachlan), reported that for the time being at least they were not directly concerned with any problems regarding the Declaration.

Referring to the principles of the Declaration, the Japanese Federation of Textile, Garment, Chemical, Distribution and Allied Industry Workers' Unions (ZENSEN) reported that there have been several cases in which Japanese unions involved themselves in disputes at overseas subsidiaries of Japanese MNEs with favourable results. ZENSEN considers that Japan-based enterprises in the textile industry appear to have taken the Declaration into consideration in their various overseas operations. Their policies seem much in line with the principles established in the Declaration.

On the other hand, both the Clothing and Allied Trades Union of Australia and the Irish Transport and General Workers' Union as well as the Federation of Korean Trade Unions noted that they had not had, as yet, much experience with the principles of the Declaration.

The State Federation of Textiles and Furs in Spain observes that the principles of the Declaration are known only to a small minority of the workers in multinational enterprises. They are informed mainly of the unions' action programmes. The Government and still less the multinationals themselves have, in the view of the Spanish trade union, undertaken no particular efforts in connection with the Declaration.

Similarly, the Trades Union Congress, United Kingdom, feels that the Declaration has had little effect on the behaviour of multinational enterprises in the textiles, clothing and footwear industries. Trade unionists in this sector are greatly concerned with the possible abuse of the Declaraction by the United Kingdom-based MNEs operating in developing countries. The TUC is of the view that certain employers have demonstrated unwillingness to observe the spirit, let alone the letter, of the Declaration.

The ITGLWF notes that its experience with the application of the Declaration is limited owing to the fact that it has been in operation for only a few years. One problem with the implementation of its principles was connected with the fact that cases in which it might be envoked in developing countries only become known long after the fact, i.e. after workers had been dismissed. By that time it was difficult to focus attention on the issues. Also, not enough publicity was made about cases of infringement. The ITGLWF also requested in a resolution adopted by its Third World Conference that the principles embodied in the Declaration should be applied.

The Trade Unions International of Textile, Clothing, Leather and Fur Workers has asked for the full application of the principles embodied in the Declaration in a memorandum addressed to several multi-national enterprises in the sector.[16]

The Declaration is followed up by the ILO periodically, in line with decisions taken by the ILO's Governing Body. Two surveys on the

effect given to the Declaration based on government reports, to be
completed after full consultation with employers' and workers'
organisations, have been undertaken so far, covering the periods
1978-79 and 1980-82, respectively.[17]   Fifty-six countries replied to
the first survey and 66 countries to the second.   However, the
information requested did not explicitly ask whether specific problems
had been encountered in particular sectors of the economy, nor did the
replies received allow a systematic analysis by sector.

An ILO procedure also exists which is concerned with disputes
regarding the application of the Declaration and which gives government:
and, in certain cases, representative organisations of employers and
workers, the possibility of raising such matters with the ILO and to
obtain an interpretation of the relevant provision(s) of the Declaratior
in the light of the issue.[18]   This procedure has not been applied thus
far in connection with multinationals in the textiles, clothing and
footwear industries.[19]

Notes

[1] Mentioning, as a good example, an enterprise not covered by the
study, Motorola Korea Co.

[2] See in this connection ILO: Multinationals in Western Europe:
The industrial relations experience (Geneva, 1976), especially
pp. 38-39;   and E. Kassalow: "Aspects of labour relations in multinational companies: An overview of three Asian countries", in
International Labour Review (Geneva, ILO), May-June 1978, pp. 273-288.

[3] ILO: Multinationals in Western Europe..., op. cit., p. 38.

[4] The ITGLWF referred in this connection to the Bata Charter.

[5] The TUI notes that the enterprises in question had not accepted
this claim, including the contents of a Memorandum elaborated by its
co-ordination committee for Europe, Africa and the Americas and
submitted to DMC in September 1979 and November 1981.   Trade Unions
International of Textile, Clothing and Fur Workers: The transnational
corporation Dollfus-Mieg and Company (Prague, no date).

[6] See Kollektiv-Arbeitsvertrag der Viscosuisse AG, Emmenbrücke,
1 Jan. 1980.

[7] See Agreement between Asahi Synthetic Fibres (Irl.) Ltd., Asahi
Spinning (Irl.) Ltd. and the Irish Transport and General Workers' Union,
1980.

[8] Procedural and collective agreement between the Nigerian Textile,
Garment and Tailoring Employers Association and the National Union of
Textile, Garment and Tailoring Workers of Nigeria, 1979.

[9] More generally speaking, international, i.e. border-crossing, collective bargaining does not exist for companies world-wide. For the question of international collective bargaining and transnational union meetings with companies, see ILO: Multinationals in Western Europe ..., op. cit. pp. 43-55. A critical analysis is found in Herbert R. Northrup: "Why multinational bargaining neither exists nor is desirable", in Labor Law Journal, June 1978, pp. 1-13. See also Rowan, Northrup and O'Brian: Multinational union organisations in manufacturing industries (University of Pennsylvania, 1982), especially Chapter V on the ITGLWF.

[10] In connection with this chapter see also ILO: Information and consultation practices of multinational enterprises (Geneva, forthcoming 1984).

[11] See in this connection doc. GB.224/MNE/1/1/D.1 (Geneva, ILO), pp. 164-169 and Analytical review, Multi-DCL-4-1983/D.2, p. 58.

[12] The ITGLWF notes in this connection that outside the zones the textile industry in the Republic of Korea counts some 170,000 union members, while there are practically none in the free trade zone.

[13] The ITGLWF mentions in this connection that restrictions for trade union organisations existed, for instance, in the zones of the Philippines and Malaysia. In Mauritius, a five-year ban on unions had recently been lifted.

[14] See in this connection the section on wages and conditions of work in export processing zones in Chapter IV of this volume.

[15] Resolution no. 10 concerning multinational enterprises in the clothing industry which requests the office "... to report on the progress made concerning the implementation of the Declaration in the clothing industry"; resolution no. 12 concerning multinational enterprises in the leather and footwear industry which requests the office "... to include among the ILO studies on multinational enterprises the leather and footwear sector, and to report the results thereof, including the application of the Tripartite Declaration of Principles concerning Multinational Enterprises and Social Policy as regards the leather and footwear industries, to the next Tripartite Technical Meeting for the Leather and Footwear Industry"; and resolution no. 78 concerning multinational enterprises in the textiles industry which requests the office "... to make every effort to ensure the full implementation of the Tripartite Declaration of Principles concerning Multinational Enterprises and Social Policy adopted by the Governing Body at its 204th Session, November, 1977".

[16] Memorandum of 19 September 1979 addressed to Agoche-Willot and Dollfus-Mieg, op. cit.

[17] See summary of these government reports found in docs.
GB/MNE/1980/D.1 and GB.221/MNE/1/1/D.1 (Geneva, ILO), as well as the
reports of the Governing Body Committee on Multinational Enterprises
(docs. GB.214/6/3 and GB.224/17/30).

[18] Details on this procedure are found in doc. GB.214/6/3 (Geneva,
ILO), para. IV.

[19] For action undertaken by the ILO in connection with this
procedure see docs. GB.221/MNE/1/3 (Geneva, ILO), paras. 4-7 and
GB.224/MNE/1/1 (Geneva, ILO), paras. 4-9.

CHAPTER VI

SUMMARY AND CONCLUSIONS

The textiles, clothing and footwear industries have been providing basic consumption goods for quite some time. It is not surprising that links between the industrialised countries and the developing world were established at an early point in this sector. For instance, United States multinationals are largely found in the Americas and Western Europe while United Kingdom and French enterprises have retained traditional ties with Asia and Africa. Japanese enterprises have up until recently established joint ventures in Asia although they are now diversifying and spreading to other continents.

The growth of textile and clothing exports have played a pivotal role in the industrialisation process of many developing countries and continued reliance is also placed on expansion in these industries for the future. The production and trade shares of developing countries in this sector (especially Asian and Latin American NICs) and Eastern European socialist countries have substantially increased while the shares of the industrialised market economy countries have decreased. By 1982, developing countries accounted for roughly 24 per cent of textile and 41 per cent of world clothing exports. In a number of developing countries, governments (such as in Brazil, Egypt, India and Mexico) have actively promoted the textile industry. A strong public-sector textile industry can be found in countries, such as Algeria and the United Republic of Tanzania. Multinationals are interlinked with these over-all developments and in the Republic of Korea they assisted with the build-up of the local textile industry; they have also played signifi-cant roles in Latin America and Africa in evolving the synthetic fibre industry.

International relocation of production has taken place, including the transfer of capacities by multinationals to host countries - although the exact magnitude of this is difficult to estimate. Concentration and multinationalisation are increasing in the textile and synthetic fibres industries, where the technological advantage of MNEs is most pronounced, as the statistics available for leading textile companies have shown; these are indications also that the role of multinationals is growing in the sector. This influence is enhanced by the fact that a number of the larger multinationals have vertically integrated opera-tions, which include the production of fibres, the manufacture of apparel and retailing activities, as well as comprehensive marketing networks. Non-capital linkages, such as licences and management contracts add to the importance of multinationals in the sector. Sales of new and used machinery by multinationals to the Third World is another factor.

MNEs have become major employers in the rapidly growing export processing zones (EPZs) in developing countries, in which textiles, clothing and electronics are the largest sectors.   In developing Asia, where EPZs accounted for more than 500,000 workers in 1980, it has been estimated that employment in textile multinationals is in the order of 200,000 (i.e. 40 per cent of total zone employment).   International subcontracting, offshore processing and the use of local inputs are major factors for the internationalisation of production.   Especially with regard to the manufacture of clothing and knitwear, these activities have grown in low-wage countries.   This is significant for indirect employment generation in these countries while affecting home country employment at the same time.   Subcontracting seems, however, to be very sensitive to economic slow-downs in the sector according to some of the replies received for the present monograph.

It ought to be recalled, however, that multinationals have, generally speaking, penetrated the textiles, clothing and footwear industries less than they have more capital- and technology-intensive sectors (such as the petroleum industry, electronics and the metal trades), in both industrialised and developing countries.   In most major capital-exporting countries, outward foreign direct investment in these industries represented by the mid-1970s only between 1 and 7 per cent of the total for the manufacturing sector.   In the case of Japan it reached 22 per cent.   Likewise, the employment share of foreign-owned enterprises in the textile and clothing industries in most industrialised and developing host countries for which data were available amounted to less than 10 per cent, and was in no case more than 25 per cent.   In most countries the bulk of production and employment in the sector as a whole is thus found in national, frequently smaller and medium-sized enterprises.

In many of the replies received for the present monograph, import competition - as a result of variations and differentials in labour cost - has been stressed as a major factor for the structural change in production, trade and employment which the sector has been experiencing throughout the world.   Imports from multinational subsidiaries located in low-wage countries to their parent companies are part of this process. Nevertheless, these "related party transactions", although they appear to be on the increase, were less important in the sector studied, as compared to industries such as machinery and scientific instruments. A few notable exceptions were footwear imports from subsidiaries to United States headquarters in the cases of Colombia, Haiti and Mexico, or clothing imports from the same countries and the Philippines.   The participating enterprises have mentioned labour cost as an important element in their motives to produce abroad.   Indeed, the labour-intensive segments of the industries concerned are undoubtedly respon-sive to wage cost developments.   Still, a detailed analysis has shown that - while trade can have an impact on certain product lines - import competition, especially from developing countries, on the whole, tended to be relatively less important for the international restructuring of the sector than productivity increases and other related factors, such as technological changes and the stagnation (if not the reduction) of consumption in the industrialised market economy countries.   This was

likewise true of capital-intensive synthetic fibre production. It is
evident, however, that none of the factors referred to above can be
looked at in isolation.

As regards future developments, a number of elements would appear
to indicate a certain slow-down of international relocation and the
multinationalisation of production in the industries concerned. These
include increasing technology intensity and slower growth, protectionism
in the industrialised countries, reduction of the export prospects for
producers in developing countries, as well as limits for import substi-
tution. Indeed, a decline in the international trade in textiles and
clothing can be observed. Exports to industrialised countries from
EPZs have also met with quota restrictions. The developing countries'
share in world textiles and clothing exports remained unchanged in 1982.
There is little doubt not only in the industrialised countries but also
in a global perspective that the sector will continue to experience
structural problems. This is especially true of the multinationals in
the sector. Market limitations and rationalisation measures in response
to competition also reduces the multinationals' capacity for direct employment generation in developing countries. Some recent studies show that
the foreign employment expansion of MNEs has tended to level off in
several instances.[1]

As a consequence of the above-mentioned tendencies, the textiles,
clothing and footwear industries have undergone a dynamic change with
employment dramatically declining in many industrialised market economy
countries. In the decade from 1970 to 1980 alone, over 1.2 million
jobs were lost in the industries studied in the then nine EEC countries
(between 20 and over 50 per cent, depending on the country) after the
considerable employment contraction which had already occurred in the
1960s. Employment has resisted much better in Canada and the United
States, where it declined by 5 and 10 per cent respectively, although
it is still continuing to decline. In spite of this, production has
not decreased much or has even increased, and so did exports, thus
confirming the above analysis of the major causes of restructuring.
On the other hand, in various developing countries, especially newly
industrialising ones, employment in the industries increased considerably, usually together with exports (such as in Brazil, Hong Kong, the
Republic of Korea and the Philippines).

Employment in multinationals - as throughout the entire sector -
has significantly declined in most of their industrialised home
countries. Thus, all participating multinationals, except one, noted
cuts in their home country employment which amounted to 25 to 60 per
cent between 1975 and 1980. During the same period, employment in
their foreign subsidiaries usually increased. From the available data
on their total activities it could be seen that employment decreased by
some 15 per cent. This came close to the overall 13 per cent employment
decrease in approximately the same years which was calculated for a
larger sample of major multinationals in the textiles, clothing and
footwear industries. In terms of production and employment MNEs in

the sector have thus become more "multinational" and the foreign content of their operations (production of overseas subsidiaries plus exports from the home country) has increased in this process. These subsidiaries, which used the same technology as the home country plants, were considered to be highly competitive by the multinationals which participated in the present study.

The analysis of the employment structure in the industries of the sector indicates that practically everywhere female workers dominate (constituting typically some 60 to 90 per cent of the labour force), except for most African countries and some Asian countries, such as Bangladesh, India and Pakistan. Low-skilled, temporary and part-time workers often account for a considerable portion of the workforce and in many countries homeworkers form a significant part. In several countries migrants are also found in greater proportions than in other industrial sectors. These groups represent a particularly vulnerable segment of the labour market which is difficult to re-employ elsewhere in the economy, especially in the present low-growth situation. While the lower-skilled labour force is in great supply in most countries, especially in the Third World, several of the participating multi-nationals referred to difficulties in obtaining technically qualified personnel in developing countries, as well as in some industrialised countries. Insufficient basic training in the countries concerned, competition among enterprises for skilled labour, low manpower mobility, and relatively low standard wages are factors contributing to the scarcity of adequate personnel.

It can be inferred from the replies received that the multinational enterprises in the sector undertake a considerable amount of training for their workers, in both the industrialised and the developing countries. As was found in an earlier ILO study,[2] training in MNEs is primarily related to the enterprises' immediate needs and is geared mainly towards higher and medium-level technical and managerial staff. The training for low-skilled manual workers is often on-the-job training and, therefore, of less general usefulness. With regard to the host country operations, training for manual workers seems very much to be left to the initiative of the subsidiaries, which takes account of the availability of suitable personnel, but - in contrast to the training provided to managers/technicians - it is not usually seen as an overall corporate function. Training in textile and clothing MNEs follows closely along these lines.

The relationships between the training programmes of multinational enterprises and national training institutions are varied. Different forms of co-operation appeared to exist practically everywhere the enterprises were located. This is also true of the co-operation offered by the enterprises to local institutions, which seems to depend much on individual initiatives of the subsidiaries in the host countries. Retraining is a particularly important function in the sector, especially in the home countries where workers are made redundant through re-structuring. It is a major concern in some enterprises (which make special efforts) but seems to be less developed in others, perhaps partly because important public programmes exist in many industrialised countries.   According to the replies received, however, training and retraining activities appear to have been reduced in recent years and in some multinationals in the sector as a result of the contraction of activity.   In general terms, the training efforts of multinationals in the sector are considered important by the host and the home countries which in many cases have introduced incentives for enterprises, both domestic and foreign, to develop training programmes.   Specific govern-ment assistance for the sector seems, however, rather more the exception than the rule although import restrictions are increasingly being resorted to.   All these measures have helped workers in adjusting to change but obviously have not had much impact on job security as such.

Participation by workers and their representatives in training activities is frequently encouraged by national law or practice and seems greater in multinationals which are more acquainted with this concept.   Still, in several industrialised and developing countries management alone appears to assume main responsibility for the formula-tion and execution of training programmes.

In determining their wages and conditions of work, the replies received showed that multinationals in the sector are much in line with the national standards prevailing in the respective home and host countries as a result of labour legislation and collective agreements negotiated either industry-wide or at the regional or national levels. Several participating MNEs reported, however, that their wages in host countries were above the statutory requirements and those fixed by collective agreements for the industry.   Employers' organisations also noted that the multinationals compared favourably with local enterprises. On the other hand, it is held by trade unions that MNE subsidiaries in the sector tend to abide, to a large extent, by minimum wage legislation in developing countries, particularly for ordinary workers.   It would seem, on the whole, that actual wages paid by subsidiaries in the host countries are rather similar to those offered by comparable domestic enterprises.   The same can be observed in the home countries.   It was noted in various replies that wages in synthetic fibre production are higher than in textiles and clothing, whereas footwear workers are normally among the lowest paid.

Concerning the systems of remuneration, the majority of participating MNEs reported that wages in the home and the host countries for manual workers were composed as follows: a portion based on a fixed salary, payments by results, and allowances and bonuses which varied.   In a number of participating MNEs, the social benefits negotiated at the individual enterprise level are above minimum legal requirements, collectively agreed or generally prevailing standards in the industries. Welfare and recreational facilities appear to be more extensive in foreign subsidiaries in the developing host countries than in local firms although they have not reached the standards of the home country

plants.   Several participating multinationals offer a system of capital
participation for managerial staff in their home countries.

Some MNEs mentioned explicitly that they do not practise any
discrimination by sex or category of workers.   It remains true that
wages for women are often found to be lower than those for men according to the experience of the trade unions.   Migrants, unskilled workers
and home and part-time workers are among the lowest paid in the sector.
Some unions reported their involvement in campaigns to improve wages
and conditions of work for these categories of workers.

In most industrialised countries, the social security practices of
MNEs are normally determined by national legislation and collective
agreements at the industrial, regional or national level which afford
workers a comparatively high standard of protection.   In various
developing countries this does not appear to be the case, and some MNEs
subsidiaries grant social security schemes over and above the local
legal requirements.

Concerning MNEs' practices in cases of redundancies, it appears
that there are few specific arrangements at the enterprise level.
MNEs usually conform to the redundancy provisions contained in labour
law or fixed by the relevant collective agreement.   However, owing to
the dramatic decrease of employment in home country plants, some MNEs
have implemented specific plans to mitigate the effects of redundancies
on workers, including training, retraining and compensation measures.
In several industrialised countries, collective agreements on protection
of workers have been concluded for the industries studied in cases of
rationalisation and technological change.   Likewise, in recent years,
improved labour legislation with respect to collective dismissals has
been introduced.

The number of working hours in MNEs, as in the industries as a
whole, is much higher in developing countries (where they occasionally
exceed 50 hours per week) than in the industrialised countries (where
they range from 40 to 43).   In the industrialised countries, weekly
hours of work in the textile industry sometimes tend to be lower on
average than in synthetic fibre production (e.g. Federal Republic of
Germany, 40.1 and 41.0 (1982); Ireland, 39.0 and 41.7 (1982); United
Kingdom, 37.6 and 39.0 (1982) - women only; United States, 40.1 and
41.5 (1980)).   As concerns other aspects of work organisation, several
MNEs reported that they did not use piece-work systems.   On the other
hand, shift work seems to be widely practised and flexible working hours
are an exceptional arrangement.   It would appear, on the whole, that in
the developing countries the larger MNEs at least, especially in the
textile industry, have better working time and work organisation arrangements than the domestic enterprises.

Shift work, night work, long working time and frequent overtime
are also found in the export processing zones, which has given rise to
concern in various replies.   As has been noted in other ILO studies,

shift work is proportionately more common in the export processing zones than in the rest of the economy, at least in Asian developing countries.[3] The nature of the type of production in the zones, in which multi-nationals predominate and in which textile and clothing enterprises hold substantial employment shares, leads to the fact that workers are mainly engaged in simple operational tasks.   As a result, the bulk of workers in the zones consists of low-skilled young females.   These characteristics largely explain the low wage rates in the zones.   Young, female and unmarried workers are also among the lowest paid in the local market outside the zones of the Asian countries.

In the field of occupational safety and health MNEs in general compare favourably with other enterprises in developing countries.   As a basic principle, MNEs apply the standards prescribed by the relevant legislation applicable in each country in which they operate.   According to some of the participating enterprises, the relevant safety and health practices found in the home countries and other places where they operate are additionally taken into account.   Several MNEs noted expressly that they follow the relevant ILO occupational safety and health standards and codes of practice.   A common feature of the majority of MNEs is the existence of joint safety and health committees which include management and workers' representatives for supervising the application of relevant standards.   When safety committees are not compulsory by law or collective agreement, their scope is usually determined at company level.

However, a number of unresolved problems are referred to in union replies.   These are connected, on the one hand, with noise, dust, fumes, toxic chemicals and unguarded machinery in certain enterprises in the sector, especially in developing countries and, on the other hand, with over-exertion in highly repetitive tasks.   In this respect, textiles appears to be the higher risk industry.   According to some union replies, the larger enterprises, multinational or national, had in general a more rational layout of their plants, which were usually cleaner and better managed than the average local enterprises in developing countries.   Also, the more recently established subsidiaries in developing countries and specifically the synthetic fibre factories were found to have more modern and thus safer equipment than the older textile plants.

Turning to industrial relations, the majority of multinationals reported that they were affiliated to one or several employers' organisa-tions in the home and host countries.   In one case, it was mentioned that there was no employers' association in a developing host country with which the MNE subsidiary could affiliate.

As regards the degree of unionisation in the enterprises, it would appear from the replies received that the situation found in the multi-nationals operating in the sector corresponded very much to the general pattern in the countries concerned.   In some cases, e.g. in Australia, France, Ireland, the Republic of Korea and Sweden, the degree of

organisation in the sector is very high: in large enterprises, including multinational subsidiaries, it may come to 80 per cent and more (and
sometimes even 100 per cent of the workforce).   As regards other
countries, great variations in the degree of unionisation can be
observed, correlating with the state of union development in general.
For instance, in developing countries, where the textile industry and
unionisation have been long established, as in India, the rate of
unionisation is usually higher than in countries where unions are of
more recent origin, such as Indonesia, the Philippines and Thailand,
although obviously other socio-economic factors also play a role.
Especially in the textile industry, unions in all parts of the world
tend to affiliate to a high degree with the international sectoral
federations.   Some of these have created co-ordination committees or
organised campaigns with respect to individual multinationals.

While certain company-wide labour relations approaches exist for
several of the enterprises studied (e.g. with regard to attitudes towards
unions, participation of employees and benefit schemes and sometimes an
advisory and co-ordination role by headquarters for major policy options),
labour-management relations, and in particular day-to-day management, is
left to the entities operating in the various countries.   Many management replies stress that national law and practice require a high degree
of delegation of decision-making powers to local management.   At the
same time, since the textile industry in particular is often one of the
initial industries in developing countries, multinationals can act as a
pattern-setter.   It was thus reported for the Republic of Korea that
foreign multinationals have introduced advanced practices of operating
joint labour-management bodies, which were unknown in the local enterprises.   On the other hand, multinationals also seem responsive to
broad changes in labour relations in the countries concerned.   Thus,
it was noted in Spain that the long-established textile MNEs seemed to
be more paternalistic in their approaches than enterprises which had
been established more recently.

The MNEs participating in the survey indicated that they conform
with national law and practice wherever they operate.   Some unions,
however, felt that a number of MNEs abided by the letter of the law only
and had to be urged to respect it also in spirit.   Most of the replies
received do not refer to union recognition as a problem for the sector
being considered.   However, workers' organisations from a minority of
countries reported serious problems of union recognition or organisation
in those countries where this question was not regulated by law.   This
was reported for some EPZs too.   It was also the experience of unions
that such problems decreased with the size of the company.   Larger
companies were normally found to be better equipped for the industrial
relations function.   There were, for instance, more frictions reported
for the clothing industry, with relatively small and sometimes family-
owned enterprises, than for the textile and footwear industries where
larger enterprises prevail.

Collective bargaining in the multinationals of the sector takes place, in line with national law and practice, either at the plant or at the industry level.   Sometimes general industry agreements are complemented by plant-level arrangements.   A tendency towards increased plant-level agreements is discernible, especially in the textile industry of various countries.   Indeed, in this industry enterprises with advanced technology and a corresponding labour force exist side by side with those using traditional production methods and thus follow differ-ent economic patterns.   It is also noteworthy that in many countries the wages and labour conditions of workers in the production of synthetic fibres are covered by the agreements in the chemical industry.   While international collective bargaining with individual multinationals does not exist for any of the MNEs in the sector (nor in any other sector), a harmonisation of union claims, in particular as regards various benefits, is aimed for by international sectoral trade union organisations.   These are often in a position to inform local unions of practices followed by the enterprise in other countries where they operate.

Information and consultation with workers' representatives are an essential element of effective labour-management relations, especially in a sector of dynamic change and international restructuring such as that of the textiles, clothing and footwear industries.   Provisions for these are most developed in the industrialised countries and established by labour legislation and/or - increasingly - by collective bargaining and apply equally to national and multinational enterprises.   In the Third World countries, information and consultation practices are generally less developed.   Thus, some participating subsidiaries note that there are no periodical or standing arrangements with unions or other workers' representatives.   With respect to these questions, the participating enterprises normally adhere to the local standards in various countries and have sometimes introduced additional innovative features of communication.   For instance, in one case a joint consulta-tion panel at the level of the group in the home country has been established, in which information is also provided about the foreign subsidiaries.   Workers' representatives noted, nevertheless, that in most cases no information was given for the enterprise as a whole and that, in general, even where detailed information/consultation arrange-ments existed, workers had no decisive influence on management decisions as such.   In the event of pending workforce reductions, however, delays may be obtained and re-employment or compensation negotiated for workers affected.   In a number of countries - especially developing host countries - information/consultation between multinationals and public authorities takes place in line with foreign investment codes or established practice with the aim of harmonising the multinationals' policies and the countries' national development plans.

The handling of grievances and labour disputes in the multinationals operating in the sector is, as are other labour relations aspects, determined to a large extent by local law and practice in the respective countries.   Several respondents refer to favourable labour dispute records for some of the participating enterprises.

As far as experience in the sector with the ILO's Tripartite Declaration of Principles concerning Multinational Enterprises and Social Policy is concerned, its value has been confirmed in a substantial number of the replies received. Employers' organisations generally observed that experience in the textile, clothing and footwear industries would indicate that most multinationals, wherever they operate, are cognisant of the desirability of following the Principles of the Declaration. It was added that many of the Principles are already reflected in local legislation or collective agreements. Some organisations mentioned explicitly that no specific problems had arisen in connection with the acceptance of the Principles. The participating enterprises either noted that these Principles were elements of policies established by them or inferred that they had not been concerned with problems regarding the Declaration.

While some trade unions confirmed that MNEs in the sector have taken into account the Declaration in their various overseas operations, others noted in their countries that the behaviour of multinationals had not been much affected by this instrument or that they had limited experience so far. Several trade union replies also revealed a feeling that the Declaration was still not sufficiently well known among workers and that this might possibly be true for other parties as well. In this connection, two international sectoral trade union organisations have requested in resolutions or memoranda that the principles embodied in the Declaration should be fully applied. It may be added that, in line with instructions received from the ILO's Governing Body and discussions in its Committee on Multinational Enterprises, the ILO will, in the years to come, make a particular effort for the promotion of knowledge about and the observance of the Declaration in all countries and sectors.[4]

Notes

[1] W. Olle: The development of employment in multinational enterprises in the Federal Republic of Germany: Results of a new survey (1974-82), Multinational Enterprises Programme working paper no. 33 (Geneva, ILO, 1984).

[2] See, in this connection, ILO: Multinationals' training practices and development (Geneva, 1981).

[3] R. Maex: Employment and multinationals in Asian export processing zones, Multinational Enterprises Programme working paper no. 26 (Geneva, ILO, 1983).

[4] See, in this connection, ILO: Improvements in the follow-up and promotion of the Tripartite Declaration of Principles concerning Multinational Enterprises and Social Policy (Geneva, doc. GB.226/MNE/1/1), and the Report of the Committee on Multinational Enterprises (Geneva, doc. GB.226/10/12).

APPENDIX I

PROFILES OF PARTICIPATING MNEs*

Asahi Chemical Industry Co. Ltd.

Asahi Chemical results from the merger in 1943 of two ammonia manufacturers, Nitron Chisso Hiryo and Nobeoka Ammonia Kenshi Company.

The company is a major manufacturer of synthetic fibres and one of the largest Japanese chemical companies.

Other products include plastics, construction materials, pharmaceuticals, medical instruments and food products.

The first overseas joint venture of Asahi Chemical Industry was established in 1961 as the Baroda Rayon Corporation Ltd. of India. This marked the beginning of a steadily growing programme of overseas joint ventures centering in the field of fibres and textiles. Foreign expansion in fibres took place in the 1960s and early 1970s through world-wide technology export (licensees) and joint ventures in Asia, Latin America and Ireland. In 1974 a particularly important joint venture was established in the Republic of Ireland for the production and spinning of Cashmilon® fibre, as a focal point for expansion into the European market. The Cashmilon® spinning and manufacturing plants started operating in 1977.

According to Asahi's sales composition, in the recent years fibre and textile importance has declined (from 59 per cent in the early 1970s to 42 per cent in 1978 and 30 per cent in 1981) as a result of falling/ stagnating sales due to the world-wide overcapacity in the fibre industry. Despite fibres and textiles' internal declining importance, Asahi Chemical remains a major manufacturer of synthetic fibres and Japan's largest producer of acrylic fibre textiles. A strengthening of this sector has been initiated through Nippon Synthetic Fibre Co. Ltd., the synthetic fibre sales company established jointly with Kanebo Ltd.

---

* Data supplied by the companies through their replies to the ILO questionnaire and their annual reports. These were supplemented by other sources, such as J. Stopford: The world directory of multinational enterprises (London, MacMillan, 1982); J. Love (ed.): Jane's major companies of Europe, 1979-80 (London, MacDonald and Jane's, 1979); and T. Ozawa: Multinationalism, Japanese style (Princeton, New Jersey, 1982).

For two other sectors, food products and pharmaceuticals, on one hand, and construction materials and housing, on the other hand, sales results increased continuously from 1976 to 1980 (respectively 4.6 per cent and 10.3 per cent in 1980).

Chemicals and plastics, after some years of stagnation, achieved a sales increase of more than 50 per cent in 1980 and hereby became Asahi Chemical's major division, with 47.8 per cent of the company's sales. In recent years, these sectors have been expanded through overseas subsidiaries and affiliates and technology export (in the Netherlands, New Zealand and the United States).

In 1980, the workforce of the parent company amounted to 13,500 and the workforce of the foreign subsidiaries to 4,908.

INDACI

INDACI (P.T. Indonesia Asahi Chemical Industry) was founded in July 1972 and operations began in July 1974. The following are the corporate data:

Capital stock:

US$8,600,000

Composition of the capital:

Japanese - 99 per cent (Asahi, 69 per cent; the other partner, 30 per cent)

Indonesian - 1 per cent

Business:

Production (acrylic yarn, spinning, dyeing, and nylon production).

Number of employees:

910

Plant facilities:

Spinning of acrylic fibre - 5,200 spindles; dyeing of acrylic fibre - 180 tons/m; production of nylon - 12 tons/m.

ASP

ASP (Asahi Spinning Ireland Ltd.) was founded in May 1974 and operations began in December 1977. The following are the corporate data:

Capital stock:

£3,000,000

Composition of the capital:

Asahi - 66 per cent

Other partners - 34 per cent

Business:

Production spinning of acrylic fibre.

Number of employees:

201

Plant facilities:

Spinning of acrylic fibre - 10,000 spindles.

ASF

ASF (Asahi Synthetic Fibres Ireland Ltd.) was founded in May 1974 and operations began in December 1977.   The following are the corporate data:

Capital stock:

£21,500,000

Composition of the capital:

Asahi - 81 per cent

Other partners - 19 per cent

Business:

Production of acrylic fibre.

Number of employees:

313

Plant facilities:

Production of acrylic fibre - 48 tons/m.

TPC

TPC (Tongyang Polyester Co. Ltd., Republic of Korea) was founded in May 1973 and operations began in February 1975.   The following are the corporate data:

Capital stock:

US$15,000,000

Composition of the capital:

Japan - 50 per cent (Asahi 50 per cent)

Republic of Korea - 50 per cent

Business:

Production (polyester filament).

Number of employees:

1,680

Plant facilities:

Production of polyester filament - 71 tons/m.

Dollfus-Mieg & Cie. S.A.

Dollfus-Mieg & Cie. S.A., DMC (France) is a holding company with interests in clothing, textiles (including accessories), industrial textiles, soft furnishings, piece-goods and printing.

The Group Dollfus-Mieg & Cie. S.A. was created in 1961 through a merger between two French textile companies founded in the eighteenth and nineteenth centuries respectively.

Starting in 1961, the company widely expanded both in France and abroad.   An alliance with the Thiriez and Cartier Bresson companies was formed in 1961, a number of weaving factories (Dechelette-Despierres, Fouillant, etc.) were taken over, as well as several companies specialising in household linen.   In 1969 and the following years, DMC strengthened its cotton-wool activities through mergers and take-overs of several French companies.   The acquisition of a 51 per cent share of Texunion (a Pricel subsidiary) was an important step in DMC's efforts to expand in textiles and other products/goods.

Abroad DMC has joint ventures, affiliates and subsidiaries all over the world.   In Europe DMC's activities outside France are situated in the Federal Republic of Germany (industrial installations) and eight other European countries.   In Africa, former French colonies, such as Morocco, Algeria and Tunisia, are host countries for DMC

investment and production.   In Latin America the company achieved a
turnover, representing 1.9 per cent of the consolidated turnover and
its main activities were in Colombia, Ecuador, Peru and Brazil, while
the only manufacturing subsidiary in Asia is in Thailand, since DMC
activities in this part of the world are mainly carried out through
licensees.

DMC activities have been restructured as the company grew, which
in workforce terms meant cuts in the French employment while employment
abroad has expanded.   To give an impression of the company's economic
importance, it can be mentioned that DMC in 1978 had 56 per cent of the
turnover of the clothing market in France, and was the leading French
manufacturer of sewing threads, lining, bedding fabrics, etc.

In 1980, the DMC Group holding was composed of three main branches:
the thread making branch - 1,026.8 million French francs (consolidated
turnover);   5,971 employees in France and 12 foreign countries;   the
Latin American branch (102.3 million French francs;   1,600 employees
in five countries);   the Texunion branch in France (1,799.6 million
French francs of turnover;   7,191 employees) and abroad (1,742.5 million
French francs of turnover;   6,193 employees in six countries including
major operations in the Federal Republic of Germany).

DMC Group's world-wide employees amounted in 1980 to 20,955, of
whom over 12,000 were in France.

Enka A.G.

Enka A.G. (Federal Republic of Germany) - for whom Akzo NV
(Netherlands) is the major shareholder (97 per cent) - is the largest
member of the Enka Group.   Enka originated in 1899 as the Vereinigte
Glanzstoff-Fabriken A.G. and established links with the Dutch AKU
(Algemene Kunstseijde Unie NV) in 1929, merging with this company,
and Koninklijke Zout Organon NV to form Akzo NV in 1969.   Besides
fibres, Akzo produces chemicals, paints and adhesives, pharmaceuticals,
detergents and a wide range of consumer products.   The Enka-Glanzstoff
Group was reconstituted in 1977 when Akzo's world-wide fibre operations
(except the American Enka Corporation) were transferred to the new
Enka A.G., which in 1978 took over 52 per cent of Akzo's stake in Enka
International Holding BV (Netherlands).

The board of directors of the two Enka companies are practically
identical.   Through or in conjunction with Enka International, Enka A.G.
has interests in - or the management responsibility for - a number of
companies throughout the world, irrespective of the degree of financial
participation (majority-owned subsidiaries are in fact rare).

The Enka Group has been able to maintain its position as one of
the leading synthetic fibre producers in the world (e.g. it accounted
for 14 per cent of Western Europe's man-made fibre production in 1980)

with extensive activities in textile machinery and engineering, plastics
and industrial chemicals, etc., carried out through joint ventures and
a range of subsidiaries in Europe, America and India. Comprehensive
changes in production and workforce cuts in its European-based factories
characterise the present restructuring period of the company.

From 1975 to the end of 1980, Enka ran up losses of 1,500 million
florin on its man-made fibre operations. Consequently, radical measures
had to be taken to reduce the loss-making activities. By 1980, synthetic fibres for textiles and carpets had been reduced only 32 per cent
of sales from a share of 53 per cent ten years earlier.

During the 1980s, Enka is aiming at cutting back its synthetic
fibre operations for textiles and carpets further to only 20 per cent
of its turnover. At the same time, cellulose-based fibres, chiefly
for textiles and industrial applications, is being reduced from a share
of 19 per cent in 1970 to 18 per cent in 1980 and 15 per cent during the
current decade.

On the other hand, Enka is developing other activities. Non-fibre
products, which were providing only 11 per cent of sales in 1970,
accounted for 18 per cent of turnover in 1980 and company plans envisage
this sector providing as much as 25 per cent of sales by the late 1980s.

The company is currently expanding its interests in areas, such as
membranes for medical and technical uses, as well as in non-woven
materials, specialised plastics, colloids, precision engineering
products and machinery for the textile, fibre and plastic industries.

In 1980, Enka's workforce in Europe was 34,070. World-wide
employment was 43,650 (non-consolidated companies included).

La Seda de Barcelona S.A.

With over 4,000 employees, LSB (Spain) is one of the largest Enka
subsidiaries.

Kanebo Ltd.

Kanebo was established in 1887 as Kanegafuchi Spinning Works and
is one of Japan's major producers of textiles. Its activities have
been developed through cotton weaving and silk spinning in the 1900s,
cotton textile finishing in the 1910s, silk weaving in the 1920s and
wool weaving, synthetic fibres and flax spinning in the 1930s. In
1963, nylon production was initiated with technology from an Italian
firm, Snia Viscosa.

The first step of the overseas operations of Kanebo Ltd. was
taken in 1953 when the company established a sales subsidiary in the

United States.   In 1956, a cotton spinning mill was built in Brazil, the first major manufacturing operation in a foreign country.   Since then Kanebo started operations in several countries, mainly in Southeast Asia and Brazil.   Most of these inroads into foreign countries were carried out during the first half of the 1970s.   It should be noted that most of Kanebo's overseas operations are in the form of joint ventures with local companies in host countries.

Textiles constituted 68 per cent of total sales in 1981 (synthetic fibres - 44 per cent; natural fibres - 24 per cent).   As a result of substantial losses in the textile sector, Kanebo in 1978 merged its synthetic fibres distribution in Japan with Asahi Chemical (Nippon Synthetic Fibre Co. Ltd.).   As another consequence, the diversification, which had started with cosmetic production, food products and pharmaceuticals (respectively in 1961, 1964 and 1966) has been increased.

In 1978, Kanebo had over 20 affiliates throughout the world, 77 consolidated subsidiaries and 49 non-consolidated.   Kanebo's employment in 1979 at the parent company amounted to 5,522 while in main joint ventures 7,968 were employed.

Lachlan Industries Pty. Ltd.
(Australia)

Corporate data -

Registration of establishment:
    February 1974

Start-up of operations:
    July 1975

Capital stock:
    A$500,000

Composition of the capital:
    Japanese partners - 80 per cent
                            (Kanebo, 60 per cent; Mitsubishi, 20 per
                        cent)
    Australian partner (ESGM) - 20 per cent

Production:
    Scoured wool - 1,800 tons/year
    Wool top   - 2,400 tons/year

Annual sales:

16,000 thousand Australian dollars

Number of employees:

85 (male 62:female 23)

Kanebo do Brasil (Brazil)

Corporate data -

Establishment:

November 1956

Start-up of operations:

April 1957

Business:

Production and sale of cotton yarn and synthetic yarn
and wadding.

Capital stock:

Cr$320,502,739

Composition of the capital:

Kanebo - 85.3 per cent

Local partners - 14.7 per cent

Plant facilities:

(spinning plant) cottong spinning machines: 111,008 spindles;
(wadding plant) wadding machines: 5 sets.

Number of employees:

1,489 (in 1979)

KTSM (Indonesia)

This company, KTSM (P.T. Kanebo Tomen Sandang Synthetic Mills)
was founded in December 1968 and operations began in 1970.   The following are the corporate data.

Capital stock:

US$9,000,000

Composition of the capital:

> Japanese partners - 70 per cent (Kanebo, 42 per cent;
> Tomen, 28 per cent)

> Indonesian Government - 30 per cent

Business:

> Production (spinning, weaving, bleaching and finishing) and
> sale of polyester/cotton fabric.

Number of employees:

> 1,360

Plant facilities:

> Spinning - 29,376 spindles; weaving - 600 looms;
> finishing - one set; dyeing - one set.

Mitsubishi Rayon Co. Ltd.

The company has its origins in the Textile Division of Mitsubishi Chemical, which after having merged during the Second World War with a fibre producer and Asahi Glass, was broken up under Allied deconcentration orders.

Its activities cover three areas: textiles, synthetic resin and others. As one of the largest manufacturers of acrylic fibre in the world, the company produces synthetic fibres, such as vonnel (acrylic fibre), polyester filament and polypropylene filament. Through interlocking shareholdings, the company is a member of the Mitsubishi Group, whose textile interests as a whole in the early 1970s included, besides Mitsubishi Rayon, the Mitsubishi Corporation and Mitsubishi Acetate (now a 100 per cent subsidiary of Mitsubishi Rayon).

The company has two affiliates abroad. It has a 4 per cent shareholding in FISIBA, a joint venture with Techem-Tecnologia e Emprendimentos Techint-Cia, Tecnica International, and BNDE in Brazil, manufacturing acrylic fibre. Mitsubishi Rayon gave technical guidance to it up until 1979. The company is also a 5 per cent shareholder of FISIPE, another acrylic fibre manufacturer in Portugal for whom Mitsubishi Rayon provides technical guidance.

The production capacity of acrylic fibre in Mitsubishi Rayon, FISIBA and FISIPE, is as follows:

Mitsubishi Rayon: 233 tons per day

FISIBA   : 10 000 tons per year

FISIPE   : 12 000 tons per year

In 1980, the workforce of the parent company amounted to 3,561.

FISIPE

FISIPE, Fibras Sintéticas de Portugal Sarl was founded on 7 September 1973 by the association of Companhia União Fabril with Mitsubishi Rayon Company and Mitsubishi Corporation. Quimigal is the major Portuguese shareholder.

The initial stock capital was 500 million escudos, with the following distribution:

Companhia União Fabril   - 60 per cent

Mitsubishi Rayon Company - 25 per cent)

Mitsubishi Corporation   - 15 per cent) 40 per cent

The stock capital was successively increased in 1975, 1977 and 1979 up to 1,250 million escudos, with the Mitsubishi's share being reduced as follows:

Companhia União Fabril   - 83.6 per cent

Mitsubishi Rayon Company - 5 per cent)

Mitsubishi Corporation   - 11.4 per cent) 16.4 per cent

Mölnlycke AB

The company was formed in 1907 as Mölnlycke Väfveri AB, a textile manufacturer. Between 1930 and 1960, ever-increasing integration of production took place from yarns and fabrics to the finished product, sewing thread, household textiles and apparel. During the same period, the company also moved into the field of hygienics. In 1975, Mölnlycke AB was acquired (100 per cent) by the SCA Group, a holding company established in 1929 for some ten wood-processing companies in northern Sweden. The Svenska Cellulosa Aktiebolaget (SCA) is the parent company.

The Mölnlycke Group now comprises seven divisions under the decentralised organisation of the SCA Group and works in product areas concerned with hygiene, leisure activities and clothing.

The Consumer Products Division develops products for baby care and menstruation hygiene. The Toiletry and Cleaning Division manufactures and markets products for hair and body care in the Scandinavian countries. The Hospital Products Division works with disposable products for the needs of the health and medical sector. The Industrial Products Division manufactures wiping and polishing materials made of tissue paper and non-woven at its own paper mills in Sweden, the Netherlands and France. Mölnlycke Marine is one of the world's foremost manufacturers of large plastic pleasure boats.

Mölnlycke Sewing Thread manufactures sewing thread for domestic and industrial use at its spinning works in Finland and sewing thread factory in Sweden. A sales co-operation agreement was signed in 1980 with one of the foremost manufacturers of sewing accessories in the United States. Melka-Tenson is a ready-made clothing company with a range consisting primarily of shirts, jackets, trousers and functional garments for active leisure. Production takes place in the company's own factories in Portugal, Finland, the Netherlands and Sweden.

The principal subsidiaries and participations include the following (wholly owned unless otherwise stated): Mölnlycke Sytråd AB; A/S Saba, Norway; Mölnlycke A/S, Denmark; Mölnlycke (Nederland) BV; Mölnlycke SA, Belgium; and Mölnlycke France SARL.

In 1980 the total workforce of Mölnlycke AB was 7,262, half of whom were working in Sweden.

Rhône-Poulenc Textile (RPT)

The parent company Rhône-Poulenc - formed in 1928 through a merger of a chemical (Société Chimique des Usines du Rhône) and a pharmaceutical company (Ets. Poulenc Frères) - is the largest French chemical company with products in all sectors of the chemical industry, particularly organic chemicals, synthetic fibres and pharmaceuticals and international operations, with 75 companies in 40 countries. Rhône-Poulenc Textile is one of the three operating groups and has world-wide responsibilities.

Synthetic fibre production was developed in the 1930s (a period of expansion as a result of internal growth for the company) through Rhodiaceta. In the early 1970s the company's operations were restructured and rationalised, as the textile manufacturing activities were merged into RPT and textile processing into Chavanoz.

The production of synthetic fibres is concentrated in France in RPT. This subsidiary is one of the major producers of synthetic fibres in the world. The main products are polyamide, polyester, acrylic, rayon and vinyl chloride fibre and yarns as well as non-wovens.

In 1975, RPT rationalised and restructured its activities. Starting in 1977, production has been limited to only three products, namely nylon, polyester and acryl, and on the other hand, highly-automated plants have been introduced in order to improve the competitive position of these products on the international market.

By the end of 1982, when the restructuring of RPT had been achieved, the new structure emerged as follows: overall number of plants - 11; and three main subsidiaries, namely:

(1) Rhône-Poulenc Fitne: three factories; main products: yarns, polyamide fibres, polyester, non-wovens "Bidim"; purchasing industries: textile industry, public works, brushes and finishing.

(2) Rhovyl: one factory; main products: chlorofibres; purchasing industries and user markets: textile industry.

(3) Cellatex: two factories; main products: rayon; purchasing industries and user markets: textile industry.

Three other subsidiaries in France: Chavanoz, Godde-Bedin, Sodetal.   One affiliate abroad: Thai Melon Polyester, Thailand (48 per cent).

In 1981, RPT's employees in France were 7,230.

Abroad, other subsidiaries of Rhône-Poulenc, such as Rhodia S.A. (Brazil), Rhodia A.G. (Federal Republic of Germany), Safa (Spain) and Viscosuisse (Switzerland), manufacture synthetic fibres.   Although these autonomous subsidiaries are part of the Rhône-Poulenc Group, they have no financial or organic links with RPT except for technical co-operation between them and RPT.

Viscosuisse

Viscosuisse is the largest textile enterprise in Switzerland. Its main products are synthetic fibres (etylsuisse and terssuisse): 96.6 per cent in 1980.   The manufacturing of artificial fibres (viscose) has been progressively reduced since 1966, the main plant in Steckborn was closed in 1973-74 and in 1980 the production of viscose was completely stopped.

Viscosuisse has two main subsidiaries in Switzerland: Hetex Garn S.A. and C. Beerli S.A.; and one foreign subsidiary in the United Kingdom: Viscosuisse Textured Yarns Ltd.

At the end of 1980, the global workforce of Viscosuisse amounted to 3,635 persons and in 1981 the workforce was 3,600.

Lotus and its parent company, Sam Hwa Ltd.

Lotus Company was established in July 1970 and registered at the Export Processing Zone Authority in the Philippines in February 1974. It specialises in leather shoes with a production capacity of 5,000 pairs a day.   Its products are mostly exported to industrialised countries.

In September 1977, Sam Hwa (Republic of Korea), which produces
sports shoes, took over Lotus, acquiring more than 90 per cent of the
latter's shares.   Lotus is Sam Hwa's only overseas subsidiary in the
footwear industry.   After the take over, Sam Hwa dispatched the
president and other key management personnel for Lotus.   Technical
advice is also being given to develop certain designs at the subsidiary
which is processing the raw materials supplied by Sam Hwa.

As of September 1981, the total employment of Lotus was 1,122.

APPENDIX II

LIST OF REPLIES RECEIVED

MNEs' replies

Name	Country
Asahi Chemical Industry Co. Ltd.	Japan*
P.T. Indonesia Asahi Chemical Industry (INDACI)	Indonesia
Asahi Spinning Ireland Ltd. (ASP)	Ireland
Asahi Synthetic Fibres Ireland Ltd. (ASF)	Ireland
Tongyang Polyester Co. Ltd. (TPC)	Korea, Rep. of
Dollfus-Mieg & Cie. (DMC)	France*
Enka A.G.	Germany, Fed. Rep.*
La Seda de Barcelona S.A. (LSB)	Spain
Kanebo, Ltd.	Japan*
Lachlan Industries Pty. Ltd.	Australia
Kanebo do Brasil S.A.	Brazil
P.T. Kanebo Tomen Sandang Synthetic Mills (KTSM)	Indonesia
Mitsubishi Rayon Co. Ltd.	Japan*
Fibras Sintéticas de Portugal, SARL (FISIPE)	Portugal
Mölnlycke A.B.	Sweden*
Rhône-Poulenc Textile (RPT)	France*
Viscosuisse A.G.	Switzerland
Sam Hwa Ltd.	Korea, Rep. of*
Lotus Co.	Philippines

---

   * Home country.

Government replies[1]

Country

Algeria	Netherlands
Australia	Nigeria
Colombia	Philippines
France	Portugal
Germany, Federal Republic of	Singapore
Hong Kong	Spain
India	Sri Lanka
Ireland	Sweden
Japan	Switzerland
Korea, Republic of	United Kingdom
Malaysia	United States
Mauritius	
Mexico	

Employers' organisations' replies[1]

Country	Name
Australia	Confederation of Australian Industry
Belgium	Fédération des Entreprises de Belgique/ Federation Beige des Industries de l'Habillement
Colombia	Asociación Nacional de Industriales (National Association of Industrialists)
France	Union des Industries Textiles (Textile Employers' Association)
Germany, Fed. Rep. of	Bundesvereinigung der Deutschen Arbeitgeberverbaenden (Confederation of German Employers' Associations)
Ireland	Federated Union of Employers (FUE)
Japan	Japan Federation of Employers' Associations (Nikkeiren)
Korea, Rep. of	Korea Employers' Federation
Malaysia	Persekutuan Majikan Majikan Malaysia (Malaysian Employers' Federation)
Mauritius	Mauritius Employers' Federation (MEF)

Country	Name
Netherlands	Verbond van Nederlandse Ondernemingen
Nigeria	Nigerian Employers' Association/ Textile Employers' Association and Manufacture Textile Employers' Association
Portugal	Confederação da indústria portuguesa
Sweden	Svenska Arbetsgivareföreningen (Swedish Employers' Confederation)
Switzerland	Union Centrale des Associations Patronales Suisses (Central Union of Swiss Employers' Associations)
United Kingdom	Confederation of British Industry

Workers' organisations' replies[1]

Country	Name
Australia	Australian Council of Trade Unions/ Clothing and Allied Trades Union of Australia
Brazil	Confederação Nacional dos Trabalhadores na Industria/Federação dos Trabalhadores nas Indústrias do Fiação e Tecelagem do Estado de São Paulo (National Confederation of Industrial Workers/ Federation of Workers in the Spinning and Weaving Industries of the State of São Paulo)
Canada	Canadian Labour Congress/Amalgamated Clothing and Textile Workers' Union (ACTWU)
France	Confédération Générale du Travail (CGT)/ Federation des travailleurs du textile et des industries rattachees (Federation of Textile and Allied Workers) Confédération Française des Travailleurs Chrétiens (CFTC) (French Confederation of Christian Workers)
Hong Kong	Hong Kong Federation of Trade Unions

Country	Name
India	All-India Trade Union Congress
Ireland	Irish Transport and General Workers' Union
Japan	Japanese Confederation of Labour (Domei) Japanese Federation of Textile, Garment, Chemical, Distribution and Allied Industry Workers' Unions (ZENSEN)
Korea, Rep. of	Federation of Korean Trade Unions
Malaysia	Kongres Kesatuan Sekerja Malaysia (Malaysian Trades Union Congress)
Nigeria	National Union of Textile, Garment and Tailoring Workers of Nigeria
Portugal	União Geral de Trabalhadores (UGT)/ Textile Trade Union (SINDETEX)
Spain	Unión General de Trabajadores (UGT)/ Federacion Estatal de Textil - piel (State Federation of Textiles and Furs)
Sweden	Landsorganisationen I Sverige (Swedish Trade Union Confederation)/ Swedish Textile, Garment and Leather Trades Union
Switzerland	Landesverband Freier Schweizer Arbeitnehmer (Swiss Federation of Autonomous Trade Unions)
United Kingdom	Trades Union Congress

International trade union organisations

International Textile, Garment and Leather Workers' Federation (ITGLWF), Brussels.

Union Internationale des Syndicats du Textile, de l'Habillement et des Cuirs et Peaux (Trade Unions International of Textile, Clothing, Leather and Fur Workers), Prague.

Note

[1] Information was requested from governments and employers' and workers' organisations in the following countries: Algeria, Australia, Belgium, Brazil, Canada, Colombia, France, Federal Republic of Germany, Hong Kong, India, Indonesia, Ireland, Ivory Coast, Japan, Republic of Korea, Malaysia, Mauritius, Mexico, Morocco, Netherlands, Nigeria, Philippines, Portugal, Singapore, Spain, Sri Lanka, Sweden, Switzerland, Tunisia, United Kingdom and the United States. The following international sectoral union organisations were also requested to supply information: International Federation of Textile/Clothing (WCL, Gent), International Textile, Garment and Leather Workers' Federation (ITGLWF, Brussels), and Trade Unions International of Textile, Clothing, Leather and Fur Workers (Prague).

APPENDIX III

ILO STUDY ON SOCIAL AND LABOUR PRACTICES OF
SOME MULTINATIONALS IN THE TEXTILE INDUSTRY
(AND CLOTHING AND FOOTWEAR INDUSTRIES)

Subject-matter guide/questionnaire

The study aims at ascertaining information with regard to social and labour policies of a sample of enterprises in the above-mentioned sector operating in more than one country. It concentrates on three main areas: (1) employment and training; (2) wages and conditions of work; and (3) labour relations. In order to obtain a balanced picture, information is sought from headquarters of enterprises and their subsidiaries; from home and host country governments; and from employers' and workers' organisations and representatives.

The following subject-matter guides/questionnaires were addressed to headquarters of such enterprises and/or their subsidiaries, employers' and workers' organisations as well as to governments with the request to supply factual information and comments, to the extent possible and where applicable, including readily available relevant statistical data, reports, collective agreements and other documentation relating to the following points:

Enterprises

1. General policy aspects

1.1 Summary description of the organisational structure of the group (parent and subsidiaries) and data on the establishment and development of operations, including factors which also help to assess the importance of the enterprise (e.g. joint ventures).

1.2 Global employment data (development during the past few years (decade) and possible future projections); distribution of employment in the home country and in host countries and its development; occupational structure; national and expatriate employment and levels in subsidiaries. (See also point 5.)

1.3 Priorities attached to social, economic and political factors when planning investment abroad.

1.4 Differences in the type of production facilities at home and abroad; location and degree of research and development activities and their repercussion on personal structure and policies.

1.5 Competitive situation in home and host countries (developed and developing) and in other major markets.

1.6 Extent to which ILO Conventions and Recommendations as well as the ILO Tripartite Declaration of Principles concerning Multinational Enterprises and Social Policy influence the formulation of labour and social policy of your enterprise.

2. Employment and training

2.1 Manpower problems encountered in the various countries where the enterprise operates.

2.2 Employment problems encountered with respect to: restructuring of activities, redistribution of production, changes in demand, declining activities in some countries or expansion in others.

2.3 Employment security arrangements concluded through collective bargaining or set up by legislation; their effect and possible problems encountered with them; any other employment level assurances.

2.4 Assessment of indirect employment effects of operations in all countries, in particular in developing host countries.

2.5 Use of employment-generating technology, both directly and indirectly, including adaptation of technology to needs and characteristics of host countries; participation, if any, in development of appropriate technology in developing host countries.

2.6 Positive and/or negative effects of operations on your home country plants' employment and structure.

2.7 Subcontracting in developing countries of work (volume and form) to other enterprises and to individuals - home work; employment generated; possible problems encountered; conclusion of contracts with enterprises in developing countries regarding the use and processing of local raw materials.

2.8 Transfer of operations (type, purpose, frequency) from one region to another in same country and from one country to another; corresponding employment effects and problems.

2.9 Collaboration and consultation, where appropriate, with competent public authorities in home and host countries and with national employers' and workers' organisations regarding enterprise manpower plans.

2.10 Types and extent of training; programmes run or sponsored in home country and host countries according to different categories and countries of operation.

2.11 Workers' participation in formulation and implementation of training programmes.

2.12 Policy regarding training of nationals and contribution to the continuous development of their vocational skills.

2.13 Contribution to national training programmes, co-operation with national training institutions, etc. (type and volume).

2.14 Assistance from governments in the organisation and implementation of training for local personnel.

2.15 Opportunities offered to local management within the enterprise to broaden experience in suitable fields.

2.16 Assessment of your enterprise's contribution to the training needs of developing host countries.

2.17 Retraining of workers affected by enterprise restructuring or closure provided by your enterprise and/or other institutions in line with enterprise and/or public policy (type and volume).

3. Wages and conditions of work

3.1 General policy on wages and conditions of work in international operations.

3.2 Major factors affecting the determination of wage rates/earnings and conditions of work in the home country and in foreign subsidiaries.

3.3 Wages, benefits and conditions of work offered in comparison with those of similar enterprises or plants by comparable employers in the country concerned (same branch or sector and size of operation).

3.4 Wage levels, benefits and conditions of work according to job categories and sex (skilled, semi and unskilled workers).

3.5 Types of wage systems and work organisation including piece work and shift work.

3.6 Social benefits including those beyond legal requirements.

3.7 Welfare and recreation facilities provided.

3.8 Redundancy benefits in the event of technological and structural changes.

3.9 Company pension funds, if any, globally or locally administered and their importance in total social security benefits available
to workers.

3.10 Safety and health standards (provide texts and examples);
co-operation with competent safety and health authorities and representatives of the workers and their organisations.

3.11 Safety and health provisions included in collective agreements and otherwise provided for.

3.12 Average weekly hours paid (or worked, specify) per worker in
various plants; other time arrangements (such as flexible working
hours).

3.13 Rest periods, breaks and relief time and annual vacation
with pay.

3.14 Initiatives regarding new forms of work organisation and
for improving other working conditions and the work environment.

4.   Labour relations

4.1 Membership in national employers' organisations and involvement in their activities in home and host countries.

4.2 Description of labour relations policies followed by the
parent enterprise and its subsidiaries. (Forms of bargaining; local,
company-wide bargaining and industry-wide bargaining; and subject-
matters dealt with at each level.)

4.3 Allocation of responsibilities in respect of labour relations
and related matters (including expansion and/or reduction of the labour
force) between parent enterprise (headquarters) and subsidiaries.

4.4 Degree of integration of subsidiaries in the labour relations
system of the host countries.

4.5 Transfer of labour relations and personnel practices from
home to host country and its effects.

4.6 Policies for intercompany transfer of employees.

4.7 Contacts by headquarters and subsidiaries with trade unions
at different levels.

4.8 Information and consultation practices.

4.9 Information provided to workers' representatives for purposes of negotiations (type, level and entity involved: e.g. company units in the country, enterprise as a whole).

4.10 Practices and machinery as regards grievances and disputes.

5. **Statistical and supplementary data (where available)**

5.1 Home country: number of plants, host countries, subsidiaries and number of plants.

5.2 Major take-overs, mergers and closures during last five years.

5.3 Joint ventures: location and conditions.

5.4 Detailed employment data for all operations (structure and trends over time).

5.5 Percentage of expatriates and levels in foreign subsidiaries and change over time.

5.6 Statistics on labour disputes (strikes and lock-outs, reasons).

5.7 Comparative data on value added per man or other productivity figures in home or host country operations which are of same or similar nature.

5.8 Please attach the five latest annual reports of your enterprise (and selected subsidiaries, if separately available).

Workers' organisations and representatives

6. **General policy**

6.1 Observations on social and labour policies of multinational enterprises in the textile industry (plus clothing and footwear industries).

6.2 Headquarters' management and subsidiary management's influence with regard to labour matters.

6.3 Role of government policy and labour legislation, including labour inspection, in social and labour matters.

6.4 Influence of workers' organisations and representatives at various levels of corporate decision-making.

7.   Employment and training

    7.1 Employment problems encountered with restructuring of
activities, modification of production, redistribution of production
facilities, changes in demand, declining activities in some countries
or expansion in others.

    7.2 Job and income security in the various plants; provisions
existing in this field (national legislation, collectively agreed and
other arrangements) and experience with them.

    7.2.1 Redundancy indemnities, retraining and other related
provisions in the event of plant and department closure.

    7.3 Training and retraining possibilities.

    7.4 Workers' participation in staff transfer in between plants
and countries.

    7.5 Workers' participation in formulating and carrying out train-
ing programmes.

    7.6 Characteristics of employment structure and problems
encountered in this connection (manpower groups with possible special
problems, e.g. women workers, young workers, etc., including persons
employed through subcontracted work enterprises/homeworkers).

8.   Wages and conditions of work

    8.1 Situation in home and host country units of the enterprises
as regards wages and other earnings; hours of work; piece work;
shift work, rest periods, relief time and paid vacation; fringe
benefits and welfare and related services, transportation, recreational
facilities, nurseries, canteens, etc.; redundancy arrangements;
company pension schemes, and so on.

    8.2 Conditions and standards of safety and health; association
of workers and their organisations in their establishment and supervision; deviations from normal standards attributable to the multinational character of the enterprise.

    8.3 Differences in wages and conditions of work (with respect to
comparable domestic enterprises in the countries of implantation of
the multinational) associated with the multinational character of the
enterprise (or to other factors; size; productivity, etc.)

    8.4 Working conditions of special groups (e.g. women, unskilled
workers, migrants, homeworkers); and efforts towards solution of
problems where found.

9. Labour relations

9.1 Structure of workers' representation (plant, enterprise, regional, national, international level).

9.2 Percentage of workforce organised in unions (in the various plants).

9.3 Arrangements for collective bargaining.

9.4 Information and consultation arrangements and practices.

9.5 Consultation with and/or participation of trade unions or other elected workers' representatives in decision-making concerning shut-downs, reduction of workforce, transfer of production and short-time working, and/or attending to the social consequences implied.

9.6 Changes in the field of labour relations, e.g. collective agreements on job security, productivity bargaining, fringe benefits, level of bargaining.

9.7 Policy of multinational enterprises in the textile industry (plus clothing and footwear) as regards trade union recognition and respect of trade union rights.

9.8 Information and co-ordination of activities of workers' representative of the various plants of the multinational enterprise, and their aims.

9.9 Particular factors affecting labour and social matters in countries of multinational enterprise implantation (such as free trade zones).

9.10 Other important social and labour issues facing workers' organisations and their representatives in the textile industry in enterprises in home and host countries.

9.11 Experience with the principles established through the Tripartite Declaration of Principles concerning Multinational Enterprises and Social Policy.

Statistical and supplementary information (where available)

9.12 Please supply statistical data and supplementary information which you consider relevant to the study as a whole. These can include comparable national data on wages and conditions of work.

Employers' organisations

10.1 Membership and involvement of multinationals in the textile industry (and clothing and footwear industries) in employers' organisations.

10.2 Influence of multinational enterprises on labour standards.

10.3 Direct and indirect employment effects of multinational enterprises in the sector considered; other relevant labour market aspects.

10.4 Training practices of the enterprises, especially in developing countries.

10.5 Wages, fringe benefits and conditions of work, including safety and health in multinational operations as compared with those in nationally operating enterprises in the same branch or sector.

10.6 Views regarding the labour relations practices of multinational enterprises in the sector concerned. Role of government policy.

10.7 Experience in the sector with regard to the principles set forth in the Tripartite Declaration of Principles concerning Multinational Enterprises and Social Policy.

Host country authorities

11.1 Government policies regarding activities of multinational enterprises in textile, clothing and footwear in your country (and the industries in general).

11.2 Where existing, special legal and administrative provisions concerning such enterprises with respect to employment, training, social and working conditions, labour relations, subcontracting and other matters.

11.3 Agreements and arrangements in practice for information and consultation with such enterprises regarding employment, training, social and working conditions, labour relations questions, etc.

11.4 Employment guarantees given by the enterprises.

11.5 Harmonisation of manpower policies of MNEs in the textile (and clothing and footwear industries) with national social development policies.

11.6 Please supply any other relevant considerations, studies and/or documents.

Home country authorities

12.1 Government policy in respect of activities of multinational enterprises in the textile industry (and clothing and footwear industries) and the industries in general.

12.2 Possible social and labour problems in connection with reduction or restructuring of activities of these enterprises in the home country; government, collectively agreed and enterprise policies regarding these problems.

12.3 Legal or administrative measures or other approaches concerning the establishment of subsidiaries abroad.

12.4 Effects of the internationalisation of production in the sector in question on the employment market in your country.

12.5 Consultations between government authorities and multi-nationals in the sector concerned regarding manpower, training, conditions of work and labour relations.

12.6 Any other relevant considerations, studies and/or documents.

Questionnaire for governments
(used for a later phase of the project)

13.1 Do government policies exist regarding the activities of multinational enterprises in the textile, clothing and footwear industries in your country (and the industries in general)?

13.2 Where this is the case, do special legal and administrative provisions exist concerning such enterprises with respect to employment, training, social and working conditions, labour relations, subcontracting and other matters?

13.3 With regard to employment, training, social and working conditions and labour relations questions, etc., do agreements and arrangements exist in practice, for information and consultation with such enterprises?

13.4 Are employment guarantees given by the enterprises?

13.5 Are the manpower policies of MNEs in the textile (and clothing and footwear industries) harmonised with national social development policies?

13.6 Do social and labour problems possibly exist in connection with reduction or restructuring of activities of these enterprises in the home country?   Are there government, collectively agreed and enterprise policies regarding these problems?

13.7 Do legal or administrative measures or other approaches exist concerning the establishment of subsidiaries of multinational enterprises abroad?

13.8 What are the effects of the internationalisation of production in the sector in question on the employment market in your country?

13.9 Please add any other considerations which you may consider relevant, and attach studies and/or documents which may be useful for this inquiry.